Race and Media Literacy, Explained (or Why Does the Black Guy Die First?)

Frederick W. Gooding, Jr.

TEACHERS COLLEGE PRESS
TEACHERS COLLEGE | COLUMBIA UNIVERSITY
NEW YORK AND LONDON

To my first fan: Thanks for the love, MA—"little to little!"
To my #1 fan: Thanks for the love, Va—"facts are facts!"

Published by Teachers College Press,® 1234 Amsterdam Avenue, New York, NY 10027

Front cover: adam bohannnon design, photo by Serdarbayraktar / iStock by Getty Images.

Library of Congress Cataloging-in-Publication Data is available at loc.gov

ISBN 978-0-8077-6940-9 (paper)
ISBN 978-0-8077-6941-6 (hardcover)
ISBN 978-0-8077-8224-8 (ebook)

Printed on acid-free paper
Manufactured in the United States of America

Contents

Acknowledgment

This book would not be possible without the patient guidance and generous support of the sagacious and scholarly couple Dr. James A. and Cherry A. McGee Banks, who I first met while presenting on this very same topic (albeit in a more succinct manner) at a conference in Haifa, Israel. This intellectual work product is living proof of our power to make connections to one another, no matter where in the world we (or Hollywood movies) may be found.

Series Foreword

Students in elementary and secondary schools spend a significant part of their day consuming and watching various forms of media. Most children in the United States spend 3 hours a day watching TV; they can spend 5 to 7 hours a day when all types of screen time are totaled (National Library of Medicine, 2023). TV watching was highest among African Americans in 2022, who watched an average of nearly 3½ hours of TV a day. TV viewing time for White, Black, and Hispanic consumers decreased from 2021 to 2022. However, the viewing time for Asian Americans grew to approximately 2 hours a day (Statista, 2023).

Movies constitute an important part of what elementary and high school students watch on TV. When viewing movies on TV and personal devices and in theaters, young people acquire images, views, and perceptions of various racial, ethnic, religious, and social-class groups, as well of images related to gender and sexual orientation. The representation of people and groups in the media is a cogent factor that can influence children's perceptions, attitudes, values, and behaviors. However, as Cortés (2000) perceptively points out in one of the earliest books published in the Multicultural Education Series, the influence of the media on students' knowledge, attitudes, and behaviors is potent, complex, fluid, and difficult to predict; it is not straightforward and clear. Cortés uses vivid examples that describe how the interpretations and meanings that children construct from media presentations are often quite different from those intended by the media maker as well as those constructed by parents and teachers.

In this illuminating, informative, and timely book, Gooding examines depictions of race within contemporary mainstream movies and their influence on society. He also describes how Hollywood mainstream movies present a limited view of people of color and a broader and more complex depiction of Whites. Gooding's descriptions of the history of African Americans in Hollywood movies are informative, edifying, and sometimes poignant. These historical descriptions convey the ways in which African Americans have been marginalized and experienced cultural erasure since the early days of filmmaking in Hollywood. *The Birth of a Nation* (1915) and *The Jazz Singer* (1927) featured White actors in blackface and egregious stereotypes of African Americans. Hattie McDaniel won an Academy Award for her role as Mammy in *Gone with the Wind* (1939). Another actress of color did not win an Academy Award until Halle Berry won for her role in *Monster's Ball* in 2002.

Movies also convey and reflect the historical and cultural times in which they are created. Woodrow Wilson screened *The Birth of a Nation* at the White House. The movie reflected Wilson's attitudes toward African Americans, and his actions gave it legitimacy and positive publicity. Although movies can be harmful and contribute to cultural erasure and exploitation, they also can foster social justice and contribute to liberation and the political efficacy of marginalized groups such as African Americans. Joe Biden screened the movie *Till* (2022) at the White House, which tells the powerful and poignant true story of how 14-year-old Emmett Till was kidnapped and brutally murdered in Mississippi by men who took the law into their hands; the men were acquitted by an all-White jury.

Gooding argues compellingly that statistical and quantitative analysis of African Americans in movies tells only part of the story and that a *qualitative analysis* of the roles and images of Blacks in movies is essential to provide a comprehensive depiction of African Americans as well as Whites in the movies. Gooding develops and describes a HARM Theory Rubric, which provides viewing audiences with "a consistent formula of their own with which to more precisely measure or evaluate the qualitative aspects of the non-White characters they encounter while onscreen" (p. 43). Writes Gooding:

> The HARM Theory Rubric helps identify and analyze the quality of non-White imagery confidently and consistently. The HARM Theory stands for Hollywood's Acting Rule for Minority (or non-White) characters and holds that *if and when* a non-White character appears within a mainstream movie, this character is likely to be compromised or marginalized in some way, shape, or form—most especially when juxtaposed against White characters within the same movie. (p. 38)

This original and engaging book about the portrayal of minoritized and mainstream groups in the movies is a timely and significant contribution to the Multicultural Education Series. The major purpose of the Multicultural Education Series is to provide preservice educators, practicing educators, graduate students, scholars, and policymakers with an interrelated and comprehensive set of books that summarizes and analyzes important research, theory, and practice related to the education of ethnic, racial, cultural, and linguistic groups in the United States and the education of mainstream students about diversity. The dimensions of multicultural education, developed by Banks (2004) and described in the *Handbook of Research on Multicultural Education, The Routledge Companion to Multicultural Education* (Banks, 2009), and in the *Encyclopedia of Diversity in Education* (Banks, 2012), provide the conceptual framework for the development of the publications in the Series. The dimensions are *content integration, the knowledge construction process, prejudice reduction, equity pedagogy*, and an *empowering institutional culture and social structure.*

The books in the Multicultural Education Series provide research, theoretical, and practical knowledge about the behaviors and learning characteristics of students of color (Conchas & Vigil, 2012; Darling-Hammond & Darling-Hammond, 2022; Lee, 2007), language minority students (Gándara & Hopkins 2010; Valdés, 2001; Valdés et al., 2011), low-income students (Cookson, 2013; Gorski, 2018), and other minoritized population groups, such as students who speak different varieties of English (Charity Hudley & Mallinson, 2011), LGBTQ youth (Mayo, 2014); and students with disabilities (Waitoller & Thorius, 2022).

The ways in which African Americans are depicted in movies are manifestations of structural and institutional racism in the United States. A number of other books in the Multicultural Education Series focus on *institutional and structural racism* and ways to reduce it in educational institutions. These books include Özlem Sensoy and Robin DiAngelo (2017), *Is Everyone Really Equal? An Introduction to Key Concepts in Social Justice Education* (Second Edition); Gary Howard (2016), *We Can't Teach What We Don't Know: White Teachers, Multiracial Schools* (Third Edition); Jabari Mahiri (2017), *Deconstructing Race: Multicultural Education Beyond the Color-Bind;* Zeus Leonardo (2013), *Race Frameworks: A Multidimensional Theory of Racism and Education*; Daniel G. Solórzano and Lindsay Pérez Huber (2020), *Racial Microaggressions: Using Critical Race Theory to Respond to Everyday Racism*; and Robin DiAngelo (2023), *Seeing Whiteness: The Essential Essays of Robin DiAngelo.*

The messages Gooding describes about how Hollywood movies portray African Americans, other people of color, and mainstream Whites are significant for teachers and other educators to consider because research indicates that many students of color and other marginalized groups have fragile and complex racial, ethnic, cultural, and national identities (El-Haj, 2007; Phinney & Rotheram, 1987; Spencer, 1982; Van Ausdale & Feagin, 2001). Positive media experiences for racialized students can help them acquire clarified, reflective, and positive identities. Students who are members of marginalized and stigmatized groups often internalize the negative attitudes, dispositions, and stereotypes of their racial, ethnic, cultural, and religious groups that are institutionalized within Hollywood movies and society writ large. In a series of pioneering studies conducted between 1939 and 1950, Kenneth B. Clark and Mamie P. Clark (1950) found that African American children as early as preschool had internalized the negative attitudes about Blacks that were institutionalized within American society. More recent research by scholars such as Spencer (1982) and Cross (1991) indicates that some African American youth still have negative racial attitudes toward Blacks.

Mexican American preschool children aged 4 and 5 years old showed a preference for White figures and evaluated lighter skin more positively than darker skin in a study by Warner and Evans (1968). Pang and her colleagues found that 4th- through 6th-grade Japanese American students scored significantly lower than White American children on three physical self-concept measures. This study indicated that some Japanese American youth during the mid-1980s had internalized negative attitudes toward their physical characteristics (Pang et al., 1985). In a CNN program that is available on YouTube, the TV host Anderson Cooper (2010) summarizes research from a pilot study by Spencer that indicates that both Black and White preschool children express more positive attitudes toward Whites than Blacks. Older Black children viewed Blacks more positively than younger children.

Media influence the self-concepts, identities, and behaviors of elementary and secondary school students in cogent, fluid, and complex ways. This original, engaging, and visionary book can help educators acquire the knowledge and skills needed to help students develop media literacy that is essential for citizens in a society in which the influence of the media is powerful, vast, and ubiquitous. I am pleased to welcome this book to the Multicultural Education Series, which it enriches.

—James A. Banks

REFERENCES

Banks, J. A. (2004). Multicultural education: Historical development, dimensions, and practice. In J. A. Banks & C. A. M. Banks (Eds.), *Handbook of research on multicultural education* (2nd ed., pp. 3–29). Jossey-Bass.

Banks, J. A. (Ed.). (2009). *The Routledge international companion to multicultural education.* Routledge.

Banks, J. A. (2012). Multicultural education: Dimensions of. In J. A. Banks (Ed.), *Encyclopedia of diversity in education* (vol. 3, pp. 1538–1547). Sage Publications.

Charity Hudley, A. H., & Mallinson, C. (2011). *Understanding language variation in U.S. schools.* Teachers College Press.

Clark, K. B., & Clark, M. P. (1950). Emotional factors in racial identification and preference of Negro children. *Journal of Negro Education, 19*, 341–350.

Conchas, G. Q., & Vigil, J. D. (2012). *Streetsmart schoolsmart: Urban poverty and the education of adolescent boys.* Teachers College Press.

Cookson, P. W., Jr. (2013). *Class rules: Exposing inequality in American high schools.* Teachers College Press.

Cooper, A. (2010, May 18). *Study shows how children view race bias.* CNN. https://www.youtube.com/watch?v=EQACkg5i4AY

Cortés, C. E. (2000). *The children are watching: How the media teach about diversity.* Teachers College Press.

Cross, W. E., Jr. (1991). *Shades of Black: Diversity in African American identity.* Temple University Press.

Darling-Hammond, K., & Darling-Hammond, L. (2022). *The civil rights road to deeper learning: Five essentials for equity.* Teachers College Press.

DiAngelo, R. (2023). *Seeing whiteness: The essential essays of Robin DiAngelo.* Teachers College Press.

El-Haj, T. R. A. (2007). "I was born here, but my home, it's not here": Educating for democratic citizenship in an era of transitional migration and global conflict. *Harvard Educational Review, 77*(3), 285–316.

Gándara, P., & Hopkins, M. (Eds.). (2010). *Forbidden language: English language learners and restrictive language policies.* Teachers College Press.

Gorski, P. C. (2018). *Reaching and teaching students in poverty: Strategies for erasing the opportunity gap* (2nd ed.). Teachers College Press.

Howard, G. (2016). *We can't teach what we don't know: White teachers, multiracial schools* (3rd ed.). Teachers College Press.

Lee, C. D. (2007). *Culture, literacy, and learning: Taking bloom in the midst of the whirlwind.* Teachers College Press.

Leonardo, Z. (2013). *Race frameworks: A multidimensional theory of racism and education.* Teachers College Press.

Mahiri, J. (2017). *Deconstructing race: Multicultural education beyond the color-bind.* Teachers College Press.

Mayo, C. (2014). *LGBTQ youth and education: Policies and practices.* Teachers College Press.

National Library of Medicine. (2023). *Screen time and children.* Medline Plus. https://medlineplus.gov/ency/patientinstructions/000355.htm

Pang, V. O., Mizokawa, D. T., Morishima, J. K., & Olstad, R. G. (1985). Self-concepts of Japanese-American children. *Journal of Cross-Cultural Psychology, 16*(1), 99–109. https://doi.org/10.1177/0022002185016001008

Phinney, J. S., & Rotheram, M. J. (Eds.) (1987). *Children's ethnic socialization: Pluralism and development.* Sage Publications.

Sensoy, Ö., & DiAngelo, R. (2017). *Is everyone really equal? An introduction to key concepts in social justice education* (2nd ed.). Teachers College Press.

Solórzano, D. G., & Pérez Huber, L. (2020). *Racial microaggressions: Using critical race theory to respond to everyday racism.* Teachers College Press.

Spencer, M. B. (1982). Personal and group identity of Black children: An alternative synthesis. *Genetic Psychology Monographs, 106,* 59–84.

Statista. (2023). *Average daily time spent watching TV per capita in the United States from 2009 to 2022 by ethnicity.* https://www.statista.com/statistics/411806/average-daily-time-watching-tv-us-ethnicity

Valdés, G. (2001). *Learning and not learning English: Latino Students in American schools.* Teachers College Press.

Valdés, G., Capitelli, S., & Alvarez, L. (2011). *Latino children learning English: Steps in the journey.* Teachers College Press.

Van Ausdale, D., & Feagin, J. R. (2001). *The first R: How children learn about racism.* Rowman & Littlefield.

Waitoller, F. R., & Thorius, K. A. K. (2022). *Sustaining disabled youth: Centering disability in asset pedagogies.* Teachers College Press.

Warner, N. E., & Evans, I. M. (1968). Perception of prejudice in Mexican-American preschool children. *Perceptual and Motor Skills, 27,* 1039–1046.

Part I

WHITE SCREENS, DARK THEATERS

Evaluating the Worth of a Motion Picture

SETTING THE STAGE

Ever since I was a kid, I have always loved the idea of "going to the movies." Not only did I relish the opportunity to leave my boring home to change my immediate surroundings, but I felt as if I were going to a special space where my dreams could be nurtured and where my imagination could be inspired. Yes, it was between the curtains on the big screen where I could watch, enjoy, and learn about the human experience as I looked to shape my own life experiences off-screen.

Yet, when I say, "going to the movies," I mean I *literally* went to the movies, often having to enlist the transportation services of a reluctant parent to get to the local theater. Way back in the early 1980s (ahem), **blockbuster** movies were only widely accessible inside of an actual movie theater for limited periods of time. Before Betamax, before satellite, before cable, before videocassette recorders (VCRs) and Video Home System (VHS) tapes, before digital versatile discs (DVDs), before video on demand (VOD), before streaming movies via the Internet, you had to physically transport yourself to the movie theater if you wanted to see a film.

Further, if you enjoyed a movie so much that you wanted to see it again—or if you simply "missed it" while it was in theaters—you could indeed rent the movie, but VHS or DVD releases often came out months after the initial theatrical release. The idea of simply whipping a "phone" out of my pocket and, after a few simple finger taps, having a new movie streaming on my own personal device honestly seemed like *Mission: Impossible*. Further, the concept that I could pause, put down, and pick up the movie again at any time was an unlikely idea from a galaxy far, far away—and one had to be willing to go *Back to the Future* to behold it!

In so many ways, going to the movies was a mini-event unto itself because there were limited windows in which I could catch them in the theater for the full movie-going experience. A movie like the 1986 blockbuster *Top Gun* was able to boast not only of its box office success but of its longevity in the theater—newspaper ads at the time touted that it was successful enough to still be in the theaters many weeks after its premiere. A movie that "bombed," or initially performed poorly at the box office, would only be in theaters for a weekend or two. At that time, movie marketing campaigns were vitally important, as they helped build anticipation for a "make-or-break" opening weekend.

To match one's building anticipation for a particular movie showing, it is hardly coincidental that early movie theaters were grand, palatial spaces constructed to reflect the magnanimity of the sublime experience one could receive. Grand lobbies, sweeping staircases, and ornate designs on the walls and ceilings are just a few features that proud movie theaters boasted inside of their edifices. While movies can indeed be shared in public parks, classrooms, or downtown squares, the original model called for a movie to be ideally released within a controlled, quiet theater space (no cell phones, please), where the screen is literally larger than life inside a darkened theater. McGinn (2005) recounts, "We are all familiar with that sense of entrancement that accompanies sitting quietly in the pierced darkness of the movie theatre" (p. 4). This unique environment is especially suited for concentrating the viewing audience's attention on the "world" portrayed within the **visible continuum,** or the known events that occur between a movie's opening and closing credits (Gooding, 2017).

Hey, let's face it—there was simply no other place on Earth where I could feel that I, too, was like Superman and glimpse for a few moments what life as a superhero would actually look like. When *Superman: The Movie* was released in 1978, I am sure there were millions of mothers across America who simply rued the day that actor Christopher Reeves swooped onto the big screen, given the fact that his handsomely heroic image would inspire millions of children to start jumping off their beds in the mistaken belief that they could fly. Or, even worse, as in the case of me and my brother, tossing our fake glasses aside as we ripped our buttoned-down shirts apart (usually reserved for Sunday-go-to-meeting to our mother's chagrin) in efforts to expose our Superman Underoos pajamas underneath (with a small cape attached via two Velcro tabs on the shoulders), much like our "friend" Clark Kent (Weiss, 2017).

Now mind you, my brother and I were readily familiar with the basic Superman premise and storyline, since we had read plenty of the comic books about our superhero prior to the movie viewing. However, seeing a "real" Superman on the big screen is what really brought Superman to life in our minds. The larger-than-life image of the man of steel, manipulating the everyday forces of nature by which I was constrained, was simply mind-blowing. Those spellbinding images dancing before my eyes within the hallowed cavern of the movie theater, combined with the invigorating theme music by legendary composer John Williams, all helped forge an indelible emotional experience that was nothing short of magical.

Little did I realize that I was perfectly primed for maximum impression. Inside of that dark theater—where the seats are (supposed to be) comfortable, with savory comfort food and favorite candies nearby—I could literally feel my curiosity taking flight with these captivating images serving as my only source of light. Thus, when Academy Award–winning film director Francis Ford Coppola once offered that "cinema, movies, and magic have always been closely associated" (Segal & Antonio, 2021, p. xi), my imagination and I could not have agreed more.

1,000 WORDS?

Further underscoring the idea that cinema, movies, and magic were closely related, my early experiences at the movies illustrated to me in living color that these pictures were clearly worth more than a thousand words. From *Superman* to *Star Wars,* I was not just entertained by these "out of this world" Hollywood productions, but rather was actually *educated* about some of the deeper meanings of life that I carry with me still. For example, I recall on one such occasion how my whole body tingled with delight at the fact that my family was finally going to go see *Star Wars: Return of the Jedi.* And this was no ordinary movie, but rather the long-awaited "final" (ahem) installment of the world-famous original *Star Wars* trilogy, 3 years after the release of its predecessor, *Star Wars: The Empire Strikes Back* (1980).

In final preparation for this noteworthy event, I made my brother quiz me with increasing frequency as the release date approached to ensure I was up to speed on all the weaponry, machinery, and alien citizenry of the then-burgeoning *Star Wars* universe. After much preparation, the moment had finally arrived! We diligently performed our ticket-purchase-let-me-stop-by-concessions-real-quick-hey-wait-does-anybody-have-to-go-to-the-bathroom ritual before locating our seats. After the 16 or 17 movie trailers had finally run their course, I settled into my seat, oblivious of the world outside of the movie theater, let alone of the people inside of the theater.

During the movie, I experienced an epiphanous moment! However, to rewind slightly, when I first saw the famed Jedi knight Luke Skywalker (Mark Hamill) in harm's way within minutes of the opening scene, I was beside myself, wracked with anxiety. Here our valiant hero was, bound and blindfolded, teetering on the edge of a desert skiff with his fate staring at him from the mouth of the hideous Sarlacc monster seated at the base of the Great Pit of Carkoon. "Oh no!" I thought. "How in the heebee jeebees is he going to get out of this one? What on Earth (or Tatooine) would I do if I were in his boots?" I was so taut with tension that I did not even notice the seemingly endless supply of Milk Duds cascading out of the crushed box in my hand onto the darkened, soda-stained movie theater floor.

But lo and behold! Little did I know that the loss of my chocolate-coated caramel candies would result in me gaining a lifelong insight. I distinctly recall how time stood still as I experienced one of my first epiphanies that I can remember—almost as if *I* were in the movies! In fact, that fateful day has led me to you, the reader, in this very moment as a media scholar who still appreciates the fact that movies are more than mere byproducts of entertainment, but can be moving works of art worth analyzing and deconstructing for deeper meaning. For, as I leaned down to retrieve my fallen Duds (five-second rule), I happened to notice my big, black, bulky, glow-in-the-dark Casio watch, and then it occurred to me: "Hey, wait a minute! The movie just started. Why would they kill off the main character less than 15 minutes into the film? He is way too important for that. Besides, *it's just a movie* and I need to be more mature [a word I had been hearing a lot lately] and realize I will walk out of this theater A-O-K."

And with this thought, I instantly relaxed and became forever transformed by the realization that I had the power of choice to determine how seriously I wanted to take in the movie imagery before me. The seeds of critical thinking were thus immaculately conceptualized. Just picture me in that darkened theater with that bulky Casio watch, unaware that I would need that light bulb flickering over my head to guide me as I went down a rabbit hole of new self-awareness and analysis. Not to sound melodramatic, but I simply did not walk out of that theater the same person.

While I have heard magical experiences can be had inside of a movie theater, what follows in this text is analysis based upon a true story upon which you may pass or reserve judgment.

JUDGMENT DAY

Fast-forward a few years from 3rd grade to 11th grade, when I find myself alone within a different, darkened theater. I distinctly recall that while I was thick in the middle of a hot and humid Philadelphia summer, I was ruminating on my decision to only wear a tank top inside of the darkened, artificially chilled environment of the movie theater. Speaking of highly anticipated sequels, before the age of "binge-watching" began via online platforms such as Netflix or Hulu, movie sequels released in the theater were the best way to "continue" the fantastical stories Hollywood created. The story I was set to continue following was *Terminator 2: Judgment Day* (*T2*), the 1991 follow-up to the iconic 1984 hit *The Terminator* starring Arnold Schwarzenegger. Just like *Star Wars: The Empire Strikes Back*, the second *Terminator* installment was hyped up in my mind as one to watch for, as I was a big fan of director James Cameron's other science fiction work, notably the 1986 classic *Aliens*, which I determined to be an absolute improvement upon the initial 1979 *Alien* film.

Cameron's computer-generated imagery (CGI) of the "liquid metal," shapeshifting T-1000 series was mind-blowing for the time. *T2* was a revolutionary movie that not only manipulated the concept of time as a weapon (à la *Back to the Future*), but it brought back alpha-male mega-movie star Schwarzenegger, who famously played the antagonist in the original movie (e.g., "I'll be back"), as the "good guy" in *T2*. I was mesmerized by the then-state-of-the-art computer graphics and was blown away by the startling visuals of seeing a freightliner semi-tow truck barrel over a bridge and into a canal viaduct just to give chase (in slow motion, mind you). Yet, while inspired and invigorated over high-intensity *action scenes*, I was also disheartened and discombobulated over seeing so-called *drama* over my Black male image onscreen.

For starters, recall that this is 2½ decades before *Black Panther* ever hit the mainstream movie screens during Black History Month of 2018. In other words, outside of the burgeoning "urban movie" subgenre in the early 1990s (e.g., *Boyz n the Hood, Juice, New Jack City, Menace II Society,* etc.) targeted mostly toward Black audiences, seeing my Black male image onscreen depicted in a prominent role within a mainstream movie was a rare event. Again, I had no problem in my youth accepting White males Christopher Reeve or Michael Keaton as my Superman or Batman. In addition to superheroes with superpowers, I also accepted White male **A-list talent** like actors Bruce Willis and Tom Cruise, whose movie characters used simple, ordinary, everyday wits to complete what we will affectionately dub within these pages as the **Hollywood Trifecta**, meaning these White males would most often: (1) get the goal (that is, accomplishing their primary objective, whether that means saving the world or vanquishing the villain), (2) get the gold (most protagonists obtained some sort of material reward or benefited tangibly from their labors), and, of course, (3) "get the girl" (need I explain?).

Even though these White male heroes looked nothing like my father, brother, uncle, cousins, grandfather, pastor, or barber—in other words, people in my everyday life whom I looked up to and who gave me advice and attention—I nonetheless accepted them as my own. I learned to "read" this visual movie language as it made me conversant with my White male friends during my private school experience—of course I saw Sylvester Stallone in *Rambo*! Of course, it was cool how he single-handedly obliterated all those men. (Wait—they were men of color? From Vietnam? But, where is Vietnam again? Those were the bad guys, right?) But as I was learning to love my own brown-skinned face in the mirror (despite the intrusive number of whiteheads on my forehead), it was nonetheless exciting to see my image on the big screen—most especially in the summer months outside of the typical 28 days of February's Black History Month. So, you can imagine how I perked up when I saw, onscreen in *T2*, Black actor Joe Morton as Miles Bennett Dyson in what can absolutely be characterized as a significant role.

If you have not seen any of the *Terminator* movies, allow me to indulge in a quick recap:

- In the original *Terminator* movie, Sarah Connor (Linda Hamilton) is a "regular" White female who becomes a damsel in distress needing to be saved from a destructive machine sent from "the future" called the Terminator. Arnold Schwarzenegger starred in the 1984 original as the titular cyborg that appears to be human on the outside but is actually a mechanized robot on the inside. The Terminator's mission is to kill Sarah because she is destined to give birth to the destined leader who will successfully defeat artificial intelligence intent upon destroying all of humankind via nuclear holocaust.
- In the sequel, *Terminator 2: Judgment Day*, it is the year 1995 and Sarah's son, John (Edward Furlong), is no longer a little kid, and the artificial intelligence network Skynet attempts again to snuff out the last remaining threat to their future by sending a new and improved T-1000 series Terminator back in time to kill John.
- In *T2*, Arnold Schwarzenegger plays a cyborg sent by "Future John" to save himself. In a "role reversal," Arnold's cyborg is identical to the one that tried to kill Sarah in the original movie but is now fighting to protect "Young John" from the newer and more powerful T-1000 series.
- In the original *Terminator* movie's climactic scene, the ruthless killing robot machine was destroyed, save for its hand. In the sequel we learn that engineers found the hand and reverse-engineered the technology, ironically forming the basis of Skynet. More specifically Miles Dyson, as Director of Special Projects at Cyberdyne Systems Corporation, is the engineer whose research unlocked the advanced Terminator robot technology for a revolutionary microprocessor that would change the world.
- Picture that! Rather than the T-1000 Terminator being the true villain despite its singular "mission" to kill Young John onscreen, *it is Black character Miles Dyson who is essentially responsible for the destruction of the entire human race on planet Earth.*

Whoa! Wait! If you think that last line is a jump in logic, simply watch the movie for yourself and follow *the movie's logic* and how it justified what I interpreted to be less than flattering treatment of my Black male image onscreen. Outside of Dyson's character, there are hardly any other Black characters with screen time, let alone with speaking lines, in 153 minutes of movie action. Recall, Black males in prominent mainstream movie roles can indeed be rare occurrences, most especially during the summer blockbuster season, but if and when they do appear, they just randomly happen to be responsible for inspiring an apocalyptic Armageddon?

BEWARE BLACK ENGINEERS

We first meet Dyson when he is in the Cyberdyne lab working on the robotic hand. We then see him subsequently inside his home, still working while absentmindedly negotiating for additional time to work from his wife, despite prior promises to spend time with both her and the kids at a local water park. Apparently, he is both excited about and committed to making a breakthrough on the new technology on which he is working. By seeing Dyson away from work, we are clued into his relatively opulent lifestyle at home.

Our Black engineer, who holds the title of "Director of Special Projects," has a nice-sized swimming pool adequate for a party of at least 25 persons, and the white and boxy contemporary architectural style of the home appears well-lit against the sleepy haze of a Southern California evening. This is by no means an "average" home, and its location in the exclusive beach community of Malibu (Eggertsen, 2017) reinforces the image of Dyson as wealthy. In continuing with Dyson's opening scene, his unnamed son is piloting a remote-controlled car, another signifier of affluence and leisure. Dyson is a well-off professional engineer living a life not normally seen by everyday Black men—onscreen, that is. Or at least he was.

Dyson is "busy" at work at a home computer (again, technology that was not common in 1991, the year of the movie's release, although the *T2* movie was set in the year 1995) when his son's car runs into his foot, an incident that ironically saves him from a bullet aimed at his head via infrared beam as he bends down to see what has disturbed his concentration. You see, Sarah Connor, as vested with permission by the universe to save humankind, took it upon herself to find the one responsible for "creating" Skynet with the rationale of eliminating him before Skynet itself could eliminate other people. Mind you, Dyson is not the Chief Executive Officer of Skynet, and whatever technology he produces as a systems engineer is within the proprietary interest of his employer, Cyberdyne Systems, technically making them the profit-seeking corporate actor responsible for massively distributing such cutting-edge technology. Not to mention there are other co-conspirators, such as the voting members of the board of trustees and scores of other employees (judging by the impressive size of the Cyberdyne building they later infiltrate) being involved in research, marketing, promoting, and developing this technology that Dyson perfects with other team members. Yet, it is Dyson and Dyson alone who is pinpointed as the primary responsible party.

Therefore, his death is justified—at least in the eyes of Sarah Connor.

Here is where, *from a logical perspective*, things get weird. Sarah, who had already committed the crime of trespassing and was hiding out in Dyson's bushes with the premeditated intent to commit murder in the first degree with a deadly weapon, not only shoots and misses Dyson, irreparably damaging his 1995 computer, but she proceeds to unleash a *Rambo*-esque full-scale artillery attack, shooting up Dyson's lovely home and terrorizing his wife and son. And, of course, by *Rambo* I refer to John Rambo, the White male, "badass" protagonist of the popular *Rambo* action-movie series starring Sylvester Stallone—a character whose *onscreen* kill count across five films from 1982 to 2018 was over 500 people, the overwhelming majority of them people of color (Kennedy, 2021). The rampant killing of people of color by the lone White male hero that audiences are supposed to root for visually communicates that the life of the surviving "hero" is more valuable—at least more valuable to the telling of the story seen onscreen.

WHOSE FAULT?

Yet, I digress—while Sarah's assassination attempt was initially unsuccessful, she continued with her attack by proceeding to enter the house, exclaiming "It's all your fault!" before shooting again at point blank range and wounding Dyson in the left shoulder. She then walks up and approaches a defenseless Dyson but for some (moral?) reason, cannot pull the trigger and kill him in cold blood in front of his family. Sarah is perhaps a sympathetic assailant after all.

Thankfully for Dyson, "Young John" and Schwarzenegger's bulky Terminator frame arrive just in the nick of time to interrupt Sarah, even as the teenaged John immediately takes charge of the chaotic situation. One of the running plot themes was the development of John's leadership, with him directing the Terminator what to do with more and more decisive authority as the movie continues. "Show me your room," he states to Dyson's son as he whisks the terrorized and confused child away, with no questions asked by either of his two legal guardians present in the immediate aftermath of a destructive and nearly deadly attack—not even, "Who the hell are you and where the hell is my child going?" or the pedantic, reflexive threat of "I am calling the cops!"

Dyson does manage to stammer, "Who are you people?" while injured, sweating, and panicked with his curiously mute wife on the floor. However, in good faith, Young John commands the Terminator to "explain" the situation (and simultaneously justify Sarah Connor's actions) with the Terminator cutting off a portion of his human prosthetic skin on his left arm to reveal the mechanical hand that Dyson is working on. However, when Young John and the Terminator first arrive on scene, it is Whiteness that is given priority. John immediately sits with his sobbing mother and comforts and consoles her, despite her failed assassination attempt but successful destruction of Dyson's home. The musical score in the background coupled with the tender closeup shots and whispered conversation between mother and son all reinforce the unspoken subtext that the feelings of the White perpetrator are more important than those of the Black victim.

We do not see a similar or parallel tender scene featuring Dyson as a victim since within the movie's visible continuum more time was spent contextualizing Sarah's conflicted emotions rather than processing Dyson and his family's reactions to Sarah's terrible actions. Based upon perspective, this scene can read as extremely traumatic for the young Black male child who witnessed his father get targeted for assassination, or perhaps it can engender sympathy from the audience who can "understand" how or why a (White) mother who desperately loves her son (and humanity) so much would be willing to kill for peace. Fortunately, Young John directed the Terminator to "help" the distressed Black couple—help that consisted of the Terminator commanding the panicked wife to apply pressure to her injured husband's wound. In "helping" Dyson, the Terminator did not physically touch or render assistance to Dyson.

After Schwarzenegger states "Listen to me very carefully" in his patented monotone, the next scene features everyone sitting down at the dinner table (complete with coffee cups), with Sarah as the exception—she is positioned higher, sitting on top of the kitchen counter, smoking inside the home (it is unclear whether she sought permission), while Sarah herself delivered the following voice-over: "Dyson listened while the Terminator laid it all down. Skynet. Judgment Day. The history of things to come. It's not every day that you find out you're responsible for 3 billion deaths. He took it pretty well." To complete the wry joke, the next line recited by Dyson was, "I feel like I'm going to throw up."

WHOSE HOUSE?

Now may be an excellent time to review and take stock of the picture that is slowly developing, even though in the middle of watching a movie such scenes may flash quickly before our eyes. Sarah ransacks and shoots up a million-dollar house, attempts to kill Dyson in his own home, wounds him, terrorizes his son, traumatizes his wife and then, without apologizing, unapologetically smokes in his kitchen while explaining to him that his life's research is fraudulent? Can you imagine? "Hi! My name is Sarah—excuse the mess. Even though I tried to kill you, I'm going to sit down and explain how your life's work is actually *more* destructive than what I did to your home and that is why I tried to kill you, no offense." To boot, the audience is not the least bit upset with Sarah because she has moral authority on her side to thwart the (indirect) "killer" of all of mankind.

If you could picture me in a director's chair presently, you should also envision me yelling "Cut!" at the top of my lungs. Because, I, for one, when reviewing this chronology of events through a racial lens find this storyline to be patently ridiculous. Given the paucity of Black characters in this movie—let alone Black characters with speaking parts—it is significant how Dyson symbolically suffers from **emasculation** on at least two levels. First, Dyson is cut down to size by having his home destroyed, which now in the audience's rearview mirror was "counterfeit" to begin with since his fortune was obtained from "ill-gotten gains" as his invention symbolized him profiting from death.

Perhaps this is a conversation for another time, but many of our "Founding Fathers" (e.g., George Washington, Thomas Jefferson, James Madison) created fortunes in part through enslavement, or ill-gotten gains, as did many of our nation's storied "Ivy League" colleges and universities (Wilder, 2013). While *T2* is "just a movie," it is interesting to note the contrast off-screen with respect to us as a society employing considerably more empathy and patience in understanding that such transactions were "complex," and that nuance is required in making full-on judgments of a person's character—at least where the victims were Black and the perpetrators were White. Yet here, Dyson—according to the Terminator's cold and calculating analysis—is the person most responsible for Judgment Day and the audience is informed that "killing Dyson might actually prevent the war." Did I issue a "spoiler alert" already? If not, the Terminator's pronouncement definitely qualifies as ominous foreshadowing!

Second, visually, Dyson is made "less-than" by sitting at his own table with his bloody shoulder in a makeshift sling, as an obvious visual cue of impairment. By being depicted with his arm in a sling, the limited mobility speaks to his curtailed potency onscreen. Consider how his immobile arm differs from the classic "stomach gash" injury trope whereby the gash allows the audience to focus on the severity of the hero's task because risk of physical harm is indeed at stake, but after conducting the private "surgery" of extricating the bullet or patching up the bleeding wound (usually shirtless, in front of a mirror either in a bathroom or hotel room since our hero must eschew traditional hospital settings that would interfere with the important task they seek to complete), the audience and even the hero "forgets" about the injury as they forge ahead to accomplish their objective despite their injury.

Or at least our valiant hero may "forget" the injury up until right after the villain is vanquished, as they might then recall the suppressed pain as they suddenly wince, touch the affected area and limp and lean on their faithful friend or paramour who emerges to celebrate and support their accomplishment as well. Subtly, Dyson's sling is a powerful visual cue that takes him out of the running so to speak as a serious contender for title of "hero." Additionally, the sling "serves as a powerful cue" that he is and will be limited in both function and power.

In contrast, to protect Arnold Schwarzenegger's Terminator character and his physically imposing alpha White male power positionality (former Mr. Universe body builder was part of his marketing packaging), even the Terminator, after willfully cutting half his arm off, is seen in the next scene wearing a black glove covering his metallic hand, accompanied with a badass black leather jacket in contrast to the obvious injury Dyson sports for all to see. The Terminator is "injured" but not incapacitated and suggesting impotence the way Dyson was.

I have so many questions. For only after a few brief moments of civil discourse at his own table inside of his recently ransacked and bullet-riddled home, Dyson instantly agrees that he must destroy his life's work! In Dyson's mind, if he was instantaneously prepared to quit his job, how was he thinking about covering those mortgage payments in about six months? Was the Terminator going to help him efficiently process the paperwork in filing the property destruction home insurance claim? Was Dyson planning on waiting to seek professional medical attention for his injury *after* he did as commanded by this pubescent, teenaged White boy (but future military leader) in the middle of the night? What happened to the "trust, but verify" mantra former California governor and President Ronald Reagan made popular during nuclear disarmament talks the decade prior (Madigan, 2017)?

Again, this is ridiculous.

But wait! The whole reason why I wrote this book is because even after the Black guy decides to leave on the spot and destroy his life's work—the same work that was so important he could hardly afford to spend any quality time with his family—it is *he* who pays the ultimate price and *dies first.*

What do I mean?

THE BLACK GUY REALLY DOES DIE FIRST

To fast-forward, Dyson sneaks our heroes into his workplace at Cyberdyne Systems Corporation, which devolves into a shootout with police (complete with helicopter). The team sets explosives to destroy Dyson's lab and the robotic arm and its technology that same night but are predictably interrupted by police with assault weapons seeing how their actions *technically* constitute a crime. For whatever reason, while everyone else is fortunately unharmed through all the shooting (of which there is plenty), Dyson is seriously wounded after having been shot several times in the open by police—but he alone has the detonator in his possession. Sarah at one point is close enough to observe Dyson's injured state, but no dialogue is shared. She instead runs out in the open to take cover with apparently more luck than Dyson, somehow managing not to get shot in the process. However, Dyson is next seen breathing heavily and dramatically (a moment that is the subject of Internet memes as of this writing) before detonating the explosive with a dead man's switch. He apologizes to the officer who discovers him, "I don't know how much longer I can hold this," before eventually slowing his pace, panting his last breath on screen. Alone. Dyson is now dead—and not just dead but blown to smithereens! *Fade to black.*

I just have so many questions. How come Dyson could not also live until the end like our heroic protagonists? If John and Sarah survive relatively unscathed, why not write the script so that Dyson also escapes? With John and Sarah, the themes of family resilience undergird the relationship's development over the course of the movie. But did Dyson not have a family too? Why did he decide to sacrifice himself? So, the White woman who tried to kill Dyson—unlawfully, we might add for those keeping score at home—is justified in surviving, living, and thriving while this Black man's death is considered explainable? Why did Dyson have to die? Is it not true that all that they needed to do was simply destroy the technology and not necessarily the man who initially "discovered" it?

Further, with Dyson sacrificing himself for the cause, Sarah's hands do not officially become stained with the blood of murder—despite her original intentions—and our central White female character is still in the clear ethically as a "positive" character for the audience to follow and support. In retrospect, the Terminator presaged Dyson's death when he intoned, "Killing Dyson might actually prevent the war." In other words, the Terminator signaled to the audience that Dyson's life was not valuable enough to preserve—at least not with all of humankind at stake. Ironically in another subplot point, Young John instructs the Terminator in a further role reversal not to shoot to kill, but simply shoot to disable offending police officers who get in their way as a mark of this noble leader's humanity. Yet, amid all this concern for preserving life, should we not also be concerned about Dyson surviving, then? In fact, the Terminator's famous first words of onscreen dialogue to Young John were, "Come with me if you want to live!" Too bad that offer did not extend to Dyson . . . or any other prominent Black male figure onscreen—especially, historically, when they share the screen with other White characters in Hollywood.

DOING THE MATH

In adding up these two movie experiences of *Return of the Jedi* and *T2* together, what do I have? I have cognitive dissonance, plain and simple. In other words, the contrast between the two character scenarios started a cosmic shift inside of me. On one hand I had White male Luke Skywalker surviving an unlikely scenario, as I intrinsically knew that his life was too important to cut short so early in the movie. On the other hand, I had Black male Miles Dyson not surviving a likely scenario, which strongly suggested to me that his life was simply not important enough to exist. Granted, there are significant differences between not killing off one of the stars of a franchise and killing off a supporting character introduced halfway through a movie, but still, you must forgive me—it was 1991 and I was young. Up until that point, seeing images of Black males on the big screen was a rare occurrence. Just think about how many movies debuted last weekend or are coming to your local movie theater this upcoming weekend where the standalone, unequivocal protagonist is a Black male . . . if these numbers are slim now, they were definitely slimmer in 1991. Thus, I instinctually took notice of my image on screen and became sensitive to its treatment. Little did I realize that the seeds were planted then for the detection of a pattern that I now share within this book.

Again, back in 1991 when *T2* first was released in movie theaters, I was a mere young lad whose daily focus was minimizing the number of whitehead pimples on my forehead out of fear of offending the young ladies who might be receptive to my jokes. It was only later in life, as I began to study American history formally en route to my PhD at Georgetown University that I acquired the language to properly describe what I saw and what I felt earlier in life. I did not suspect how early this cognitive dissonance along the lines of race began.

I knew that I was feeling something, but I did not know exactly how to precisely express it. Having spent the better part of 2 decades studying racial imagery in movies and popular media, I now have the words to best describe *analytically* what I was feeling, and I wish to share much of this vocabulary within this space here. In other words, just like Indiana Jones (another White male childhood hero), I feel that I have braved numerous challenges to bring back to the public incisive analysis and user-friendly vocabulary that will make sense of the racial imagery we see onscreen. More importantly, my findings will aid and assist readers to explore the mainstream cinematic universe for themselves to discover more evidence of the pattern I have detected as "hidden in plain sight."

Moreover, this text challenges audiences to take an in-depth look at the global and pervasive influence of Hollywood by parsing out the complex web of historical, institutional, and financial factors that influence the portrayal of race in mainstream movies. This discussion goes "behind the scenes" to explore the ways in which these images are consciously created, manipulated, and distributed for public consumption to audiences in virtually every country around the globe. This in-depth look at the entire movie industry illustrates in clear detail how Hollywood glamorizes images of Whiteness, which often excludes or appears at the expense of non-White representation. Unlike many "anecdotal" treatments on race, readers will leave with concrete concepts and a uniform vocabulary with which to recognize and further analyze these formulaic images.

Race and Media Literacy, Explained represents a cutting-edge analytical approach for the 21st century, picking up where academic texts like Donald Bogle's seminal 1973 book *Toms, Coons, Mulattoes, Mammies, and Bucks: An Interpretive History of Blacks in American Films* left off. Further, traditional research regarding racial imagery in movies typically adopts a historical approach to blatantly disparaging images from Hollywood's early years. Yet, a strength of *Race and Media Literacy, Explained* is that it utilizes a structured framework that identifies and outlines contemporary patterns of marginalizing roles for non-White characters, many of which fall outside of traditional **stereotypes**.

Talking about race can be so incredibly awkward at times—but it does not have to be! Often, many restrict themselves from fully participating in these necessary dialogues because of a profound fear of "saying the wrong thing" (MPR News Staff, 2016). While laypeople have the option to demur or avoid discussions about race, our educators do not have the same luxury. As individuals responsible for preparing a new generation of thinkers prepared to innovate improved solutions for the society we share, inevitably, the topic of race must not only be broached, but broached productively.

Effective educators must learn to communicate effectively about race relations. Thus, if an educator is to be fully prepared to engage with contemporary and diverse student bodies—complete with varied needs and experiences—then it is to their advantage to have updated tool kits designed to help them reach their audiences. In keeping with this interdisciplinary approach, contemporary students' learning needs now consist of being able to see the world reflected to them in dynamic and innovative ways. After all, educators must keep pace with a growing appetite for such substantive discussions since as reported in *Forbes*: "six in 10 Gen Zs and 56% of millennials say that systemic racism is fairly or very widespread throughout society" (Deloitte, 2021, para. 4).

This book, therefore, offers 12 clear, cogent, and concise racial rubrics that help users of mainstream media more readily discern patterns "hidden in plain sight." While this book primarily leverages mainstream movies as the medium of analysis since they are ubiquitous in their distribution and unparalleled in their cultural significance and social impact, the rubrics apply to other forms of mainstream media as well (e.g., television, print media). I aim to assist educators to reconsider and think critically about both the quantity *and quality* of non-White images circulated throughout mainstream media. To this extent, the book's provocative title references a well-known rhetorical question asked within the African American community to express quizzical frustration with disparate treatment of non-White images onscreen. When "the Black Guy" or another non-White character dies early or graphically within mainstream movies, subtle, yet significant statements are made about the lesser valuation of non-White imagery in contrast to "normal" White images. Such statements remain largely unexplored until now.

Specifically honing media literacy skills in the classroom when it comes to race is imperative given younger populations' increased use and reliance upon media generally. For example, the Statista Research Department in December 2023 reported that for millennials (i.e., persons born between 1980 and the early 2000s), "due to the rapid development of technology in their lifetimes, the Internet has become a key part of their daily lives" (Statista, 2024). Millennials are therefore "teaching" educators—provided they are willing to listen—to adapt their pedagogical approaches that are more responsive to the contemporary student's needs. Today's student simply craves and responds to media—most especially media easily accessible through their phones. Printed books will simply not be the only vehicle by which students learn the further we head into the future.

While print books have not been fully replaced and will not be anytime soon, there is still recognition of "a publishing industry in transition—one that's modernizing in response to evolving reading habits" (Howe, 2017). Increasingly more people turn to and rely upon social media (e.g., TikTok) as a means of information gathering, if not for purposes of being influenced (Schulz & Guynn, 2022). Increasing practical media literacy skills through mediums like mainstream movies will help educators to remain relevant and resourceful in light of the fact that millennials "spend more time with their phones than they do with significant others, parents, friends, children or coworkers" (Hill, 2016).

There is no doubt that the Internet continues to help connect people and ideas virtually instantaneously in dynamic new ways. But with so many more information sources sprouting up as more individuals create spaces for their voices through podcasts, vlogging, blogging, or social media stories posted publicly on the Internet, much information online is disorganized and littered with flat-out inaccurate data or information requiring updating. So, what is a qualified educator to do?

With this book, educators can now leverage mainstream media "in real time" to reach learners effectively, instead of dusting off examples from 20 years prior, which may have been an effective example when the educator was busy learning their craft. The consistent, easy-to-learn and hard-to-forget racial rubrics are applicable to contemporaneous material and are flexible enough to adapt to new media consumed by their students, rather than be fixed and restricted to older examples with which the educator is familiar. Educators will then be better equipped to consider whether current images of diversity depicted represent an improvement, or, based upon patterns of the past, merely represent familiar tropes in new forms that escape censure and judgment?

To effectively reach today's students, educators will quickly learn the six standard archetypal patterns for non-White characters and six standard prototypical patterns for White characters in mainstream movies, as discussions of racial diversity often bizarrely overlook and exclude the dominant racial group. With the analytical framework serving as the foundation for the discussion, the next logical step is for educators to then help their students make connections in seeing some of the very same patterns off screen and within their classrooms. Unlike many "anecdotal" treatments about race, readers will leave with concrete concepts and a uniform vocabulary with which to recognize and further analyze these formulaic images.

Ultimately, my analysis will show that non-White characters are simply not as valuable or important as their White counterparts onscreen, and we must reconcile with this bigger picture before we can alter it. After all, *if a picture is worth a thousand words, then how much is a moving picture worth?* We all share the same mainstream movies, but do we all share the same experience? *Spoiler alert:* the answer is a polite "no."

The *bottom line* is that although Hollywood is a White-dominated industry, it consistently produces lucrative mainstream movies designed to appeal "universally" to racially diverse audiences around the world. Nevertheless, Hollywood mainstream movies routinely present a limited view of minorities, in stark contrast to the broadly developed spectrum of White characters. Given Hollywood's extensive reach and economic impact, the consistently marginalized non-White images in mainstream movies reflect and reinforce messages of racial imbalance worldwide.

Behold! How we arrive at this bottom line is what I deign to explain in the pages that follow. I look forward to starting a conversation about the value of Blackness specifically and the quality of non-White imagery onscreen generally. Unlike the fragile fate of so many "Black guys" on screen, I trust you will survive to the end of this book unharmed.

CHAPTER 1

Have We Seen This Movie Before?

WDF?! (WHY DIE FIRST?!)

Awww maaaaaan! "But why does the Black guy die first?!" Feel free to skip ahead if you have heard this rhetorical question before. If not, then you are in for a treat. By way of explanation, this entire manuscript will not parse out in excruciating detail all filmographic instances where a Black character met their demise "first" onscreen in contrast to other key characters. Nor does this book exclusively analyze whether Black bodies have been disproportionately targeted within movies from the horror genre—Robin Means Coleman and Mark Harris aptly handle that task in their February 2023 offering, *The Black Guy Dies First: Black Horror Cinema, From Fodder to Oscar* (Coleman & Harris, 2023). Rather, what interests me most is a larger, substantive conversation about the value and visibility of non-White images within mainstream movies generally.

The book's parenthetical subtitle, *(or Why Does the Black Guy Die First?)*, comes from a general frustration that whenever there is a mixed or interracial cast of characters within a mainstream movie, a visual vocabulary not so subtly emerges whereby White characters are accorded more value. This hierarchy is communicated primarily through **character arcs**, or the trajectory of a character's range over time. Typically, more important characters experience greater arcs built directly through large amounts of screen time and dialogue. Such arcs increase in complexity when the audience learns more about the character's backstories in relation to the overall plot. Thus, this book will leverage character arcs as a qualitative means of measurement when assessing the relative value of characters seen onscreen.

Further, asking "But why does the Black guy die first?!" speaks to a larger, existential question about the expressed value of their life itself. For in essence, this manuscript's central thesis rests upon the foundation of **psycho-segregation**.

Allow me to explain.

By way of "backstory," the social concept of segregation was unfortunately normalized and legalized within the United States with the divisive late-19th-century Supreme Court decision that allowed for "equal but separate accommodations for the white and colored races" (*Plessy v. Ferguson,* 1896). Many American history classrooms, if and when they adequately spend time on the topic, often display black and white photographs to illustrate the publicly enforced social code of segregation. As you read this sentence, what likely comes to mind is a visual of two water fountains adjacent to one another: one that appears to be the height of modern technology (at least in the 1950s) complete with a refrigeration system to cool the water with the singular word "White" on the wall above it, next to a more threadbare, nonrefrigerated water fountain with a mere saucer-basin left to expose more of the same wall that also posts the singular word "Colored" above it.

This picture of social discrimination and racism during the Jim Crow era—while historically accurate—needs to be updated in living color. Thus, the principle of **Racism 2.0** holds that the practice of racism within society has not changed so much in substance as in form, and therefore merely has been updated over time. Hence, when it comes to race and media literacy, it is important to distinguish between the two types of racism that we are looking for when critically analyzing mainstream media. Examples of "traditional racism" within mainstream media are overt, obvious, and offensive. Think of a "period piece" film set in 18th-century America in the Southeast (i.e., during the era of enslavement) that employs a White character spewing vile epithets while exhibiting a masochistic violent streak toward a Black female character (see *12 Years a Slave* for an Academy Award–winning example). While these images certainly illustrate the concept of racism, if this is the only type we are searching for, then much will be missed.

However, in contrast to "old" racism that is overt, obvious, and offensive, Racism 2.0 is much more subtle, suave, and sophisticated in its character (see Table 1.1). This new extrapolation is therefore more difficult to discern and discuss. This manuscript will serve as a guide, leveraging analytical rubrics to help uncover and discover subtle, suave, and sophisticated racialized patterns seen within mainstream movies, but remain conspicuously "hidden in plain sight." In contrast to only seeing "racism" as embodied by the stereotypically rabid plantation owner, our media literacy can be increased to also understand the devaluation of others based upon race (i.e., "racism") by also analyzing *Why does the Black engineer character Miles Dyson in the movie* Terminator 2: Judgment Day, *die first?*

The rhetorical question, "But Why Does the Black Guy Die First?!" has been asked informally as an "inside joke" over the years (at least within my circles) and has even been leveraged outwardly in marketing campaigns that subversively sought to get contemporary audiences to think about similar questions of value. For example, in the June 2023 release *The Blackening*—a comedic spoof on the horror genre starring seven Black friends who find themselves facing down a killer during a weekend getaway (of course, in a cabin)—the movie's own official website includes in its summary paragraph the caveat that: "*The Blackening* skewers genre tropes and poses the sardonic question: if the entire cast of a horror movie is Black, who dies first?" (Bergeson, 2023).

Part of *The Blackening*'s marketing campaign also featured the phrase "We can't all die first" in big, block letters above the ensemble cast on advertising posters. While on one hand the movie's in-house marketing team is leveraging a fresh, tongue-in-cheek approach to boost ticket sales of their edgy comedy, at the same

Table 1.1. Differences in Types of Racism

Racism	Racism 2.0
• Overt • Obvious • Offensive	• Subtle • Suave • Sophisticated

time their strategy is not based upon a joke. The sardonic question of "who dies first" is based upon an existing Hollywood horror movie trope that apparently exists because presumably, the marketing team is banking on the idea that before investing millions of dollars in promotional materials, enough people have noticed the persistent "truth" of this pattern (i.e., of Black characters being discarded early) over time for it to become predictable and cognizable. To wit, I also offer a "Top Ten" list of *nonhorror* movies whereby Black characters indeed made early exits in comparison to their White onscreen counterparts, thereby communicating volumes about their relative worth, but if you are not skipping ahead, these movie "killers" will be revealed in the book's final chapter.

Overt and obvious racism has often been measured using quantitative means. Statistics and data often are leveraged to provide evidence of racism, just as future Supreme Court Justice Thurgood Marshall did when illustrating that "separate but equal" was a legal fiction because even if separating members of society by race is morally questionable, the disparate spending rates per pupil within educational systems demonstrated local government's repeated failure to be equal in distributing financial resources between Black and White students (Ifill, 2021). An example of using a quantitative approach to measure racism in mainstream media currently would be the Hollywood Diversity Report issued by UCLA's Entertainment & Media Research Initiative as it tabulates the percentage of non-White versus White directors, writers, and leads within Hollywood movies (Ramón et al., 2023).

To best measure the "new" forms of racism that are more subtle, suave, and sophisticated, we must take care to employ both quantitative *and* qualitative means. Therefore, the analytical rubrics provided in this book are designed to increase one's media literacy by heightening one's awareness of more qualitative means of measurement. "But Why Does the Black Guy Die First?!" can also represent a substantive question about social worth because early Black deaths (or of people of color)—while previously the source of macabre "inside jokes"—can serve as a revealing qualitative marker of the value and visibility of Black life.

The book's undergirding premise of psycho-segregation means that while society no longer *physically enforces segregation* the way it did under the "old," Jim Crow-esque racism, the "new" challenge posed by Racism 2.0 is a society that struggles with *psychological segregation*, whereby the lower quality of images depicting non-White people that we ingest mentally communicates inferiority or lesser value. Repeated consumption of these racially devaluing images then fosters barriers in the mind; thus, after sufficient mandatory "diversity training" at work, an individual will sign off on the company's policy that they will eschew blatant racial discrimination but may unwittingly commit a racially based microaggression later that same day based upon a false assumption that they *privately held in their mind*.

To those looking to increase their media literacy when it comes to race, one must understand that racism is not just limited to Jim Crow-esque examples of a starkly separated society blemished by "separate but equal" park benches, water fountains, public restrooms, and seating sections on busses. The harsh segregationist themes of exclusion have given way to more subtle themes of expendability. Fewer instances of overt racism within society (due to policy or culture changes) do not necessarily mean less racism within society; racism has not evaporated insomuch as it has *evolved*. This book therefore forces us to reconcile with the more difficult questions regarding how our definitions of racism can actually be expanded—namely, thinking beyond the limited construct that only verbally hurling a racial epithet qualifies as racist behavior.

But what if they still think it?

Or what if they still see it?

Even better, what if they still see it in a movie?

But how much is a moving picture worth anyway?

And what if that moving picture is a mainstream movie?

BUT WHAT IS A MAINSTREAM MOVIE?

The *average* cost to produce and market a major movie is roughly $100 million (Mueller, 2022), with some movies like *Pirates of the Caribbean: On Stranger Tides* inching closer to a nearly half-a-billion-dollar budget at $410.6 million (Munson, 2022). Practically speaking, with such significant sums of money invested and expended with no guarantee of a return on investment, what then is the most practical course of action? It follows that with several competitive movie studios juggling multiple investments on multiple film projects simultaneously, any idea offered to help minimize risk while maximizing profits sounds like a good idea. In other words, while mainstream movies have continued to evolve over the years, **major movie studios** still largely adhere to formulaic patterns to improve their chances for financial success.

The analysis within these pages applies primarily to **mainstream movies**, or those movies that have the highest level of visibility within contemporary pop culture, as they have the greatest potential to reach the **greatest possible audience**. Often, the greatest possible audience is not found, but rather created. Major movie studios factor into their budgets millions of dollars and months of lead time in order to prepare people for the possibility of getting excited about handing over their hard-earned dollars to the studio once the movie product is ready for sale. The ability to begin promoting on a national scale several months before a movie's scheduled release not only signals a healthy marketing budget; it also signals the studio's faith in a movie to penetrate the **mainstream pipeline** successfully and recoup significant investment costs. The extended length of time studios use to market movies is significant because it virtually guarantees repeated exposure to movie ads prior to the theatrical release. Consider how Disney's 2010 release of *Tron: Legacy,* according to the *New York Times,* culminated 3½ years of advance marketing, or "priming the audience pump" (Barnes, 2010). Further, with the greatest possible audience (and revenues) in mind, a studio's desire not to "offend" audiences may impact creative decisions—especially if dealing with concepts or ideas that challenge the "average American" to think critically about race-related issues that may be uncomfortable or cause "drama."

There are six major mainstream movie factors that clue the audience member into the fact that a significant investment was made in the movie and, therefore, steps will be taken to recoup its investment. Moreover, these factors clarify the threshold ground rules for applying the HARM Theory rubrics to be discussed at length in Chapters 3 through 14. The six mainstream movie factors at a glance are:

1. Full-length release
2. Widespread distribution
3. Production/marketing costs
4. Large box office sales
5. A-list talent
6. Mainstream media exposure (Gooding, 2017, p. 16)

Additionally, bonus mainstream movie factors help clarify in more detail the criteria for whether the movie is a mainstream movie. Bonus mainstream movie factors include:

1. Adaptations
2. Themed attractions
3. Promotional tie-ins
4. Merchandising
5. Oscar "bounce"

For the reader's convenience, Table 1.2 briefly details why each Mainstream Movie Factor and Bonus Movie Factor is significant (Gooding 2017, pp. 30–34):

TAKE IT FROM THE TOP

Race can be such a polarizing topic that valid arguments made about questionable or offensive material are frequently swept up and then swept aside in a sea of emotion. My analysis is unique because it is designed to provide movie watchers with a consistent rubric that allows everyone to engage dispassionately in a constructive dialogue without sugarcoating the harsh realities of the disparities seen throughout Hollywood. Mainstream movies are a shared social experience of significant value; they are important tools used both to inform and influence cultural identity. As it stands, American mainstream movies are seen and enjoyed by diverse audiences not just in America, but all over the world. I apply my racial analysis exclusively to mainstream movies (as opposed to independent films or "made-for-TV" movies) because they have consistently demonstrated the greatest potential for societal, cultural, and financial impact.

Yet, in applying our racial rubrics (explained in Chapter 2) to the frame of Hollywood mainstream movies, the question then becomes, *but which movies*? How can the integrity of such analysis be credible without randomly isolating and targeting select examples for scrutiny? Hundreds of mainstream movies are released annually, with Statista Research Department remarking that "in 2022, a total of 449 movies were released in the United States and Canada, up from 406 in the previous year. Still, the 2022 figures amounts to about 56.7 percent of the 792 titles released

Table 1.2. Mainstream Movie and Bonus Factors

Factor	Significance
Full-length release	A full-length feature typically ranges from 90 minutes to 3 hours in length. A **first-run movie** is first exhibited to the public in a movie theater after a heavy promotion schedule. Such a movie typically is released either on a Wednesday or a Friday in movie theater chains across the country, for which moviegoers must pay admission for the viewing privilege.
Widespread distribution (within the United States)	Given that there are nearly 6,000 theaters in the United States as of 2020, a movie that penetrates at least a third of those theaters will qualify as being nationally distributed in the United States (Statista, 2023a). Based upon distribution models, some movies like *Pacific Rim* (2013) can actually outearn domestic box office sales, as it earned just over $100 million domestically but $309.2 million abroad (Epting, 2020).
Production/ marketing costs	In addition to, or even apart from, having high-quality content, one simply must have a high-quality production and marketing campaign to position the movie for optimal success. The average cost of producing and marketing a movie is roughly $100 million. This high financial bar sends a loud and clear message that not everyone can afford to show and tell their story on the mainstream stage.
Box office sales	Gross box office receipts are an effective tool to assess the preferences of the viewing audience. Top-grossing mainstream movies now routinely make hundreds of millions of dollars at the box office, sometimes within a single weekend (e.g., *Star Wars: Episode VII—The Force Awakens*)! Not to injure or insult any purists reading this text, but "the bottom line" is one key factor those within the industry use as a metric with which to measure and adjudge a movie's "success"—technical innovations with new camera techniques and stellar costuming and set design and crisp acoustics aside, if the movie simply does not sell, it is adjudged a "fail." Opening weekend box office sales are frequently referenced in making this determination.
A-list talent	With all due respect to Lady Gaga and Bradley Cooper, *A Star Is Born* onscreen, but not usually in lower-budget productions with "unknown" talent. Typically, to shore up the significant investment, studios go out of their way to inform the public that their high-quality production that people should pay for has top-notch A-list talent worth spending one's time with. This goes hand in hand with marketing for if a studio spends $20 million on one A-list actor alone, chances are high they are going to invest considerable funds to ensure that they recoup their investment provided the movie is marketed and promoted on a large, global scale.
Mainstream media exposure	Mainstream media consists of a dizzying array of information channels, structured and designed to reach the greatest possible audience through established nationwide marketing and distribution networks. There are television shows, newspapers, magazines, and radio programs accessed by vast numbers of people throughout the country, thereby serving as a means of sharing information, centralizing thought and organizing loose societal networks.

Bonus Factors	Significance
Adaptations	An adaptation occurs when a new movie idea is crafted from an already established or well-known book, television show, or comic book. While the Top Ten list can thank Marvel comic books for at least four entries with the *Avengers* series and *Spider-Man: No Way Home* entries (see Table 1.3), some of the most well-known movies in cinematic history, such as *The Godfather, The Wizard of Oz*, and *The Lord of the Rings*, were built on the backs of known commodities already introduced into the mainstream pipeline.
Themed attractions	The creation of a theme park ride solely scripted around a recently released movie indicates that the movie referenced is well within the mainstream pipeline—millions of dollars are invested in the hopes that millions of fans are familiar enough with the movie to be inspired to come visit their locale and spend hundreds of millions of dollars. Think of the Wizarding World of Harry Potter installation at Universal Studios theme parks or the Avengers Campus at Disney's California Adventure Park as a couple of significant examples that demonstrate this phenomenon. Even if one has not seen these movies, if they plan for months to take a family a vacation for thousands of dollars, whether they like it or not, these movie outlets will be there.
Promotional tie-ins	National promotional tie-ins bolster a movie's marketing efforts since the studio and the corporate partner can promote each other's product either independently or jointly. The promotional tie-ins also illustrate how corporate partners must be involved early on in the movie-making process. For example, not only did the original blockbuster 1993 hit *Jurassic Park* garner attention for its not-so-subtle product tie-ins with products like the Ford Explorer, but the 2015 *Jurassic World* marketing campaign was even more explicit in making such connections with corporations like Mercedes-Benz having standalone ads exhorting viewers to "Watch the new GLE Coupé in *Jurassic World* in theaters June 12th," along with a website promoting the tie-in, just in case potential viewers were liable to think the connection or product placement was coincidental (Harwell, 2015).
Merchandising	If a movie is popular with the paying public, then studios will maximize the movie's popularity by keeping the movie alive in the minds of moviegoers for as long as possible with lucrative licensing deals. For instance, as popular and "successful" as the 2017 surprise-hit racially themed horror movie *Get Out* was, few sightings of *Get Out*–themed bedsheets in national big-box chain stores like Target have been made in contrast to bedsheets (aaaaaaaaand blankets, beach towels, towels, bathing suits, swim bags, sunglasses, wrist watches, puzzle sets, board games, plush toys, socks, flip-flops, lunch boxes, backpacks, action figures, LEGO® playsets, coffee mugs, ink pens, hats, t-shirts, desk lamps, water bottles, refrigerator magnets, headbands, etc.) featuring *Star Wars* characters.
Oscar "bounce"	The Academy Awards are regarded as the most prestigious awards in the movie business. In an industry of so many people, only a select few are rewarded with an Oscar, an exclusivity that only adds to its prestige and value. Sponsored by the Academy of Motion Picture Arts and Sciences, this annual televised event has taken on global proportions, commanding top dollar ranging between \$1.6 million and \$2.1 million for 30-second commercials for those vying to advertise during the ceremony's internationally televised broadcast (Bradley, 2023).

in 2019, before the COVID-19 outbreak" (Statista, 2023b). With such a high volume of cinematic releases, can one be consistent with such sensitive racial analysis? Can one determine that one movie is representative over another across multiple genres featuring different actresses and actors filtered through a myriad of various directors' visions?

Well, pardon the random movie reference that merely includes the word "yes" in response to the rhetorical question posed in the prior sentence, but the good news is, *Yes Virginia, there is a Santa Claus*! Quite simply, many of the questions in the foregoing paragraph can be answered with a common metric any traditional moviegoer can leverage, namely the movie's performance in the original venue specifically built and designed for it to literally illuminate and stimulate audiences of all ages all over the world: box office ticket sales. While box office revenue is certainly not the only metric by which we can and should measure movies, it is a mighty and influential one. After all, the bottom line is *the bottom line*. Part of the bottom line is that with movies requiring such significant investments of time, money, and energy to produce, we as consumers and fans must not lose sight of the fact that these movies made for our consumption are not made purely for altruistically artistic purposes. Rather, movies are made to make money.

Thus, measuring how much revenue a movie generates provides generous clues as to its cultural value, significance, and influence. To demonstrate the strength and viability of the racial rubric (i.e., archetypes and prototypes), we will apply it to the Top Ten–grossing films of all time at the time of publication (Table 1.3). The list is procured from experts at Box Office Mojo (n.d.), which is powered by the recognized authority on movie information, the Internet Movie Database (IMDb), and incorporates international ticket sales. If the problematic patterns appear in the Top Ten films, then likely the rubric will apply to other movies that garnered smaller audiences. By focusing on the Top Ten films, understandably such films may not be fully reflective of the breadth and depth of the entire cinematic experience. But recall, the focus of this text is on *mainstream movies,* which already precludes a significant number of excellent documentaries, made-for-television releases, or independent films by innovative filmmakers. Again, the bottom line is the bottom line.

N.B.: Although this list is not dated, the movie with the latest release date is *Avatar: The Way of the Water,* December 2022.

As opposed to the horror, drama, or romance genres, most of the Top Ten–grossing films of all-time internationally fit the family-friendly, catchall category of "action/summer blockbuster." Even if you have not seen a single film from the Top Ten, chances are you know someone in your family or circle of friends who has seen at least one of the movies on the list. Even without having seen any or all of the Top Ten titles, the chances are very high again that you have heard of the movie or seen some public manifestation of it commercially through some of the mainstream movie bonus factors detailed in this chapter (i.e., merchandising, spinoffs). In other words, these Top Ten movies remind us of how ubiquitous movies can be and how they can penetrate and influence our daily life even if we have not undergone the formal viewing experience.

Thus, to stem off critiques that the rubric described in this book is applied selectively to hand-picked examples (which still would not negate nor alter the

Table 1.3. Top Ten Highest Grossing Films of All-Time Internationally (as of June 2023)

	Title	*Gross*	*Year*	*Studio*
1	*Avatar*	$2,923,706,026	2009	20th Century Studios
2	*Avengers: Endgame*	$2,799,439,100	2019	Marvel Studios
3	*Avatar: The Way of Water*	$2,315,057,233	2022	20th Century Studios
4	*Titanic*	$2,261,385,180	1997	20th Century Studios
5	*Star Wars VII: The Force Awakens*	$2,071,310,218	2015	Walt Disney Studios
6	*Avengers: Infinity War*	$2,052,415,039	2018	Marvel Studios
7	*Spider-Man: No Way Home*	$1,921,847,111	2021	Columbia Pictures and Marvel Studios
8	*Jurassic World*	$1,671,537,444	2015	Universal Studios
9	*The Lion King*	$1,663,075,401	2019	Walt Disney Studios
10	*The Avengers*	$1,520,538,536	2012	20th Century Studios

problematic nature of any scenes analyzed herein), the author had little influence or jurisdiction over which films made the overall Top Ten list. If examples of non-White archetypes and White prototypes are found in these highly successful films, then perhaps we must ask ourselves more critical questions as to how and why potentially problematic racial patterns can and do remain hidden in plain sight. As the book explains and illustrates how archetypes and prototypes operate, all examples will be furnished from the list of Top Ten movies to underscore that many of us viewers worldwide have been more exposed to this pattern than we might care to admit.

The rubric also can be applied to mainstream movies outside the Top Ten list, but the focus must remain upon mainstream movies as films made exclusively for television, foreign productions, and independent releases operate by different financial constraints that affect the content differently. In other words, a niche independent film that is neither built nor designed to reach the greatest possible audience is more liberated to explore more serious themes and not have cookie-cutter denouement by movie's end the way more mainstream movies are designed—with some notable Hollywood directors like Martin Scorsese referencing Marvel films (of which four made the Top Ten list) as "formulaic fairground rides" (Salmon, 2019).

While we are on the topic of Top Ten movies, not a single one of the Top Ten–grossing movies worldwide have a non-White *human character* who receives "top billing," or is the primary protagonist of the film. As the author of *Black Oscars: From Mammy to Minny, What the Academy Awards Tell Us About African Americans* (Gooding, 2020), I am especially sensitive to the fact that hardly any of the 10 selections have many prominent Black characters that influence the plotline or story development. The trilogy of *Avengers, Avengers: Infinity War,* and *Avengers: Endgame* mostly employed ensemble casts, which included Samuel L. Jackson as

Nick Fury and Chadwick Boseman as Black Panther, but both roles were neither central to all three movies nor as high-profile as Robert Downey, Jr.'s Iron Man, Tom Holland's Spider-man, or Chris Hemsworth's Mighty Thor. Both *Avatar* and *Avatar: The Way of Water* movies have Sam Worthington's Jake Sully starring as the White male protagonist who also serves as the movie's central hero with his supporting love interest voiced by Afro-Latina actress Zoe Saldaña (as an aside, Saldaña's character was only seen in alien form, whereas Sam Worthington's central character was seen in both human and alien form).

The oldest blockbuster on the list, *Titanic*, likely will have defenders point out that it would be anachronistic to have Black passengers on board a luxury ship in 1912 (due to racial restriction of resources). Although Haitian Joseph Laroche was reportedly one of the only Black people onboard, Laroche was not a character expressly featured in the only Top Ten movie made in the 20th century (Course, 2016). In *Spider-Man: No Way Home*, Tom Holland's leading love interest was played by Zendaya, an actress who claims both African American and German/Scottish mixed-race ancestry, while his proverbial "best friend" was played by Hawai'ian actor Jacob Batalon. Do note that Holland's love interest also fulfills the pattern whereby a woman of color approaching the White aesthetic in appearance may be deemed more marketable with higher profile opportunities in contrast to other non-White women who have less ambiguity in approaching White physical features. Black French actor Omar Sy made crisp and brief appearances in *Jurassic World* but was certainly conspicuously absent during the movie's climactic scenes. None of the non-White actors listed above could be mistaken as lead protagonists based upon their character arcs, screen time, and dialogue or presence within promotional materials.

Out of the Top Ten, the movie with perhaps the greatest degree of representation of non-White characters would be the 2019 remake of *The Lion King,* which had a predominately Black cast with the two leading roles of African lions Simba and Nala voiced by talented entertainers Donald Glover and Beyoncé. However, if the reader is inexplicably somehow unfamiliar with these films, both the original 1994 *The Lion King* film and its remake a quarter of a century later do not feature live human characters onscreen since they are both animated movies, with the 2019 remake benefiting from computer graphic animation (nor are human characters depicted in the movie itself). Not to mention, as a testament of *The Lion King*'s global reach, even though the remake "only" took in $1.6 billion at the box office, the storied franchise itself earned an additional $8 billion at box offices around the world from its live stage adaptation. Placing matters further in perspective, the stage adaptation has "made almost as much as every single Star Wars film combined" (Seymour, 2017).

However, I wonder whether the box office sales would have been similarly robust if movie audiences had to connect Black voices with Black bodies onscreen, as opposed to being filtered through the "protective layer" of computer graphic–animated lions onscreen. In other words, would a movie comprising a majority of (live, human) "Black guys" in the cast ever break into the Top Ten–grossing list of all time simply because audiences worldwide were able to connect with Black characters as people?

To answer the question formulating on many minds, the 2018 *Black Panther* does indeed come in at number 15 on the list! However, while this data point is certainly noteworthy and encouraging with respect to the future diversification of Hollywood, we also must be clear-eyed about what factors have precipitated this success. With both *The Lion King* remake and *Black Panther* releases, while considerable funds were invested in production, the risk of rejection was mitigated by the fact that these two financially successful movies featuring majority non-White casts were already part of globally successful franchises with plenty of name recognition and exposure. Particularly with *Black Panther,* it is also important to note that it was the 18th movie released from the Marvel Comic Universe, with the first release coming a decade earlier with the initial installation of the 2008 *Iron Man.* Finally, with *Black Panther*, the fictional character was first introduced via comic books in 1966, over half a century before the 2018 movie release. In contrast, Top Ten movies like *Titanic* or the *Avatar* series simply featured new stories revolving around White characters that became instant hits.

But I digress—for whatever it is worth, the voicing of Simba and Nala throughout the whole movie was a possible correction from the original 1994 box office smash that featured White actors Matthew Broderick and Moira Kelly as the principal voices of adult Simba and Nala (although Black voice actors played young Simba and Nala, and other prominent non-White actors such as Whoopi Goldberg, James Earl Jones, Cheech Marin, and Robert Guillaume had significant speaking parts in the original 1994 version as well). Even though part of the marketing campaign was the Walt Disney Company corporation's first foray into storytelling in "Africa," which we know to hold a special significance for many people of the African Diaspora, including Black Americans, Disney has not been shy about leveraging this *Lion King* product and cultural and symbolic themes from Africa for other product offerings, with its (double negative alert) noninexpensive Disney's Animal Kingdom Lodge properties.

And last, but not least would be *Star Wars Episode VII: The Force Awakens*, which does indeed include prominent characters outside of the common White male protagonist model that has rendered Hollywood so much financial success over the years. Of course, the new badass Jedi to be anointed is our White female heroine, Rey, as played by British actress Daisy Ridley. Alongside her are her two male friends, Poe and Finn, played by Guatemalan-born Oscar Isaac and British Nigerian John Boyega, respectively. Poe's character never directly references "Guatemalan heritage" throughout all the intergalactic happenings in the movie, and therefore if an audience member did not know his background ahead of time, they just might assume that he was "White" or "White passing" given his physical appearance. Boyega, on the other hand, is visibly identifiable as being non-White onscreen.

A simple YouTube search will reveal how numerous "critics" with ample time on their hands apparently have made critiquing Finn's dubious role a pleasurable pastime. While many viewers might be overinvesting their energies in such critiques, in their defense, Finn's character simply did not live up to the hyped expectations Disney set in motion with its strategic marketing campaign that heavily suggested a much more substantive, nuanced, and involved role for Finn. Boyega apparently agreed with this assessment and based upon his own direct experience ended up offering a critique of his own.

After maintaining years of silence in the name of solidarity and teamwork, in the aftermath of George Floyd's senseless murder at the hands of an unflinching Derek Chauvin in May 2020 that sparked international protests and dialogues about race, Boyega then stated publicly, "What I say to Disney is do not market a black character as important and then push them aside" (Famuerwa, 2020). To Boyega's point, while the movie may have been marketed as a progressive departure from the traditional White alpha male character serving as the central "tent pole" supporting the story's central narrative, a simple look at movie posters and trailers will tell you what you already know: Finn may play a significant role, but he does not play the role of primary protagonist. That honor goes to our heroine and largest face of the campaign, Rey.

Notwithstanding the foregoing, I wish to stress that the Top Ten list is merely a starting point in a conversation in attempts to find a **common denominator** to which many can relate: the common denominator of ticket sales. These movies, of course, are not indicative of the ever-expansive breadth of options available to global consumers—but that is precisely the point. In light of the increased number of choices, these 10 movies from a fiscal standpoint rise to the top in terms of patronage and support at the box office. Yet as an aside, the Top Ten list provides an opportunity to reconcile with the fact that only a limited number of entities are producing high-performing movies at the highest levels—apart from *Jurassic World,* which was produced by Universal Studios, the other nine titles in the Top Ten list were produced or distributed in part or wholly by outfits currently owned by Walt Disney Studios. (N.B.: As of 2019, 20th Century Studios is owned by the Walt Disney Company while Columbia Pictures is owned by Sony, thereby explaining why as of print *Spider-Man: No Way Home* is not available on Disney+ like all other Marvel movies; see Table 1.3) (Littleton, 2019; Sandwell, 2022).

Again, the Top Ten list may not be *dispositive* of what millions of viewers digest from Hollywood on a daily basis, but given their significant levels of global penetration, the list is at least *indicative* of some of the more popular types of mainstream images audiences consume worldwide. We know that such images are circulated widely, but what we want to explore further is what these images mean when analyzed from the perspective and framing lens of race.

As presumptively more people have seen the movies enumerated in the Top Ten all-time highest grossing list than, say, the Top Ten independent movies as voted by critics, which would be inherently more subjective and evaluative, there likely is more potential for these movies to enjoy increased coverage, exposure, and influence.

Hence, if a movie makes it to the all-time Top Ten box office gross list, that is a pretty solid quantitative indicator that the movie is not only popular but is part of **mainstream culture**. Potentially, the greater the revenue a movie generates, the greater its potential for influence and exposure of the symbols, images, and messages contained therein. So, when these movies are totaling billions at the box office to global audiences, the question is in addition to a (hopefully) entertaining display, what is it that people see when it comes to race? Is there a sincerity of diversity or a mere illusion of inclusion? While we may have differing ideas on what race means, there is nothing to quibble about with the numbers—and our society (and media) often makes a big fuss over a movie that makes a lot of cash. After all, as some wise men from Staten Island said it best many moons ago: "Cash rules everything around me (C.R.E.A.M.)" (WuTangClan-VEVO, 2014).

Yet, if the expression "the bottom line is the bottom line" bears any merit, then Hollywood audiences have demonstrated that at least when it comes to the Top Ten-grossing movies of all time, most of the movies included in this rarefied air consist of storylines that showcase or feature primarily White characters. These movies are not necessarily classified as "White movies," but rather are known collectively as **mainstream movies.**

MAINSTREAM RACISM IN BLACK AND WHITE

I will never forget when my good friend Khalid Patterson posed to me many moons ago the riddle of, "If mainstream Hollywood *was* racist at some point in time in the past, then when exactly did it stop being racist?" This inquiry made a deep impression on me as we began analyzing movies critically even before I became a graduate student—when all I had were rough-cut theories and ideas that required further testing. However, if asked to pick definitive "start dates" for racism making itself manifest in Hollywood, there are at least two key dates that should be remembered and stored to rote memory: (1) 1915 as the release year for Hollywood's first groundbreaking feature length movie, *The Birth of a Nation*, and (2) Hollywood's first talking picture ever created, *The Jazz Singer,* released in 1927. While both movies are still widely circulated and discussed for their historically significant contributions to the canon, both movies also are considered "racist" for a myriad of historical, content-related reasons that film historians could lecture about for hours on end. For whatever it is worth, **minstrelsy** and offensive, problematic, racist visual iconography is ensconced within Hollywood history.

Further, with the acceptance of minstrelsy and blackface within early Hollywood, many White performers abused their dominant power position within a Jim Crow society to not just "poke fun" of other members of society, but to weaponize entertainment as a means to express that an entire race of people were inferior and not worthy of dignity nor respect within mainstream society. To further add insult to injury, many Whites profited off this widespread minstrelsy practice as a key ingredient of cultural appropriation. As a direct result of this economic exploitation, millions of Whites have made billions of dollars from this shameful practice over the years both in and out of Hollywood. Sadly, it is not an exaggeration to state "millions made billions" when accounting for the sheer volume of minstrel-based products produced over a century starting in the 1830s with Thomas Dartmouth Rice being known as the "Father of Minstrelsy" with his introduction of the blackface character "Jim Crow" in the aftermath of the Civil War up until the 1950s with public performances by the blackface troupe

Vernon & Ryan (Jim Crow Museum, 2020). Products ranged from live shows to books to amateur blackface kits to art to trinkets to food products and more (University of Chicago, 2013).

Considering Hollywood's birth during the Jim Crow era, is it truly any surprise that given the heavy proliferation of insulting non-White imagery that permeated the most popular mainstream media channels at the time (i.e., newspapers, printed products, music, live performances, etc.), that as technology evolved, so would the magnitude of the insult? Meaning, once society transitioned from static images to moving pictures, the potential to move audiences toward distorted images only increased in ease and efficacy. While the technology changed (and improved) over time, the minds behind the technology remained relatively static. While the movie industry was borne about in the 1920s not long after the still photograph camera was invented, this advanced technology was nonetheless used to reanimate and, in many ways, reinforce, older, antiquated ideas that first infected society in the early 17th century (Hannah-Jones, 2019).

When viewed from a different perspective, movies like *The Jazz Singer*, which popularized blackface minstrelsy globally, merely made visible and tangible problematic ideas about the presumed lower value and visibility of Black Americans first made popular some two centuries earlier. Two centuries before *The Jazz Singer* even came to be, in 1727 there was no still camera, let alone movie cameras laying around—yet the idea of presumed Black inferiority in relation to Whites was most definitely in existence, if the Middle Passage and Triangular Trade involving the sale of enslaved Black human beings are credible data points (National Park Service, n.d.). The point is that even as society adapted and improved over the years, the thought of publicly portraying Black Americans as equals was an obvious omission. Technology improved, but the White gaze behind it did not.

Early American film reflects this problematic perspective—which is clearly and literally seen in "black and white." Not only is early American film punctuated by film that is technically devoid of color and presents as the colors black and white with numerous shades in between, but the term "black and white" can refer to a simplistic dynamic between two perspectives. Early filmmakers leveraged this psychology to make clear—with minimal shades of gray—who was more attractive and therefore more valuable, or superior.

The key for such "black and white" thinking was contrast and juxtaposition—when considering Hattie McDaniel's "breakthrough" performance as the first non-White individual to win an Academy Award for her role as Mammy in *Gone with the Wind*, it was for an image that contrasted heavily against the White standard of beauty. Scholar Charlene Regester notes that "In many films of the pre-1960 period, the physicality of the Black actress as shadow was used as a contrast to enhance the whiteness (sexuality and beauty) of the leading white actress" (2010, p. 250). Thus, while Scarlett O'Hara represented the paragon of beauty and femininity, Mammy (as was her assigned character name) was darker skinned, more heavyset in weight, less polished in grammar, and constantly had her hair covered in a bandana; there was no "competition" between the two images and the movie creators could wash their hands of any wrongdoing, as they were merely fulfilling the fantasies of paying Jim Crow audiences.

RACISM: NOW IN LIVING COLOR

The Jim Crow era, an extended period of legalized racial segregation within the United States over roughly the first half of the 20th century, is known for separating White people from visibly identifiable people of color in all aspects of public life. Within mainstream media, the Jim Crow era is unfortunately frequently distilled down to mere access to public bathrooms, water fountains, and park benches. Yet, Jim Crow was comprehensive in character and overwhelming in its execution. Jim Crow apparently was so intense with its racial segregationist policies that the Third Reich studied 1930s American Jim Crow policies, and "inspired" Nazi architects took notice (Little, 2017).

While numerous aspects of public life were (and continue to be) racially segregated (e.g., analysis of residential segregation sponsored by the University of California–Berkeley found "more than 80% of large metropolitan areas in the United States were more segregated in 2019 than they were in 1990"; Semuels, 2021), the formal period of Jim Crow is bracketed by two U.S. Supreme Court cases beginning at approximately the turn of the 20th century with the *Plessy v. Ferguson* Supreme Court decision and concluding roughly at the century's midpoint with the 1954 *Brown v. Board of Education* decisions (*Plessy v. Ferguson*, 1896; *Brown v. Board of Education*, 1954). Again, racial discrimination most certainly exists outside of this 58-year period, but this reflects the years when discrimination was legally recognized as standard social practice. In fact, this legal system was so robust, Nazis and South Africans were both inspired and took note of American legalized discrimination tactics.

However, many civic books when discussing this period often focus on only one aspect of discrimination by publishing black-and-white photographs of disparate water fountains side by side. Jim Crow was much more damaging than an individual having an inferior bathroom to use, being limited to the balcony of a movie theater, or having a certain park bench upon which one could sit. Jim Crow was much more expansive, encompassing, and insidious. Jim Crow affected economic and political opportunities as well.

The aim of such legalized tactics was effectively to communicate that Blacks were simply not deserving of equal treatment—as the "separate, but equal" mantra was always a false premise. There is no way two water fountains of different size and functionality could be considered equal—everyone looking at the two side by side understand this. However, as times have changed, so have the methodologies and instrumentalities of racial discrimination. Unlike denser matter that remains obstinate in its ability to change quickly (e.g., a rocky boulder), new forms of racial discrimination will be demonstrated to be quite fluid in form within these pages, meaning that similar to water, racism can "take the shape of its container"—kinda sorta like the shapeshifting T-1000 Terminator series!

Numerous policies have come and gone creating new "containers," or new approaches to racial conflict. However, despite innovative, daring, and groundbreaking attempts, racism stubbornly and persistently works its way into the implementation and execution of said policies whenever people are involved. Hence, what viewing audiences must be keenly aware of is that not all symbols and messages need to or necessarily will expressly communicate that White characters are "more valuable" than non-White characters. However, based upon the cumulative effect of mainstream movie images, a question for audiences to consider is to what degree do consistently devalued images of non-White characters affect what people see and expect of others outside the movie theater?

In other words, the blatantly racist portrayals of *Birth of a Nation, The Jazz Singer,* or *Gone with the Wind* indeed reflect a more overtly racist era in society generally. But contemporary movies, while not employing such overt, obvious, and offensive symbols, nonetheless communicate messages of inferiority or lesser value of non-White characters—especially when juxtaposed with White characters within the same visible continuum. This psycho-segregation is key to still having audiences walk out of theaters with roughly similar ideas about value and difference (with respect to race) without having to pay the "penalty" of having been associated with vitriolic or highly problematic material that would easily draw public criticism.

Thus, racism as we knew it is no longer *en vogue*; it is currently downright unbecoming to appear in public as not having tolerance or to harbor disdain for diversity. In contrast to blistering 19th-century U.S. Supreme Court decisions that infamously declared that Black people "had no rights which the white man was bound to respect; and that the negro might justly and lawfully be reduced to slavery for his benefit" (*Dred Scott v. Sanford*, 1857, p. 407) most of us are now more sensitive to the idea that people of different races should be respected in our new age. Racism 2.0 therefore refers to the stubborn persistence of negative, disparaging narratives of old that are more refined and stylized and thus less obvious and overtly offensive in appearance. Present discrimination is much more subtle, suave and sophisticated in appearance and thereby more difficult to detect, let alone gain consensus upon.

Racially problematic thought patterns have been updated (i.e., 2.0) to increase capacity and efficiency while minimizing cost and waste, much like our quieter, faster, sleeker, and cleaner high-speed trains in contrast to the loud, lumbering, and pollutive locomotives of old. While American society has made significant social improvements specifically around the topic of race over the years, current data suggest that there may remain a smidgen of room for improvement.

It is true that many Americans and several pockets of America still observe "poor habits" from the past—whether consciously or unconsciously—that perpetuate class, gender, and racial discrimination against other Americans. Such discrimination is implied generally by statistical data but seldom acknowledged directly among individuals who have been raised by their parents not to "see the color of another's skin" but to see "the content of one's character" instead (Associated Press, 2013). Within these pages, we aim to tackle this issue very directly. For there was indeed a time when America and Hollywood were racist. It is now time to explore whether our present-day mainstream Hollywood movies are free from racism or whether, under the principles of Racism 2.0, the same tropes are being sold as a sequel at a theater near you. Another way to frame the inquiry is to ask more directly: If Hollywood's first groundbreaking feature-length movie, *The Birth of a Nation* (1915), and Hollywood's first talking film ever created, *The Jazz Singer* (1927), could be considered "racist," since they both featured White actors in blackface, then when exactly did Hollywood stop being racist? Feel free to pick a year, any year actually, between 1927 and present day.

Although the United States is still predominately White, it has grown more diverse at a breathtaking pace in recent decades. Whether Hollywood will reflect America's newfound diversity remains to be seen. As it stands, American mainstream movies are seen and enjoyed by diverse audiences not just in America, but all over the world. There is no debating that mainstream movies are time-consuming, multi-million-dollar projects that require the coordinated effort of many different companies, agencies, and individuals. Due to the size, scale, and cost of creating mainstream movies, everything you see onscreen has a function and a reason for its placement. The purpose of this book is to stimulate a broader discussion about the significance of race within contemporary mainstream movies and their impact on mainstream society.

Regardless of whether you are an aspiring academic or an avid moviegoer, all audiences are welcome to participate in this dynamic discussion. If you are looking for a place to analyze and discuss racial images that you may or may not have seen in your movie, then consider yourself seated in the right theater. Mainstream movies are a shared social experience of significant value. They are important tools used both to inform and influence cultural identity.

The formulaic nature of mainstream movies is driven by the ever-pressing need to consistently reach a mass audience. When a Hollywood studio takes a risk by investing hundreds of millions of dollars into a single movie project, it also seeks to minimize that risk by going with "what works" to improve the movie's chance of becoming profitable. It is, after all, the entertainment *business*. This formulaic nature of mainstream movies is part of the underlying reason why Hollywood relies on a consistent pattern of racial imagery. During a movie, viewers must somehow process the various racial images they see, whether consciously or unconsciously. The concepts within this book will enable and empower readers to identify non-White character patterns beyond a context of loosely organized and isolated examples. Many viewers are misled because they only look for blatantly obvious caricatures that are indisputably offensive. It is now high time to learn the subtle yet significant ways in which movies communicate coded messages about race often "hidden in plain sight." Moreover, with a firm understanding of Hollywood's racial patterns, you will be liberated from having to "see every movie" to competently discuss race in the movies.

By the book's conclusion, you will find that although Hollywood is a White-dominated industry, it consistently produces lucrative mainstream movies designed to appeal "universally" to racially diverse audiences around the world. Nevertheless, Hollywood mainstream movies routinely present a limited view of minorities, in stark contrast to the broadly developed spectrum of White characters. Given Hollywood's extensive reach and economic impact, the consistently marginalized non-White images in mainstream movies reflect and reinforce messages of racial imbalance worldwide.

CHAPTER 2

Value and Visibility

NOTHING NEW TO REPORT

There is no debating that mainstream movies are arduous, time-consuming, multi-million-dollar projects that require the coordinated effort of many different companies, agencies, and individuals. Due to the size, scale, and cost of creating mainstream movies, everything we see onscreen has a function and a reason for its placement. Few accidents are assumed. Whenever we watch a polished, final movie project onscreen, very little of what we see is the product of mere happenstance and coincidence. With so much invested and on the line for a Hollywood production, we assume that at least one person has thought about anything that one's eye can see onscreen—even racially problematic material. Many Hollywood studios are well aware of the marketing strategies they employ based upon demographic information, and leverage race where convenient for profit, consistent with the principles of *institutional* racism.

Yet, the conundrum is that if we were to sit down and take a poll of Hollywood professionals and inquire whether they as *individuals* purposely wish to create products that racially demean or devalue non-White participation onscreen, chances are low that many will answer definitively in the affirmative. Thus, while numerous Hollywood professionals are quite conscious about their craft and are aware of patterns and formulas for "what works" at the box office, there simultaneously exists a "blind spot" or inability to see "hidden in plain sight" how racially disparaging tropes within mainstream movies stubbornly persist. How do we explain this *Blindspotting*?

This tension between institutional and individual racism leads us to a question that some may consider *An Indecent Proposal*: namely, "What is the reason racially problematic portrayals exist?" For our purposes, even in adopting an optimistic viewpoint that most creatives in Hollywood do not intend to appear as racially intolerant or insensitive, we must reckon with the impact of numerous racially problematic cinematic scenes that have been produced by Hollywood corporate studios that we must presume know *exactly* what they are doing. I proposed that we can reconcile this tension by employing what I call the *3Es framework* when it comes to race relations. Quite simply, the 3Es holds that most people in the world are indeed good people (although conceivably, Dallas Cowboys football fans are likely one of the most glaring exceptions to this premise), but that they are limited by the 3Es—a lack of education, exposure, and experience (Gooding et al., 2023).

Education represents information—and accumulating factual information by way of data (e.g., primary and secondary sources) is a solid foundation with which to start. Yet, political skirmishes in populous states such as Texas and Florida over critical race theory and Advanced Placement African American History demonstrate that deciding *which facts* to educate the youth with are still in contention, with numerous education advocates simply wanting to reconcile by telling the holistic truth (Zahneis & Supiano, 2023).

The next step in the 3Es progression is *exposure*, which is the next level of understanding. Exposure can mean extended conversations, additional readings, musical and artistic works, cuisine samplings, or specific opportunities to deepen one's connection to the material. More importantly, as one begins to apply the education or information acquired above rote recall of certain facts and dates, one is now in position to convert the information into knowledge.

The third and final step is *experience*, arguably the most difficult but most meaningful step of the 3Es, for a meaningful experience requires that one relinquish control, immerse oneself in a live scenario that allows them to internalize what they know to be true. Arguably, this is what so many youths in society desperately miss—structured substantive opportunities to apply what they learn about others outside of their originating identity framework (think of the small percentage able to take advantage of the blessings of study abroad). Often, through shared experiences, one's knowledge is now converted to a budding wisdom. The hope is that one will grow wise enough to simply respect another's culture—refraining from adjudging whether it is superior or inferior, but merely appreciating that it is simply *different* from one's own.

Thus, when a lack of the 3Es is properly taken into account, we can see how intelligent and well-intended creatives can nonetheless fall prey to subtle, yet significant patterns when it comes to prioritizing dialogue, overall screen time, and more developed character arcs for White characters at the expense of non-Whites onscreen. While creatives may have collaborated with the best of intentions to actually *include* people of color within mainstream movies, if they still quietly struggle with the 3Es, and lack education, exposure, or experience, then limited thoughts and ideas about racial difference will make themselves manifest in the final product. To wit, the Writers Guild of America and the Directors Guild of America are *still* very much White-dominated in membership, at 82.1% and 90%, respectively, as of 2020 and 2017 (Robb, 2022; Handel, 2018)—just as they were when founded decades ago during the Jim Crow era. Jim Crow has thankfully come and gone, but the lack of diversity in these key organizations that shape the vision and labor tasks of mainstream movie productions may now be exposed as a contributing factor.

Of course, a movie that only has White creatives working on it is not inherently racially problematic, *per se*. However, the lack of input or feedback from other perspectives can mean that a seemingly innocuous scene that has "humorous dialogue" aimed at a non-White character onscreen can land differently if the non-White perspective is never actually considered. Again, this is not to say that *evil* people are working on these movies, creating these scenes—however, many people may be uneducated, unexposed, and inexperienced when it comes to meaningful and substantive interactions with non-White individuals. Hence, this struggle with the 3Es is a contributing factor to the stubborn persistence of racially problematic patterns.

After all, if there is any entity acutely aware of the need for continued growth, it would be Hollywood. It is telling to see how many reports have been issued and continue to be issued by prominently positioned organizations involved in the movie-making process with roughly similar messaging: Hollywood can do better when it comes to racial diversity. Below is a sampling of several high-profile reports over the years—observe and see to what degree true, innovative, substantive change has taken root versus similar remakes merely being produced by Hollywood with different actors, as if this were the 11th installment of the *Fast & Furious* franchise (the 10th installment, *Fast X*, was released in May 2023 with a production budget of only $340 million).

For instance, in a 2019 report sponsored by the Annenberg Foundation and the University of Southern California's Annenberg School of Communication Inclusion Initiative that studied inequality in 1,200 popular films by examining portrayals of gender, race/**ethnicity**, LGBTQ status, and disability from 2007 to 2018, project lead Stacy L. Smith offers insights such as that only two-thirds of the top 100 films of 2018 contained Black females at all, which was an improvement over the fewer than half that included Black females in 2015 (Smith et al., 2019).

But even still, these glaring reports only tell part of the story. Many of these reports quantify diversity by measuring how many of a particular racial grouping are participating by virtue of their percentage. For example, Latinx characters only represented 5.3% of all of the speaking characters the study analyzed for an 11-year time period. Given the growth, significance, and continuing contributions of Latinx Americans to society, these numbers are still sobering, but we must go further still. Producing and reproducing reports from a quantitative standpoint will only advance the conversation but so far. What also needs to be included is a *qualitative* analysis—thus, many of these reports purport to measure diversity, but they may more accurately be tracking the more tangible concept of numerical *presence* rather the larger concept of *participation*.

During the Jim Crow era, theaters throughout the South, such as The Carolina in Durham, North Carolina, designed special balconies (i.e., "the buzzard's roost") to separate Black audience members from White attendees. Additionally, other theater owners "built special partitions, maintained Blacks-only entrances, or allowed special late night showings, known as 'midnight rambles,' to maintain racially separate viewing" (Newton, 2023), all of which added up to "connoted public humiliation" as succinctly described by scholar Charlene Regester (2005, p. 115). But notice that when it came to commerce and capital exchange, the rules of racism started to become pliable and bend in the wind. The theater did not interpret Jim Crow as a strict ban on Black patrons, but rather "Whites only" meant only Whites could watch the movie as an audience without restrictions. The theater still took money from Black patrons at full price—a detail not to overlook given that Black patrons were technically receiving less value for their money with more limited options and inferior service (to reinforce the idea that they themselves were inferior).

Similarly, Hollywood producers would be foolhardy to limit their audience and therefore curtail their profits by stating that only certain members of the population could pay for the privilege to patronize their product. Granted, a movie made with a certain genre in mind (i.e., romantic comedy) may not possess universal *appeal*, but no movies sold to the public are subject to selective repeal. Thus, a romantic comedy movie may be greenlit by producers with the knowledge that their finished product may not appeal equally to all audiences, but this will not prevent the moviemakers from accepting proceeds from anyone outside their target demographic. It follows that numerous movies have been made without non-White characters, writers, producers, or directors present, but nonetheless remain available for non-White audience members to patronize.

Worse is that during Hollywood's early years, diversity on screen was statistically severely limited when Jim Crow politics affected most areas of public working life. If the 2023 Hollywood Diversity Report (Ramón et al., 2023) is to be believed when it reports that "only 1.7 out of 10 theatrical film directors are people of color" (p. 23), then one can only imagine how much more stultifying the environment was for a non-White individual during Hollywood's nascent years during the institutionally discriminatory Jim Crow period. Due to a limited, incorrect, and racist worldview, many depictions were problematic. And that is *if* we are counting numbers strictly. Plenty of ink has been spilled documenting that non-White individuals played "less of a role" in the creation of mainstream movies—both in front of and behind the camera.

These quantitative data are certainly helpful, but not holistic. Quite simply, in addition to the quantity, we must also look at the *quality* of character images seen onscreen.

INTRODUCING THE HARM THEORY RUBRIC

In terms of the psycho-segregation concept discussed in Chapter 1, and being able to have novel movie images penetrate and push audiences' collective minds in new directions toward true acceptance and belonging, the following racial rubric is offered to measure concretely not just the quantity of non-White roles in a movie (which still provides a key piece of information), but also the *quality* of the role. The HARM Theory rubric helps identify and analyze the quality of non-White imagery confidently and consistently. The HARM Theory stands for **Hollywood's Acting Rule for Minorities** (or non-White characters) and holds that *if and when* a non-White character appears within a mainstream movie, this character is likely to be compromised or marginalized in some way, shape, or form—most especially when juxtaposed against White characters within the same movie. The clause *if and when* is employed only because many a successful mainstream movie may be bereft of significant non-White participation (think *Titanic* or *Oppenheimer*). The HARM Theory rubric comprises two character subsets based upon the simplified multiverse of White characters (prototypes) and all other non-White characters (archetypes).

This formulaic nature of mainstream movies is part of the underlying reason why Hollywood relies on a consistent pattern of racial imagery. Although Hollywood is a White-dominated industry, it consistently produces lucrative mainstream movies designed to appeal "universally" to racially diverse audiences around the world. Nevertheless, Hollywood mainstream movies routinely present a limited view of non-White characters, in stark contrast to the broadly developed spectrum of White characters. This is no trifling matter; given Hollywood's extensive reach and economic impact, the consistently marginalized non-White images in mainstream movies reflect and reinforce messages of racial imbalance worldwide.

Hence, to break down this formula further, there are six characters patterns for non-White figures called **archetypes** that are consistently marginalized in contrast to White characters onscreen. Conversely, there are six White character patterns that typically work cohesively to glamorize their presence in contrast to all others depicted onscreen, called **prototypes**. The purpose in learning these patterns is not to then make broad, generalized, and sweeping statements about how the entire movie or all of Hollywood is "racist" per se. If anything, precise command of these racial rubrics will assist the reader in being able to recognize that which is racially problematic without losing sight of "the bigger picture."

In turn, each archetype and prototype will receive specialized attention and analysis through their own individualized chapters, but a simple listing of the two sets of rubrics and their overarching themes are also succinctly provided in Figure 2.1.

Do note that neither archetype nor prototype classifications are mutually exclusive, meaning that a non-White character can exhibit traits from more than one archetype group. For instance, if a non-White individual only appears onscreen for one fleeting minute to utter a self-deprecating punchline, then it is possible that their character may qualify as both a Background Figure due to limited screen time in addition to possibly qualifying as a Comic Relief Figure due to the humorous nature of the line—most especially if tinged with some racial overtones.

Moreover, throughout this book, I contextualize the six principal non-White character patterns, or archetypes, by analyzing these roles in concert with broader character patterns that Hollywood employs to glamorize White characters, which we refer to as prototypes. It is far too easy for individuals to compartmentalize and dismiss the black-and-white images of "old" Hollywood footage as passé without stopping to seriously consider how the substance of these disparaging racial patterns of the past continue today, albeit in a different form. Traditionally, mainstream movies have been an almost exclusively White domain. Many "classic" Hollywood movies,

Figure 2.1. Archetype and Prototype Themes at a Glance

Archetypes	Central Theme
Angel Figure	Helpful, not helped
Background Figure	Counted, not included
Comic Relief	Funny, not serious
Menace to Society	Hot, not cool
Physical Wonder	Specimen, not special
Utopic Reversal	Empowered, not powerful

Prototypes	Central Theme
Assumed Affluent	Ability to access
Family Tied	Ability to bond
Hero	Ability to succeed
Intellectual	Ability to solve
Manipulator	Ability to navigate
Romantic	Ability to love

from *Miracle on 34th Street* to *Singin' in the Rain*, did not feature any non-White characters prominently.

Yet, this is not to say that Hollywood did not feature non-White images in its early history—far from it. The first ground-breaking feature length movie, *The Birth of a Nation* (1915), and the first talking film ever released, *The Jazz Singer* (1927), both featured White actors in blackface. In both movies, as with many others throughout the early history of Hollywood, non-White characters were openly denigrated by the stereotypical images that they embodied. Almost always, the quality of non-White roles in Hollywood mainstream movies was inferior to the roles of White heroes and protagonists. In fact, this inferior status was not just tacitly acknowledged, but rather it was openly celebrated.

For instance, Hattie McDaniel was rewarded for her rendition of a sassy but servile "Mammy" figure in *Gone with the Wind* with a highly coveted Oscar for Best Supporting Actress—becoming the first non-White actor to ever win an Academy Award in the process. Fast-forwarding to today's current movie climate, the quantity of non-White images has certainly increased and evolved. However, the true quality of this evolution remains the billion-dollar question. Despite Hattie McDaniel's "breakthrough" victory in 1939, more than six decades passed before another non-White actress won an Academy Award, when Halle Berry claimed the Best Actress prize in 2002 for her role in *Monster's Ball*—a role that some may argue was not that much more flattering than McDaniel's with respect to "traditional" racial imagery seen onscreen.

Speaking of which, although I am a Black author, and there is indeed an overwhelming number of examples of "traditional," disparaging, race-related imagery with Black characters onscreen, one additional contribution of this work is the more general application of these principles of qualitatively valuing character contributions onscreen for non-White and White characters—this is not a work that focuses solely on the Black American experience, unlike another work of mine, *Black Oscars: From Mammy to Minny, What the Academy Awards Tell Us about African Americans*. Therefore, for every archetype discussed, four different examples will be provided to demonstrate the ubiquity and pervasiveness of the HARM Theory rubric patterns: Asian, Black, Latinx, and Other. These four categories, along with the fifth category of White, comprise **Hollywood's Racial Makeup.** Let me take this time now to acknowledge that there are some practical limitations in grouping vast groups of people within "catchall categories." However, I find it most effective to analyze race through the paradigm that *Hollywood provides us* as viewers.

For our analytical purposes here, the Asian category in this instance is synonymous with East Asian culture (e.g., Chinese, Japanese, or Korean) and can also include Pacific Islanders. With respect to traditional stereotyping within Hollywood, "Asian" does not necessarily signify someone who hails from India or Pakistan, even though individuals from South Asian countries are often racially grouped within the general catchall category of "Asian" as well. The Black category includes those hailing from the mother continent of Africa as well as her descendants from the African Diaspora, wherever they may be found (e.g., Caribbean, African American, etc.). The Latinx category includes those persons of Hispanic descent and includes references to both

Latinx and Hispanic heritage, which in Hollywood parlance typically boils down to the character employing some aspect of the Spanish language (or an accent that signifies they are a native Spanish speaker) onscreen. The "Other" category includes the smaller yet recognizable racial and ethnic groups that appear infrequently onscreen, although Native Americans and Middle Easterners comprise the largest groups within this Other category. Here is where those appearing as East Indian or South Asian would be categorized. Finally, the Other category will also include characters who appear racially ambiguous onscreen that do not otherwise satisfy the other four categories. The "White" category includes all ethnic classifications and differentiations that share White aesthetics and phenotypes that are not of Latinx descent.

By examining the dynamic relationships between non-White and White characters onscreen, we can unlock substantive meaning beyond superficial comparisons. To truly appreciate the full gravity of the situation, we must understand to what degree non-White images are marginalized versus White images that are glamorized. Only by combining our analysis of both archetypes and prototypes together may we more effectively approach the question: "When exactly did Hollywood stop being racist?"

SIXTH SENSE: I SEE WHITE PEOPLE

What is particularly novel about the prototypes analysis is that it restores balance to a traditionally skewed conversation that has hitherto not made much sense. Non-White individuals routinely bear the burden of "proving their case" of discriminatory depictions, with the unspoken and oft unchallenged presumption that Whiteness is the typical centralizing starting point by which difference is measured. With this calculus in mind, discussions and debates can rage on for days without any direct or explicit analysis of the bedrock Whiteness that is responsible for the debate in the first place. Consider by way of brief historiography just how many works to date either (1) address the concepts of race or diversity in film from broad, generalist perspectives or (2) focus exclusively upon prioritizing the lens of a particular non-White group, typically with an agenda of highlighting a history of disparaging racial images *in contrast to* or *juxtaposed against* more favorable depictions of White characters onscreen. For the generalist approach, several stellar books that come to mind include the following:

- *America on Film: Representing Race, Class, Gender, and Sexuality at the Movies*, by Harry M. Benshoff and Sean Griffin
- *Reading Race: Hollywood and the Cinema of Racial Violence*, by Norman K. Denzin
- *Reel Inequality: Hollywood Actors and Racism*, by Nancy Wang Yuen

Conversely, as a counterpoint to the generalized approach of analyzing *Everything Everywhere, All at Once*, several researchers have made significant contributions that heighten our media literacy awareness of how the larger machinery of Hollywood has collectively contributed to a mosaic of consistently problematic images for particular non-White groups when viewed through the White (male) gaze:

- *Feminist Film Studies*, by Karen Hollinger
- *Making the White Man's Indian: Native Americans and Hollywood Movies*, by Angela Aleiss
- *Reel Bad Arabs: How Hollywood Vilifies a People*, by Jack G. Shaheen
- *Reel Latinxs: Representation in U.S. Film and TV*, by Christopher González and Frederick Luis Aldama
- *Slanted Screen: Asian Men in Film and Television*, documentary by Jeff Adachi
- *Toms, Coons, Mulattoes, Mammies, and Bucks: An Interpretive History of Blacks in American Films*, by Donald Bogle
- *Yellowface: Asian Whitewashing and Racism in Hollywood*, documentary by Clara and Julia Kuperberg

I, too, am no stranger to this approach, as I also contributed through the very specific lens of studying African American imagery within Hollywood with the 2020 release, *Black Oscars: From Mammy to Minny, What the Academy Awards Tell Us About African Americans*. Yet here, *Race and Media Literacy, Explained* seeks to add additional balance to the growing conversation by providing analytical rubrics that apply to multiple groups of non-White individuals and by underscoring the strength of a holistic analysis by including Hollywood's most dominant racial group both in front of and behind the camera: *White people*.

Thus, White characters, despite their overwhelming dominance onscreen since Hollywood's *Inception*, ironically have avoided racial scrutiny due to their ubiquitous presence. In fact, White character presence has been so constant and consistent that it represents the visual norm, the baseline by which difference is measured. We all know that, in totality, Hollywood movies are dominated with White character imagery—what is unknown is just to what degree. It is difficult to find data accurately totaling the number of movies made. Further, even though Hollywood started making movies during the Jim Crow era and many a film was shown in racially segregated theaters, the movie products themselves were neither advertised nor promoted as being for "Whites only." For, if there one place where Hollywood treated everyone equally—it was at the box office.

White characters are frequently glamorized in relation to non-White characters in three general ways: (1) more screen time, (2) more meaningful dialogue, and (3) more complex character arcs that demonstrate change over time. The result is often a richer, more intimate, and more complete picture of White characters with which the audience can relate. For movies with majority-non-White casts, or movies that have a majority of Asian Americans, Mexican Americans, or Black Americans without significant White character presence, quite frankly, the moviemakers have no choice but to develop and elevate the characters seen onscreen from two-dimensional to three-dimensional portraits. Unfortunately, non-White characters frequently suffer from being more two-dimensional—they may have some screen time and dialogue, but the area where they often falter is the lack of character arc development over time—*most especially when paired in movies with other high-profile White characters.*

Typically, when studying or discussing non-White participation in mainstream movies, individuals will use quantitative metrics. Non-White progress is usually quoted as a percentage increase within a particular statistical category. What is not in dispute is that Hollywood now features more minorities in more movies than at any other point in its history. Discussing statistical increases only tell part of the story however, therefore with the HARM Theory rubrics (i.e., archetypes and prototypes), viewing audiences now have a consistent formula of their own with which to more precisely measure or evaluate the qualitative aspects of the non-White characters they encounter while onscreen.

It may sound unpleasant, but the hard truth is that the HARM Theory rubrics essentially revolve around the age-old tensions concerning power and control. Such themes can readily be found in narrative stories, from old imaginative fairy tales to blockbuster summer mainstream movies. When it comes to increasing one's media literacy for understanding the role race plays onscreen, a simple way to ground oneself before perhaps getting lost in the analytical weeds is simply to ask, "What does this role say about power and control?" Onscreen, many non-White characters are far removed from the centers of power and control or are not depicted as having agency let alone full dominion over other people or systems, whether the systems are economic, militaristic, or political. But White characters are frequently depicted as having more agency and consequently exercising more power and control onscreen by movie's end—which is often the reason why we showed up to the theater in the first place.

In addition to the archetype and prototype patterns that will receive the bulk of attention in this book, there are additional factors that conspire to elevate and enrich Whiteness we see and experience onscreen: the **White Beauty Standard** and the **asymptote.** The White Beauty Standard is the worst kept secret in Hollywood: namely that while objectified, White individuals are elevated as the paragon, or standard bearers, of beauty, and that all others are measured against this standard. There are two problematic issues with this framework. First, this standard is exclusive and exclusionary for anyone who in reality does not identify as White, and second, this standard is misleading insofar as it is partially fabricated. Going with the second point first, the star system was invented by savvy Hollywood studios around the 1930s (McDonald, 2002). The system consisted of movie studios being intentional and strategic in publicly propping up mostly White, larger-than-life, desirable *personalities* that fans could lavish with admiration and adulation—as opposed to critically concentrating wholly on the skills of these actors as *performers*. Furthermore, the star system helped promote "collective escapism at its highest level when considering the public's desire to fawn over glamorous celebrity red carpet wardrobe choices in tabloid magazines and on social media" (Gooding, 2020, p. xv).

On one hand the star system was simply a clever means to spark interest and patronage for upcoming movie products; by formulating a relationship with the actor or actress and not the movie, fans would "follow" the actress and most likely support whatever movie project in which she next appeared, rather than critically evaluating each movie product individually. For instance, a Greta Garbo fan might faithfully see her latest movie, thereby generating additional revenue for the studio, even though poor movie reviews may suggest that watching the movie would not be the best expenditure of time or money. On the other hand, the star system created a "golden cage" dynamic whereby for certain actors and actresses to be deemed worthy of public studio support and financial backing, they had to meet certain standards of appearance and decorum. During Hollywood's early years, coinciding with the Jim Crow era of institutionalized racial discrimination, all of the stars who were amplified, glorified, adulated, and exalted just also happened to be White.

SEEING (WHITE HOT) STARS

Over time, the star system leveraged the White Beauty Standard to slowly carve out the idealized images audiences grew accustomed to seeing onscreen: slim figure, waif-like shape, wispy hair (Howard, 2018). As White women who did not conform to this ideal profile were rarely propped up as stars, one can only imagine how it was even more difficult for someone who was not White to fit the bill. With the advent of roughly half of all films transitioning from traditional black-and-white imagery to color (or Technicolor!) by the mid-1950s, the additional criterion of reflecting attractive femininity as blonde was unofficially added. Famed film director Alfred Hitchcock was renowned for employing blonde, White women in his movies; even leveraging blonde star Janet Leigh's shower murder scene in *Psycho* (1960) into one of the most shockingly famous Hollywood scenes of lore—akin to how a blonde Drew Barrymore made a similarly shocking and early exit in the initial installment of the *Scream* series in 1996.

Additionally consider the large amount social currency still accorded to the image of a blonde, White female, with several movies flagrantly marketing and promoting movie products that literally contain the word "blonde" in the title, from Reese Witherspoon's *Legally Blonde* franchise, to Oscar winner Charlize Theron's *Atomic Blonde,* to Ana de Armas's 2023 Academy Award–nominated Best Actress role in *Blonde,* to Nicole Kidman, Charlize Theron, and Margot Robbie all teaming up for *Bombshell.* These financially successful movies help make beauty standards proven to be economically remunerative—and therefore prized by Hollywood studios—that much more unattainable for non-White women. Lest we forget to include the 2023 full-length cultural phenomenon *Barbie*, starring Margot Robbie, based upon the storied franchise in existence ever since 1959, generating over a billion dollars' worth of sales in 2020 alone (Gilblom, 2021).

In the shadow of this white-hot spotlight, the asymptote concept slowly emerged (Gooding, 2017, p. 62). Just like in algebraic mathematics, an asymptote refers to a line that approaches a curve but will never touch it. Similarly, those non-White women who approach the White standard of beauty are typically rewarded accordingly—even though they will never touch nor directly reach the line or become White. Consider how 1950s Black actress Dorothy Dandridge was celebrated as much for her talent as her appearance; she had mixed race ancestry (from both parents) and therefore was possibly more appealing to White audience's sensibilities during the Jim Crow era. Yet shameful and painful stories such as the Hotel Last Frontier draining the pool the day after Dandridge touched it was proof that she was never fully accepted in spite of her approaching the White aesthetic more so than a darker-skinned Hattie McDaniel, for instance (Gooding, 2020, p. 57).

Additionally, numerous actors and actresses have taken measures personally to approach this standard—whether it be straightening or lightening one's hair, changing eye color, or any other cosmetic change designed to appear more "attractive" under the glare of the Hollywood spotlight. Additionally, numerous actors have leveraged **masking**, or the practice of manipulating their "government names" to appear more marketable, or culturally "vanilla" and devoid of obvious cultural references that may take their image outside the realm of traditional Whiteness. Jewish actors like Natalie Portman (Natalie Hershlag) and Winona Ryder (Winona Horowitz), Latinx actors like Charlie and Martin Sheen (Charlie and Martin Estevez), or Black actors like Jamie Foxx (Eric Marlon Bishop purposely chose an androgynous moniker) have all chosen their stage names to increase their odds of getting that callback and breakthrough—which is not too far from the concept of Lakisha and Jamal receiving fewer callbacks from résumés nationwide as "every measure of economic success reveals significant racial inequality in the U.S. labor market" (Bertrand & Mullainathan, 2004, p. 991).

As a result, it is not surprising that some non-White actors will attempt to leverage the best career move for themselves, even if it means consciously changing their appearance or identity to improve their appeal to the mainstream. Efforts by non-White actors to establish their "Americanness" often encourages an acknowledgment of a simplified heritage, free of ties to anything but America. However, the resulting invisibility of the non-White actor's "original" race is what becomes problematic. Ultimately, the message communicated to aspiring actors is that non-White marginalization is simply more marketable.

THE CURIOUS CASE OF WHITE WOMEN

Furthermore, macro approaches to race are simply unable to provide the level of detail necessary to appreciate how the larger machinery of structural and institutionalized ideas of racial difference can be framed differently based upon the primary subject. Further, these generalized treatments run the risk of conflating similar, but separate and distinctly nuanced experiences that each deserve their own analysis. For instance, in addressing the disparate treatment of female characters onscreen overall, what remains hidden in plain sight is the fact that generic terms like "gender" or "women" mask as euphemisms for the specific grouping of "White women."

There is no dispute that White women are indeed objectified and subjugated onscreen. However, as the mothers, grandmothers, sisters, daughters, and spouses of the racial demographic historically recognized as the most economically and politically dominant within American society (i.e., White men), White women enjoy a *special relationship* given the "roles" they play within the daily lives of White men. This means, while exploited, they are exploited in different ways that ironically still privilege their existence over other non-White men and women due to the structural permanency of their more intimate relationships. White women not only *are indeed victims* of misogynistic power imbalances onscreen in relation to White men, but they also *are indeed benefactors* of the racial power imbalances non-Whites suffer onscreen in relation to both White men and women.

Jim Crow created a conspiracy whereby male and female members of society were protected from embarrassing, violent, or even deathly treatment if they identified as White. Cynthia Skove Nevels (2007) provides the eye-opening account that unfortunately for victimized Blacks, "Americanness" was demonstrated through anti-Black cruelty, with Italian and Irish immigrant descendants trying to assimilate to the concept of Whiteness going as far as participating in violent lynching acts. Jim Crow was about race, not gender. Therefore, White women, benefited (and continue to benefit) from a racist society *that is also systemically sexist.*

Thus when White women "identify" with the experience of discrimination, their experiences battling objectification and subjugation are verifiably valid, yet these experiences simply differ from that of an individual who under the auspices of intersectionality, would have to juggle objectification and subjugation in addition to racial discrimination. Scholars like Kimberlé Crenshaw remind us of the necessity of factoring in both race and gender when attempting to digest patterns of how non-White women are portrayed both in spite of and despite their gender (Coaston, 2019). Thus, to place "gender" in the same phrasing as "race" potentially can confuse audiences to read the two struggles as flatly synonymous. *Race and Media Literacy, Explained* uncouples the perhaps unintentional, yet impactful "norming," or flattening of different experiences while still allowing for intersectional analysis.

COMING SOON

What follows are 12 separate chapters covering two groups of rubrics for both archetypes, which highlight patterns of marginalization for non-White characters, and prototypes, which highlight patterns of glamorization for White characters. Each chapter begins with a brief thumbnail sketch called the "30-Second Spot," followed by the "Trailer"—a bullet-point analysis of the archetype or prototype—and the "Main Feature Analysis," which offers more exposition on some key, related concepts. Included in each chapter is an element called "Black Mirror," which engages with the idea that it is no longer effective to only talk about non-White images in a vacuum; their relationship with the most dominant image source, or White characters, must constantly be borne in mind. Then, examples of each highlighted archetype or prototype from our list of Top Ten movies (see Table 1.1) are included. Each chapter in Part II then concludes with "Questions for Questing," which may be engaged at any time at any level for those interested in continuing this critical conversation.

Now! Get your popcorn and take your seats. "May the force be with you" as you enter Part II, or the book's second act.

Bottom Line #1

[Part 1, *White Screens, Dark Theaters*: Introduction–Chapter 2]

Although Hollywood consistently produces lucrative mainstream movies designed to appeal universally to large, broad audiences of all races, it remains a White-dominated industry.

Part II

COLOR ME BAD: ARCHETYPES AND PROTOTYPES

CHAPTER 3

The Angel Figure Archetype

30-SECOND SPOT

- Solicited/recruited by White protagonist for advice/assistance
- Character's principal purpose/aim is to assist White protagonist
- Minimal familial or personal relationships onscreen outside of relationship with protagonist

TRAILER

- WHO: non-White character (archetype)
- WHAT: since they are solicited/recruited by the White protagonist for advice/assistance, they are helpful to White protagonist whose needs are paramount, not vice versa.
- WHEN: look for this character to be established typically after the protagonist is introduced in the movie; depending upon the depth of the sacrifice, the Angel Figure's sacrifice may come toward the movie's climax.
- WHERE: as the advice/assistance is of value to the White character, look to the protagonist's dialogue or actions in response to evaluate the significance of the help rendered.
- WHY: this character's principal purpose/aim is to assist the White protagonist and demonstrate value through usefulness while simultaneously demonstrating racial comity.
- HOW: the isolation and focus of this supportive role is increased when the character has minimal familial or personal relationships onscreen outside of protagonist.

MAIN FEATURE ANALYSIS

The Angel Figure. Traditionally found in a servile position, this character is known for rendering some type of aid or assistance to the protagonist who is most likely White. Recall that the archetypes are not mutually exclusive, so it is not uncommon to see this character presented in different formats—meaning that a non-White character can not only serve as an Angel Figure, but say in the case of Peter Parker's "best friend" Ned from *Spider Man: No Way Home,* they can also exhibit characteristics of a Comic Relief archetype as well. The phrasing of "servile position" does not necessarily mean that this character is depicted in an actual service capacity like a butler or a maid—although those movies do exist—but generally speaks to an imbalanced power dynamic onscreen, whereby the non-White character appears to be working to accomplish whatever it is the White protagonist wants.

However, there are several movies from the 21st century starring non-White individuals in literal butler or maid service capacities:

- *The Butler* (2013)
- *The Help* (2011) (Octavia Spencer = 2012 Academy Award winner, Best Supporting Actress)
- *Spanglish* (2004)
- *Maid in Manhattan* (2002)

The Angel archetype is often endowed with admirable qualities: strength, empathy, caring, and resourcefulness. These qualities are not inherently disparaging by any stretch of the imagination. However, when such attributes are present solely to provide a White character with help or support, these attributes adopt a hollower meaning. Ultimately, despite the many ways in which the Angel is presented, this non-White archetype is largely limited to a service role for a principal White character. Even though it appears that this character is "involved" in the movie's storyline, the Angel's only purpose is to assist the central White characters in fulfilling *their* purpose.

In broader terms, if Whites are typically centered as protagonists in mainstream movies (Smith et al., 2019), then when and if a non-White individual appears onscreen, one must critically inquire as to what the function and purpose of that character is. Meaning, while it may seem dispassionate or cruel to do so, every character one sees onscreen can be seen as a tool for accomplishing a job, or as a paint brush that helps add color to the canvas. As viewers, we often become emotionally attached to or invested in certain characters. But if we were purely analytical, we can qualitatively measure whether every major character onscreen exists on account of their own merits or is merely present onscreen as a "foil" to help us learn something new about the protagonist, who is most often White.

The Angel Figure serves a dual purpose. Not only are they literally helping the White protagonist, but they also help the audience believe (or fantasize) that perhaps racial tensions are not as fraught as they may appear—at least outside the theater—under the auspices of racial comity. Yet, racial comity does not equal racial status. As White characters serve as our protagonists most of the time, most non-White Angel Figure archetypes are solely onscreen to provide aid or assistance to the protagonist. Creative backstories may help explain the non-White best friend who goes "way back" with the protagonist, but ironically enough, the Angel Figure or non-White character will appear onscreen socially isolated with minimal developed relationships outside of the protagonist. But notice, the non-White character's isolation justifies or explains the Angel Figure's myopic dedication to the protagonist, even if the relationship appears to be a "one-way street." For these so-called relationships are not depicted as balanced nor reciprocal; it is the non-White Angel Figure who sacrifices something very personal to them in order to keep both the movie and the relationship going—even if it is their own life!

What is inherently problematic about the Angel Figure is that on a surface level, it appears that non-White individuals are contributing members to the movie's story development in a meaningful manner. But in actuality, they are glorified assistants. Rather than being present for their unique, quirky identity that the audience may grow to like, the value of this person is more explicitly coded as help, or, more specifically, this non-White character's actions are designed to help "prop up" the (more important) White protagonist with a more complex and developed character arc.

The resulting effect for the viewing audience is a neatly packaged and sanitized presentation of race relations. Off-screen, the reality is that with many White people "increasingly choosing to self-segregate into racially isolated communities" (Chang, 2018), numerous White moviegoers may not be in close contact or community with other non-Whites. Within the fantasy space of a fictional movie, White viewers can perhaps better understand a White character's relationship with another person of color onscreen and not be troubled by it, but just so long as the White person is within a recognized position of power and control. Hence, visually there is no threat insofar that the non-White individual adheres to the wishes or command of the White person. The facile acceptance of the supportive and helpful Angel Figure contrasts sharply from the amount of cognitive dissonance that may result from seeing an intimate interracial relationship onscreen, where historically laws have been passed to "protect" Whites from getting to know non-Whites too intimately.

In order not to over-esteem superficial changes over time, leveraging the HARM Theory rubric to analyze Angel Figure characters for their root function may be helpful. Take, for example, the historical Mammy stereotype within Hollywood film. According to the BBC, the mammy is traditionally defined as "a dark-skinned, overweight woman, wearing a headwrap and shawl, the mammy is employed by a white family to care for their children and is utterly devoted to her charge" (Jones, 2019, para. 2). Mind you, the headwrap's purpose was not necessarily to keep "wild hair" in place, but rather was made to mute the Black character's sexuality in contrast to the "more attractive" White female character glamorized onscreen. Thus, as Hollywood moves forward in time, it might be patently offensive to cast a Black female character who *appears* like a mammy figure opposite a White female A-list actress in a contemporary movie given the weighted, historically racist implications associated with the mammy image. Yet, is it equally as offensive if a contemporary Black female character *approaches* the same function as the archaic mammy trope, albeit while appearing more palatable to audiences' naked eye?

For example, in the 2008 *Sex and the City* movie, Black songstress Jennifer Hudson (which makes her a crossover star who is not a "classically trained" actress) is cast as Sarah Jessica Parker's *personal assistant.* While it is not a criminal act for Hudson's character Louise to work for Parker's character Carrie, do note that the job of a personal assistant is different in title and task than that of an associate director or a manager—subordinate titles that still carry augmented levels of power and more responsibility than a mere personal assistant. However, more important for analysis is how, although not cast as a mammy character, Hudson's personal assistant character may not only fulfill the Angel Figure archetype but also may still end up performing the same function onscreen as a traditional mammy figure. Adding to the irony of Hudson's subjugated role is her decorated status off-screen.

Since the *Sex and the City* movie was adapted from the successful HBO series bearing the same title, Parker likely had more acting "chops" than Hudson if going by the sheer number of filmed production appearances for a series that ran for 6 seasons from 1998–2004. Yet, an argument could be made that at the time of the movie's casting, Hudson potentially "outclassed" Parker as she was the only Oscar winner on set after claiming Best Supporting Actress for her role in the 2006 movie *Dreamgirls*. Yet, in her very next feature film appearance, Hudson is seen aiding and assisting Parker onscreen—albeit while more fashionably dressed than McDaniel's Mammy character from *Gone with the Wind*.

At the root, by natural order of power and control, Hudson's character is supposed to carry out the wishes of her supervising employer if she expects to get paid. Parker supervises Hudson and therefore tells her what to do. Nonetheless, whether it is McDaniel as an "official" mammy in 1939 or Hudson as a "personal assistant" nearly 70 years later, viewers of both movies end up seeing Black females in character roles subordinate to more powerful (and more sexually liberated) White women. Further, viewers from both movies see Black women portray characters whose primary purpose is to take care of or provide personal attention to the White woman's more important needs. Thus, while Hudson's personal assistant character is dissimilar from McDaniel's mammy role by *definition and appearance*, as seen in Table 3.1 the HARM Theory rubric helps expose the underlying power dynamic between the Black and White female characters as similar in *function and performance* onscreen in relation to their White counterparts.

Under the auspices of Racism 2.0, it would be overt, obvious, and offensive to cast an obsequious Black woman kowtowing and catering to a White woman, dressed as a maid or a Mammy figure in the "modern era" (i.e., after the year 1995, or within 3 decades of the publication of this book). Technically while that did happen with the Academy Award–winning 2011 movie *The Help*, the movie was nonetheless set in a historical period whereby racism was still wrong, but ruled the day quite openly. Naturally in order for *The Help* movie to be "accurate," demonstrating the power imbalance onscreen between White and Black women would be a natural, logical step in telling the story—a story that nonetheless features Emma Watson's White female Skeeter character as the most developed protagonist.

After all, "we must also remind ourselves that such movies are *not* documentaries and are Hollywood studio productions made not just for art's sake, but to turn a profit for their investors" (Gooding, 2023). With a period piece like *The Help*, "history" may be wielded as a defense to such a modern movie made for profit. For perhaps it is a separate question to pursue, namely, what these films say about the value and visibility of Black female imagery if Black actresses are *still* winning Academy Awards from portraying maids onscreen over 70 years apart (i.e., 1939

Table 3.1. Consistent Power Dynamic Between Black and White Women

	Gone with the Wind (1939)	*Sex and the City* (2008)
Black female character	*Mammy* (Hattie McDaniel) • Professionally subordinate to White woman • More heavyset and darker skinned than White woman • Isolated from others onscreen outside of relationship with White woman • Very little character arc development	*Louise* (Jennifer Hudson) • Professionally subordinate to White woman • More heavyset and darker skinned than White woman • Isolated from others onscreen outside of relationship with White woman • Very little character arc development
White female character	*Scarlett O'Hara* (Vivien Leigh) • More sexually liberated • Enjoys elevated status above Black female and provides instruction to Black female • Considers black female a "confidant," or friend despite power dynamic in her favor • Significant character arc development	*Carrie Bradshaw* (Sarah Jessica Parker) • More sexually liberated • Enjoys elevated status above Black female and provides instruction to Black female • Considers black female a "confidant," or friend despite power dynamic in her favor • Significant character arc development

Best Supporting Actress Hattie McDaniel for *Gone with the Wind* and 2011 Best Supporting Actress Octavia Spencer for *The Help*)? More bluntly, as the mainstream movie *The Help* is not a documentary, what is so entertaining about seeing suffering, subjugated Black women onscreen?

Thus, while it may be more "offensive" to stylize a Black woman in a maid outfit trailing and serving a White female downtown in an urban, bustling modern metropolis in a 2008 movie, an affluent, put-together, take-charge, confident, and sexually liberated White woman having a personal assistant to help keep her life organized makes much more sense. Mind you, the personal assistant just happens to not only be Black in identity but is one of the few if not the only Black character onscreen with a speaking part in the entire movie. Merely characterizing the relationship as voluntary, or as a neutral byproduct of unseen market forces, as if it were the natural order of affairs, is perhaps less offensive. Hardly any news articles published reviewing the movie at the time even mentioned or spoke to this angle. But just as with a brilliant Shakespearean reference, the ever-present "racial angle" is there to be uncovered or discovered at any time. But we still get the same basic idea—we see that the body of Jennifer Hudson, one that embodies an Academy Award–winning performance, is junior to and takes direction from Parker's character onscreen. Period.

This scenario speaks to another concept that we will briefly make mention of here—that is, many historians characterize their profession as chronicling "change over time" (Andrews & Burke, 2007). I would like to challenge this approach directly by reminding all who will listen that history is best understood as balancing that which changes over time against that which remains *consistent over time*. Whenever race relations receive historical treatments, often much emphasis is placed upon the "change," at the expense of appreciating what remains consistent. Here, although the appearance, form, and formal relationship between the Black woman and White woman has changed from *Gone with the Wind* to *Sex and the City*, what remains consistent is the underlying power dynamic. Hence in addition to questioning what is different, Table 3.1 helps us ask what is structurally consistent about these two different pictures from two different eras some 70 years apart.

Ultimately, in both movies, a more "powerful and attractive" White female is telling a Black female character with significantly less screen time and dialogue what to do. The Black and White female characters are therefore not seen as equal within the visible continuum. While Hudson's physical appearance onscreen may not trip the same *"This is racist!"* alarm bells as the clearly problematic imagery that Hattie McDaniel's headwrapped Mammy character would, the thrust of both Black female character roles relative to White women remains consistent. What also remains consistent are romantic racialist overtones whereby the Black character is wanted, but not needed as a true and personal confidant and connection—Sarah Jessica Parker's Carrie character has her other White female friends for that emotional and intellectual "heavy-lifting."

Further, the White woman's more powerful positionality and direct role in the Black female's subjugation can be masked under principles of "niceness" (Castagno, 2019), where audiences do not think twice about the power imbalance since the White female is so nice to the Black female. Yet, all is "nice" only because the predominant power dynamic goes relatively unchallenged during the visible continuum. This power dynamic privileging White women over Black women onscreen may be better camouflaged under the "best friend" scenario seen in the 2020 movie *Like a Boss,* starring Tiffany Haddish, Rose Byrne, and Salma Hayek. While both a Black and a White female were partners in business together, Haddish provided mostly comic relief—when it came to the "heavier emotional lifting" of figuring out specifically what to do with the business, the plot shifted to go through the White female's character arc and dialogue.

In the neo-modern era, Jim Crow segregation only grows more distant in the proverbial rearview mirror as society steadily hurtles down the road to racial progress. And of course, in referencing "Jim Crow," we refer to the period of intense racial segregation that wrought significant social, economic, and political consequences for non-Whites generally, but Black Americans more specifically.

But if only life were truly that linear.

Instead, we must consider the cyclical nature of time while reconciling with its fluid nature to potentially change. Meaning, when traditional historians approach history, it is mostly a chronological approach that has a set beginning and a specific ending resulting with a bracketing of periods to make the larger concepts more digestible along a linear path. In other words, in referencing racial progress, one would not be faulted for concluding that America has improved over time. New social policies introduced in the 1960s helped redress problematic policies approved in the 1860s, and likewise newer policies introduced in the 2020s improved upon policies from the 1960s. Yet, despite these new and improved policies serving as indicators of social progress over time, many American neighborhoods, work environments, and educational institutions are just as racially segregated as they were during the Jim Crow period (Semuels, 2021). The reasons for continued segregation patterns within society are complicated and manifold and not the essential thrust of this chapter. However, the result is that racial equity is still not experienced universally.

What is universally true about Hollywood is that the first Academy Award ever bestowed to a non-White individual was Black female actress Hattie McDaniel for her role as "Mammy" in the 1939 hit movie, *Gone with the Wind*. In that movie, McDaniel played an enslaved maid. Her official character name lacked the sophistication and dignity of a first and last name, and she was objectified by being named solely for her function—which was a matronly figure whose sole responsibility was to look after and care for members of the O'Hara household. Such assistance came in the form of laborious tasks such as cooking, cleaning, and doing the laundry in addition to abstract tasks of providing companionship and counsel. All the while, it was quite easy to spot McDaniel's "Mammy" character in contrast to Vivien Leigh's protagonist, Scarlett O'Hara, because she was visibly identifiable as more dark-skinned, heavier in weight, and perhaps less beautified as she was always depicted with a bandana atop her head, covering her hair. Scarlett O'Hara represented the idealized feminine figure popular in early American film: incredibly slim, flowing hair, and White.

Even though McDaniel was largely typecast for all of her working career playing similar subjugated roles, she once famously quipped, "Why should I complain about making $7,000 a week playing a maid? If I didn't, I'd be making $7 a week being one" (Gooding, 2017, p. 52). This rationale of potentially justifying a problematic narrative onscreen so long as there was a sufficient "payoff" may well be instructive. For, with many contemporary American audiences, many films sell very similar narratives—that Blacks on sight have a role, which is to aid or support the principal, or more important White characters—but the "payoff" to the audience is higher when no one has to feel guilty reconciling historically problematic images. In other words, making movies in the modern era about Black maids may well be anachronistic and can court castigation from the viewing community (even though a movie about Black maids won an Academy Award in 2011). However, a contemporary movie where the Black character appears to fulfill *a very similar function* of caring for and exclusively helping the White protagonist is tolerated, especially if the Black character is elevated to the status of "best friend."

By merely changing and massaging job titles and physical appearances, many audiences readily accept Angel Figure archetypes, even though their function differs little from the more offensive servitude tropes established in earlier American film. For example, another high-profile Angel Figure servitude example would be Da'vine Joy Randolph's role as Mary Lamb in *The Holdovers* (2023), which also fulfills the familiar caretaker role that Hollywood has consistently carved out for Black women.

As a (heavyset) Black female "cafeteria administrator," Lamb's function is literally to serve the students at a preppy New England boarding school, and her character is not cast as a colleague equal in rank to fellow classics professor and principal protagonist, Paul Hunham, as played by Paul Giamatti. As Randolph won the 2023 Golden Globe Award for Best Supporting Actress for her role, she arguably still would have been capable of delivering the exact same heart-warming performance in a higher-ranking position onscreen. In addition to literally serving others, Lamb also fulfills the Angel Figure role due to her praised performance as a grieving mother who is able to relate to and comfort a young man with a troubled soul in Angus Tilly, as played by Dominic Sessa. Perhaps the moviemaker's defense would be that in order to be "accurate," Lamb's subjugated position is consistent with social relations in 1970, the year the movie is set. But for an industry that gave us *Abraham Lincoln: Vampire Hunter* (2012), Hollywood's creativity knows no bounds, except perhaps when it comes to the bodies of non-White characters.

But you have seen this all before. Three key components with which to qualitatively "measure" an Angel Figure would be: (1) complexity of their character arc (or lack thereof), (2) evidence of **one-way culture sharing,** and (3) to what degree this non-White character facilitates **catharsis** for the White protagonist by virtue of the Angel Figure's contribution. Catharsis can be achieved through the non-White character providing some aspect of their culture, like the samurai sword in the 2003 film *Kill Bill,* bequeathed by Japanese actor Sonny Chiba's Hattori Hanzō character to Uma Thurman's (blonde) Bride character. This giving act also represents one-way culture sharing because often the White protagonist gives nothing back of equal or greater value to assist the non-White character. Or, catharsis can be achieved by the Angel Figure character saying the right thing at the right time, effectively giving a part of themselves, like (Academy Award–nominated Best Supporting Actor) Brian Tyree Henry's James Aucoin character did to Jennifer Lawrence's Lynsey in the 2022 film *Causeway.*

BLACK MIRROR

Under the HARM Theory rubric, just as archetypes are designed to marginalize non-White participation and prototypes are designed to glamorize White participation, it is important to bear in mind that every archetype has a corresponding prototype with which to juxtapose behavior observed onscreen. For instance, the Angel Figure is likely best contrasted against the Hero or Manipulator prototypes insofar that rather than sacrifice something significant to assist or aid another character to accomplish a goal, the White character possesses sufficient agency to seek out and eke out a solution for themselves. We often forget that the whole point in patronizing a superhero or a prominent protagonist (e.g., Indiana Jones) is to see the hero survive. Far too often, non-White characters do not go the distance (hence the subtitle of "Or Does the Black Guy Die First?") as a larger commentary on *visible value,* or the quality of images communicated during the visible continuum.

ANGEL FIGURE ARCHETYPE EXAMPLES FROM THE TOP TEN

Asian

Film: Spider-Man: No Way Home *(2021)*
Top Ten Ranking: #7
Character: Ned (Jacob Batalon)

A simple example of an Asian American character (from the Top Ten list) fulfilling the Angel Figure archetype would be that of Ned in *Spider-Man: No Way Home.* Jacob Batalon provides emotional support to Peter Parker as the requisite "best friend." However, Ned never helps to the point where he would be considered a major influence on the principal action, which would elevate his status to that of protagonist. For example, Ned helps free Dr. Strange from the Mirror Dimension—this was a product of him "fooling around" and bringing in two additional Spider-Men to the present. By opening a portal for Dr. Strange, Ned contributes by facilitating the presence of the individual who can and does put everything back in its place, even though Ned personally lacks the power or expertise to do it himself—or at least we do not see Ned behave this way during the visible continuum.

Black

Film: Star Wars VII: The Force Awakens *(2015)*
Top Ten Ranking: #5
Character: Finn, formerly FN-2187 (John Boyega)

The Force Awakens provides an example of an Angel Figure by way of Finn. In numerous scenes, Finn appears not to be behaving out of a personal connection to the overall mission but appears driven solely to help the protagonist, Rey, with no true objectives of his own to accomplish. To wit, several YouTube videos exist where fans have spliced together numerous clips where Finn is screaming Rey's name at the top of his lungs, desperate to be of help or assistance to his friend (and not love interest).

Latinx

Film: Avatar *(2009)*
Top Ten Ranking: #1
Character: Trudy Chacón (Michelle Rodriguez)

In *Avatar*, during the battle of Home Tree, fierce fighter pilot Trudy Chacón, played by Latina actress Michelle Rodriguez, fulfilled the Angel Figure archetype in two key ways. First, she made a strategic decision to rebel, or purposely contravene her militaristic authority chain with the thought that such a sacrifice would assist with the overall cause to protect Pandora from exploitation of resources. Saving Pandora also was White protagonist Jake Sully's principal cause, which Chacón joined. *Spoiler Alert:* Second, as an otherwise skilled and crafty pilot of the designated Samson rotorcraft vehicle, she also made a strategic decision to sacrifice herself and her flying aircraft to help further the fighting cause, dying (first?) in the process.

Other

Film: Avatar *(2009)*
Top Ten Ranking: #1
Character: Eytukan (Wes Studi)

Also in *Avatar*, Native American actor Wes Studi voices the role of the Omaticaya clan leader who, under his and his spouse Mo'at's instructions, agreed to help train outsider Jake Sully (played by White male protagonist Sam Worthington) in the ways of the Na'vi as opposed to rejecting him outright. Sully proved to be an astute learner—apparently—and mastered the ways of Na'vi well enough to become the eventual leader of the clan by movie's end. *Spoiler Alert:* Eytukan does not survive the movie as clan leader.

Questions for Questing	
Define	• Define the Angel Figure archetype. • List 2-3 examples of Angel Figures you have seen within the past year. • Which Top Ten Angel archetype example stands out to you the most?
Discuss	• What is the most memorable sacrifice that you recall seeing an Angel Figure make? • Which stereotypes are the Angel Figure most closely associated with? In which ways is the Angel archetype more acceptable and less offensive? • Which Top Ten Angel Figure examples had you seen before? Did you notice this archetype upon your initial viewing? If not, do you agree or disagree with the analysis?
Decide	• What usually happens to Angel Figures after they render the protagonist aid? • Are Angel archetypes encouraging or condescending? • To what extent have you seen the same non-White actors reprise the same archetype in different roles? Just by way of example, with this Angel Figure definition in mind, consider to what degree there is variance or change in these supporting (as in, not leading) roles by Morgan Freeman listed in chronological order: » *Driving Miss Daisy* (1989) » *Robin Hood: Prince of Thieves* (1991) » *The Shawshank Redemption* (1994) » *Bruce Almighty* (2003) » *Million Dollar Baby* (2004) » *Batman Begins* (2005) » *Wanted* (2008)

	» *The Dark Knight Rises* (2012) » *Lucy* (2014)
Discover	• *Bulletproof Monk* (2003) [Asian: Chow Yun-Fat as Monk with No Name] • *The Green Mile* (1999) [Black: Michael Clarke Duncan as John Coffey] • *The Legend of Bagger Vance* (2000) [Black: Will Smith as Bagger Vance] • *Shall We Dance* (2004) [Latinx: Jennifer Lopez as Paulina] • *Windtalkers* (2002) [Other: Adam Beach as Private Ben Yahzee]

CHAPTER 4

The Background Figure Archetype

30-SECOND SPOT

- Little to no dialogue
- Minimal screen time
- Little to no bearing on plot development

TRAILER

- WHO: non-White character (archetype)
- WHAT: minimal presence and effect upon plot although technically included
- WHEN: look for this character to be established early in the movie; such characters typically recede to the peripheral as the audience focuses in on the principal (i.e., White) characters who do most of the emotional and intellectual "heavy lifting" onscreen as the movie plot develops.
- WHERE: most especially in action/blockbuster movies that feature large "realistic" crowds (i.e., urban setting)
- WHY: this character's principal purpose is to provide the "illusion of inclusion," or provide a reminder that the visible continuum is not completely devoid of diversity.
- HOW: these characters are easily disposable and expendable with relatively flat character arcs.

MAIN FEATURE ANALYSIS

The Background Figure archetype, although not terribly significant in terms of storyline impact or dialogue, is nonetheless important for Hollywood. While current statistics show that Whites are frequently overrepresented in movie roles relative to their percentage of the population, few mainstream movies completely exclude non-White characters. Hence, many moviegoers may see or hear a non-White character for a few moments onscreen and walk away with a more favorable impression of non-White participation than what is truly offered by Hollywood. Background Figures therefore demonstrate that Hollywood studios are in fact making efforts to include "diversity," albeit in a manner that limits sustained and substantive participation by non-White characters. Background Figures represent a low-risk, low-cost investment in a superficial display of visual diversity that nonetheless allows studios to channel most of the mainstream movie's plot development through central White characters.

What is inherently problematic about the Background Figure is that it merely facilitates the "illusion of inclusion." Even though such characters may have screen time or dialogue to suggest relevance and presence, such time and dialogue is very limited in contrast to the (White) protagonist. On a surface level, it may appear that non-White characters are contributing members to the movie when they are glorified props in essence. Rather than be present for their unique, quirky identity that the audience may grow to like, the value of this person can be more explicitly coded as merely setting the stage. Similar to the Angel Figure archetype, Background Figures pose little threat and minimize cognitive dissonance by *including* non-White imagery without *incorporating* non-White power and control. Background Figures therefore provide diversity in more manageable dosages for Hollywood studios that may be skittish about upsetting established formulas.

Thus, seeing one lone "Asian best friend" out of a group of several friends (think *Pitch Perfect*) is fine and does not pose a significant risk. But flipping the script and having a blockbuster film featuring mostly Asian friends co-mingling with a solitary A-list White star might be a different proposition. Now studios would have to answer the question of whether "too much diversity" would be a barrier to the movie performing successfully at the box office without the typical heavy-handed focus on White character relationships. For those keeping score at home, this is why the 2018 romantic comedy hit *Crazy Rich Asians* is so remarkable—its $239 million performance at the box office was considered a breakthrough success, illustrating that a movie with a majority-Asian cast can be financially viable in the open market. Still, it is important to note that the cast did not feature any White A-list actors, and its excellent $239 million box office take still is shy of *The Proposal*'s (2009 romantic comedy) $317 million take or *A Star is Born*'s (2018 musical romantic drama) $436 million take showcasing White protagonists.

In the neomodern era, society is still not fully racially integrated. Therefore, in a mainstream movie featuring a White protagonist, non-White presence will be explained, and the relationship will be exercised to demonstrate racial comity. Of course, if a movie like *The Last Samurai* (2003) is set in Japan, it would make sense to employ actors of Japanese descent seeing how samurai soldiers are geographically and culturally specific to the island nation of Japan. Or, if a movie like *The Great Wall* (2016) takes place in China, it would make sense to employ numerous actors of Chinese descent seeing how the Great Wall of China is geographically and culturally specific to the large nation of China. Yet, in the *Great Wall* movie, White male actor Matt Damon is prominently featured as the face of the movie even though there may be a higher quantity of Chinese American Background Figures than in a typical mainstream movie. Nonetheless, the quality of such representation may be low if Matt Damon is the sole, dominant star. Perhaps we should be grateful—after all, it is not as if Damon actually attempted to *play an Asian character* the way White actress Scarlett Johansson did in the 2017 *Ghost in the Shell* movie, where Johansson played the role of a unequivocal Japanese protagonist, Motoko Kusanagi (Fang, 2018).

I strain and struggle to think of the possibility of a movie being made, possibly entitled *Mount Rushmore*, where a foreign Chinese national is primarily responsible for battling ancient spirits around an American national monument. If anything, if anyone does hear any controversy surrounding Mount Rushmore, it might be the spirits and souls of the Lakota People, indigenous to the area we now call South Dakota, who remind us that the Black Hills were once occupied and happily inhabited before they became a rock-graffiti tribute to four White males who previously served as president of the United States. And not to leave Tom Cruise out of the discussion, but he as the central White male in the movie *The Last Samurai* was literally the last samurai. I similarly strain and struggle to envision Hong Kong movie star Jackie Chan starring in an analogous role as *The Last American Green Beret.*

Movies that have large numbers of non-White characters do not automatically receive high marks based upon quantity alone. We must also consider how many movies may have high numbers of participation, but only as low-quality Background Figure fodder—or more specifically, cannon fodder—secondary to a more specific (and important) cause as determined by our protagonist. Consider these movie examples that feature large quantities of non-White actors, but the quality of these Background Figure roles is quite low in contrast to the more central White characters seen onscreen:

- *Rambo: First Blood, Part II* (1985) = Vietnamese casualties
- *Traffic* (2000) = Mexican casualties
- *Extraction* (2020) = East Indian casualties

Further, Background Figures help facilitate depersonalization of "the Other." In the 2020 Netflix movie *Extraction,* A-list White male Chris Hemsworth (N.B.; He also played the blond Norse "god" *Thor* in the Marvel Cinematic Universe) totaled a "kill count" of 183 persons—virtually all people of color—as he was justified in doing whatever was necessary to rescue the son of a drug lord in the country of India (Oleksinski, 2020). I struggle to think of a financially successful mainstream movie (recall, the movie just cannot get made; it has to have an audience that patronizes it) that features a male of color indiscriminately killing nearly 200 background White characters on screen all by their lonesome within the span of two hours to protect or avenge just one person they care about. For whatever reason, that movie has not been made yet.

BLACK MIRROR

Under the HARM Theory rubric, just as archetypes are designed to marginalize non-White participation, and prototypes are designed to glamorize White participation, it is important to bear in mind that every archetype has a corresponding prototype with which to juxtapose behavior observed onscreen. For instance, the Background Figure likely is best positioned opposite the Family Tied prototype because the Family Tied character reminds us of the power of connection and what people are willing to sacrifice and go through to honor, respect, and uphold one's family structure despite internal disagreement or external threats that consist of superhero villains, global shifts in weather, or attacking aliens trying to interfere or get in the way. Conversely, with the Background Figure, while their character does indeed offer limited screen time and dialogue, it is usually insignificant to overall plot line or story development, essentially rendering their contribution as maybe an instrumentality of diversity, but not instrumental to the most important thematic questions regarding power and control in the movie.

The Background Figure reminds us of how infrequently this happens for non-White characters—most especially in a movie with a mixed race, or mostly all-White cast. When productions have mostly non-White characters, such as *Boyz N the Hood, Joy Ride, Like Water for Chocolate*, or even *Crazy Rich Asians* as referenced earlier, non-White characters must be developed for the movie to make sense and experience denouement. It is when races are combined and are asked to share in the visible continuum that a racial hierarchy quietly emerges. The Background Figure reminds us of to what degree diversity is taken for granted onscreen when it comes to measuring more effectively not just the quantity but also the quality of diverse representation onscreen.

BACKGROUND FIGURE ARCHETYPE EXAMPLES FROM THE TOP TEN

Asian

Film: Star Wars VII: The Force Awakens *(2015)*
Top Ten Ranking: #3
Character: Admiral Statura (Ken Leung)

In *The Force Awakens*, Admiral Statura is played by Ken Leung. Leung plays his part well, but only has brief windows in which to do so. He is only onscreen for a few limited moments and offers sparing dialogue that, if necessary (e.g., only four lines in a movie lasting 2 hours and 16 minutes in length) (McKnight, 2015) could be trimmed or cut from the movie without altering the fundamental thrust of the story—in other words, this character is essentialized, but is not essential.

Black

Film: Avengers: Endgame *(2019)*
Top Ten Ranking: #2
Character: James Rhodes (Don Cheadle), Sam Wilson (Anthony Mackie)

In *Avengers: Endgame*, the mighty Thanos must be dispensed with once and for all, after having killed off half of Earth's population in *Avengers: Infinity War*. While arguably Rhodes and Sam play more than just rudimentary background roles, their roles are still not as prominent and they take a backseat to some of the other more prominent White character heroes seen onscreen. While the initial 2012 *Avengers* was a different story, by the time the Avengers franchise developed and moved on to the more popular and financially significant third and fourth movies (which both eclipsed $2 billion at the box office, ranking in the Top Ten grossing movies of all time), Samuel L. Jackson's initially relevant Nick Fury role appeared to diminish as the stakes grew higher toward the finish. More specifically, Fury was relegated to a non-fighting, Background Figure role in *Avengers: Endgame* when he simply made a brief, nonspeaking cameo as one of the last people depicted at Tony Stark/Iron Man's funeral by Stark's cabin by the lake.

Latinx

Film: Spider-Man: No Way Home *(2021)*
Top Ten Ranking: #7
Character: Flash Thompson (Tony Revolorio)

Guatemalan American actor Tony Revolorio plays Flash Thompson in *Spider-Man: No Way Home*. Born in Anaheim, California, under the name Anthony Quinonez, Revolorio plays a smaller role than he did when he established his classic high school bully persona in the 2017 *Spiderman: Homecoming*. In *Spider-Man: In No Way Home*, Revolorio has a brief moment in the spotlight when he appears to have limited screen time and dialogue looking to frame his relationship with Peter Parker as a "friendship" and profit from it with the sale of his book to onlooking paparazzi as Parker attempts to inconspicuously attend school after his identity has been revealed.

Other

Film: Avatar *(2009)*
Top Ten Ranking: #1
Character: Dr. Max Patel (Dileep Rao)

East Indian actor Dileep Rao plays the Background Figure of Dr. Max Patel in *Avatar.* Patel offers a few lines sprinkled throughout in brief spurts but is not present during any of the key climactic scenes toward the end of the movie.

Questions for Questing

Define	• Define the Background Figure archetype. • List 2–3 examples of Background Figures you have seen within the past year. • Which Top Ten Background Figure archetype example stood out to you the most?
Discuss	• What is the most memorable line that you recall seeing a Background Figure recite? • Which stereotypes is the Background Figure most closely associated with? In which ways is the Background Figure archetype more acceptable and less offensive? • Which Top Ten Background Figure examples had you seen before? Did you see the archetype the first time around? If not, do you agree or disagree with the analysis?

Decide	• What usually happens to Background Figures after they appear onscreen? • Are Background archetypes needless or necessary? • To what extent have you seen the same non-White actors reprise the same Background Figure archetype in different roles?
Discover	• *Blood Diamond* (2006) [Black: unnamed teenage and child amputees] • *Déjà Vu* (2006) [Other: Nadia Shazana as Trauma Nurse] • *Harry Potter and the Sorcerer's Stone* (2001) [Other: "diverse" group of friends playing Quidditch] • *Old School* (2003) [Other: Sarah Shahi as Erica] • *Snow Dogs* (2002) [Other: Graham Greene as Peter Yellowbear]

CHAPTER 5

The Comic Relief Archetype

30-SECOND SPOT

- Ethnicity/culture serves as fodder for humor
- Non-White's culture-specific traits and/or characteristics contrasted against "normal" White behavior
- Non-White conduct marked by exaggerated facial expressions, voice intonations, and physical gestures

TRAILER

- WHO: non-White character (archetype)
- WHAT: utterances, outbursts, facial expressions, or physical movements that depart from the "more serious" plot line
- WHEN: look for this character's comedic traits to be set up during their establishing scene; similar to Background Figures, such humor helps these non-White characters psychologically recede to the peripheral as the audience focuses in on the principal (i.e., White) characters who do most of the "more serious" emotional or intellectual "heavy lifting" onscreen. Further, Comic Relief archetypes are quite common and popular most especially in action/blockbuster movies that require moments of levity in the face of otherwise serious circumstances such as the "end" of the world due to an impending alien attack (think of Will Smith's Captain Steven Hiller's comedic lines as he "slaps" or knocks out an alien creature with his bare hands in the 1996 hit *Independence Day*).
- WHERE: as 120 minutes is a "long time" to remain hyper focused on a cataclysmic, if not depressing event (e.g., the destruction of the entire universe if our tormented Thanos were to have his way), humor or comic relief is often leveraged as a tool to "break up" the action. Observe the type of gags made by and about White protagonists versus the type of jokes made by and about non-White characters. For example, in *Avengers,* one of the gags for a principal White character was that in his establishing scene, Steve Rogers (aka Captain America) was so focused and pumped up about defending America that he obliterated the punching bag in front of him when initially approached during a recruiting visit from S.H.I.E.L.D. Director Nick Fury. While this display of strength would certainly be mildly surprising for any

first-time viewer, adding to the gag is that, while talking nonchalantly to Fury, Rogers casually walks over to a large pile of replacement punching bags on the floor and picks up another to replace the damaged one (on account of his routine passion and strength) as an impressed Fury continues his recruiting pitch. Conversely, in the same movie, a comic relief moment showcasing a non-White character features Fury addressing the World Security Council with slightly less than professional language when he says to the (all-White) body that even though he recognizes they made a decision, he chose to ignore it since it was a "stupid-ass decision"—a line that likely elicited some smiles and laughs from the viewing audience as cursing is part of Samuel L. Jackson's casting profile (Moen, 2022).

- WHY: this character's principal purpose is to help release tension surrounding larger issues likely driving the main action of the movie.
- HOW: as this archetype frequently displays intersectionality tendencies with Background Figures, the cost of using this character for comic relief is that without many additional lines or screen time to counterbalance or outweigh the light-hearted lines, the potential exists that audience members may not take this character as seriously as those with more developed character arcs.

MAIN FEATURE ANALYSIS

Comic Relief characters often retain and exhibit many elements of stereotypical roles recycled from a seemingly bygone era in Hollywood. However, the sting of such stereotypical conduct is diffused or blunted under the auspices of humor, parody, and burlesque. The ironic result is that non-White audience members often pay to see humor marketed through mainstream movies at their own culture's expense. Non-White characters are certainly not above satire. However, their historically low levels of **racial capital** in Hollywood call into question whether non-Whites are still being left out of the joke.

Two key concepts to bear in mind when contemplating this deceptively complex archetype are: (1) contra-juxtaposition, and (2) minstrelsy. **Contra-juxtaposition** consists of an exaggeration of an existing non-White stereotype contrasted against "typical" White middle-class norms—the more that the non-White deviates from the norm, the more humorous the situation is intended to be.

Minstrelsy was a wildly popular form of entertainment that denigrated Blacks and lampooned their status as victims of systemic racism dating back to the early 19th century and stretched into the mid-20th century. Minstrel shows frequently featured both Whites and Blacks who donned "blackface" make-up. Currently, patently offensive blackface performances are all but an afterthought in today's modern cinema. However, the notion that non-Whites—Blacks in particular—engage in unflattering and wildly overdramatized scenarios designed and conceived primarily by Whites for laughs, hearkens back to the principle undergirding minstrelsy that uses humor as a wedge rather than a bridge for racial understanding.

While considered relatively outdated as a product of a bygone era, occasionally we are reminded of minstrelsy's curiously stubborn allure—whether it be Governor

Ralph Northam of Virginia defending his 1980s yearbook photos to comedienne Sarah Silverman in 2016 posting a "joke" about "menstrual cramps" (London, 2019; Silverman, 2016) to Robert Downey, Jr. receiving a Best Supporting Actor Academy Award nomination for playing the role of a Black character onscreen in blackface in the 2008 film *Tropic Thunder*. Downey defended his role, indicating that after taking a poll of his "Black friends," no one raised an objection, thereby mitigating his need to address or atone for his performance that historically was deemed offensive. Said Downey, Jr.: "90 percent of my black friends were like, 'Dude, that was great'" (Chiu, 2020). Again, the movie *Tropic Thunder* was presented under the auspices of comedy.

While minstrelsy is less en vogue today (except for some people on Halloween, without fail) (Eddington, 2022), the question is whether the same idea of exaggerated gestures and expressions is achieved through more sophisticated Comic Relief archetypes. Consider early in comedian Kevin Hart's career the type of comedic roles he took on, and consider to what degree Hart is simply "being funny," and to what degree his actions and mannerisms are reminiscent of the racist caricatures of old—bug eyes; loud, screaming intonations; and exaggerated expressions (in alpha order):

- *The 40-Year-Old Virgin* (2005)
- *Central Intelligence* (2016)
- *Get Hard* (2015)
- *Jumanji: Welcome to the Jungle* (2017)
- *Little Fockers* (2010)
- *Ride Along* (2014)
- *Soul Plane* (2004)

The object here is not to legislate what is and what is not objectively funny as one's sense of humor can vary dramatically based upon personal experience. But rather the point is to highlight how Hollywood, an industry that has over 90% White writers, composing joke threads that make light of non-White character's isolated presence or culture, even for the limited time that they have onscreen, contributes to larger patterns of non-White imagery devaluation.

BLACK MIRROR

Under the HARM Theory rubric, just as archetypes are designed to marginalize non-White participation, and prototypes are designed to glamorize White participation, it is important to bear in mind that every archetype has a corresponding prototype with which to juxtapose behavior observed onscreen. For instance, when analyzing the Comic Relief archetype, which speaks to themes of "not getting it" or not being treated as seriously, this archetype differs markedly from the Intellectual or Manipulator prototypes. The Intellectual counters the Comic Relief in that rather than elicit laughter over not knowing how to do something, or lacking expertise, the Intellectual is able to improvise and devise solutions to pressing problems. Similarly, rather than elicit humorous merriment from one's inability to perform competently under pressure, the Manipulator demonstrates an unusual ability to still accomplish their important objectives.

COMIC RELIEF ARCHETYPE EXAMPLES FROM THE TOP TEN

Asian

Film: Avengers: Infinity War *(2018)*
Top Ten Ranking: #6
Character: Ned (Jacob Batalon)

In *Avengers: Infinity War*, all of our famed superheroes are pressed into action once they realize that there is an imminent global threat. Spider-Man is one not to neglect his superhero duties and therefore while on a school bus with other school-aged children commands his friend Ned to "create a distraction" so that he can surreptitiously slip out relatively unnoticed and tend to his superhero duties of saving the world from maniacal domination. Instead, Ned blurts out, "We're all gonna *die*!" which although is a serious statement, was included for comedic effect given the predictable panicked reaction in response. Implied in Parker's request to Ned for a distraction was a solution that would not cause panic or alarm, even though it was effective enough to allow Parker to slip out the bus window undetected.

Black

Film: Star Wars VII: The Force Awakens *(2015)*
Top Ten Ranking: #5
Character: Finn, formerly FN-2187 (John Boyega)

In *Star Wars VII: The Force Awakens,* Finn is parched after crossing the desert sands of Jakku on the heels of his crash-landing escape from the First Order early in the movie. Poe Dameron (played by Latinx actor Oscar Isaac), who piloted a stolen TIE-fighter while Finn manned the guns, was nowhere to be found after the crash. Finn finds and takes Poe's fighter jacket (for protection from the unforgiving desert sun, perhaps?) and sets off for the next sign of civilization. We next see Finn stumbling about in a village, quietly whispering, "Water, water."

As a qualitative measure of his resourcefulness, Finn indeed solves the problem of finding water. The only issue is that rather than display any savvy negotiating skills or even low-level criminal trickery (or even *the force?!*) to obtain potable water from another villager presumptively with no currency, the only source of water he finds is an open trough whereby a large, gigantic pig-like creature called a Happabore is busy consuming water as well. In fairness, Finn does in fact ask out loud, "Is there water?" but appears to be admonished or rebuffed—albeit briefly—on three separate occasions by alien village traders before hearing the sound of water. At the trough, the massive, elephant-sized Happabore appears busy ingesting water, with its oversized snout dominating its physical appearance.

Nonetheless desperate, Finn proceeds to run over to the trough and drink from it—and visibly gags to confirm the audience's suspicions that the water is most likely unclean, most especially if being indiscriminately utilized by an otherworldly, oversized pig-like beast. As an aside, in our universe on planet Earth, many humans refuse to eat swine-related products due to the belief that pigs are unclean since they are known to eat filth. So, imagine the image of a pig-creature writ large and Finn's conscious decision to drink from the same source and what it says about Finn's ability to solve problems (i.e., find water) in the most effective manner.

To add insult to injury, as if this compromising moment was not embarrassing enough—for we all perhaps can relate to instances where we had to suffer through discomfort and can laugh at it in retrospect—the Happabore knocks Finn on his backside while Finn is still on his knees drinking (ironically, the stout but large beast is standing on all fours). What also may qualify as comic relief is that this scene merges into the next chase scene, further demonstrating the limits of Finn's ingenuity. After being knocked over from the trough, Finn looks up and witnesses Rey being physically assaulted by village traders. Alarmed, he races over to presumably help, but stops short when he sees that she is more than capable of defending herself as she quells the fracas and defeats at least two perpetrators all by her lonesome. Finn's reaction of "Huh!" may also be interpreted as a wry joke referencing the incorrect assumption of men to assume that women are somehow more fragile and are in constant need of male assistance.

A chase scene ensues when Rey, who is accompanied by Poe's droid BB-8, is alerted by the droid that nearby Finn is wearing Poe's jacket. Having been spotted, Finn decides to run when Rey charges after him. He attempts to elude her by running through a labyrinth of traders only to be caught by surprise and knocked on his backside again. Rey clearly outsmarted Finn in the run and chase game, and is seen standing over him with her long, pole weapon bellowing the inquiry, "What is your hurry, thief?" The final piece of comic relief comes when BB-8 jumps into the fray, so to speak, while Rey is explaining BB-8's spotting of Poe's jacket, by extending its electric charger and shocks Finn briefly, as a humorous way to administer discipline.

All of these jokes are on Finn. In contrast, Rey's character has a completely different relationship with humor onscreen. If anything, her most humorous moment came from her ability to prove the legendary Han Solo wrong by fixing the Millennium Falcon's inability to go into hyperspace by "bypassing the compressor"—in other words, it was funny how competent she was as opposed to the audience laughing at Finn's incompetence.

Finally, what perhaps is not as humorous is the idea that Finn is essentially the only Black male with a speaking part in the third *Star Wars* trilogy (Episodes VII, VIII, and IX). For the first trilogy (Episodes IV, V, and VI), that distinction went to Billy Dee Williams' Lando Calrissian character. For the second trilogy of movies (Episodes I, II, and III), perhaps that distinction goes to Samuel L. Jackson's Mace Windu character (with no disrespect to Hugh Quarshie's Captain Panaka), provided the animated Jar Jar Binks is not counted as a Black male, although the character was voiced by Black male actor Ahmed Best. In other words, even in the wide, expansive, visually diverse, and creative universe of *Star Wars,* where aliens and humans seemingly coexist, there still only appears to be room for one Black male at a time. Thus, Finn's isolation only increases the impact of his limited character arc; please see Finn's entry under the Utopic Reversal archetype for additional analysis on his inability to grow with the force. Finn on his backside was an inside joke, perhaps? For literally, that is how he was seen in his last scene onscreen from *Episode VII*, on his back, knocked unconscious.

Latinx

Film: Spider-Man: No Way Home *(2021)*
Top Ten Ranking: #7
Character: Flash Thompson (Tony Revolorio)

In *Spider-Man: No Way Home*, Tony Revolorio makes the most of his few minutes by adding comic relief. His character is supposed to be "over the top" as a persistent antagonist of charmed hero Peter Parker. Revolorio was also mentioned earlier as his Flash Thompson character also served as a Background Figure. Even though he was attempting to exploit Peter Parker by selling a book with the claim that the "Spider-Man" concept was his idea, it was presented as humorous how ridiculously opportunistic he was to illustrate the lengths that some will go just to profit off another. N.B.: There are hardly any Latinx characters in the entire *Avengers* series; Scott Lang's "best friend" and former cellmate Luis (Michael Peña) from the original standalone *Antman* movie series did not make it into the *Avengers* movies although Antman's romantic counterpart Wasp (Evangeline Lilly) and their daughter Cassie (Emma Fuhrmann) did.

Other

Film: Avatar *(2009)*
Top Ten Ranking: #1
Character: Dr. Max Patel (Dileep Rao)

Dileep Rao plays Dr. Max Patel in *Avatar.* Patel offers a few lines and is not present during any of the key climactic scenes toward the end of the movie. Although it is not "slapstick" comic relief per se, Rao's character contributed to a lighthearted moment in an indirect way. When White male protagonist Jake Sully first "transfers" into his avatar, as an immobile individual who uses a wheelchair in real life, Sully was quite excited over the prospect of being able to stand and walk—even if inside a 10-foot-tall bluish body.

Upon first regaining consciousness in his avatar for the first time, Jake is predictably a bit wobbly with his balance inside of the laboratory. Dr. Patel instructs Jake through an elevated glass panel, "Listen to me! You're not used to your avatar body. This is dangerous." Jake responds with a smile, "This is great," and proceeds to ignore Dr. Patel's admonitions and storms his way outside, taking in the natural environment of Pandora for the first time, tasting newfound physical freedom perhaps. Seeing Jake's childlike joy over being able to run freely contributes to the lighthearted mood, which was only made possible by his perhaps "innocent" but nonetheless insubordinate actions against Dr. Patel. Coincidentally, for whatever reason, the initial avatar transfer and Jake's reaction was overseen by Dr. Patel and *not* Dr. Grace Augustine, played by White A-list actress Sigourney Weaver. Perhaps the scene would have landed differently, and not as lighthearted and humorous, if Jake had directly contradicted the authority of an accomplished White female doctor onscreen.

Questions for Questing	
Define	• Define the Comic Relief archetype. • List 2–3 examples of Comic Relief figures you have seen within the past year. • Which Top Ten Comic Relief archetype example stood out to you the most?
Discuss	• List the last movie you saw that contained a race-based joke. • Which stereotypes is the Comic Relief figure most closely associated with? In which ways is the Comic Relief archetype more acceptable and less offensive? • Which Top Ten Comic Relief examples had you seen before? Did you see the archetype the first time around? If not, do you agree or disagree with the analysis?
Decide	• How many non-White comedians are known for "straight-man humor" as distinguished from exaggerated expressions and actions? • To what extent have you seen the same non-White actors reprise the same Comic Relief archetype in different roles? • Should Comic Relief archetypes be regarded as humorous or humorless?
Discover	• *The 40-Year-Old Virgin* (2005) [Black: Romany Malco as Jay] • *Austin Powers: Goldmember* (2002) [Asian: Carrie Ann Inaba as Fook Yu; Diane Mizota as Fook Mi] • *Doctor Dolittle* (1998) [Latinx: John Leguizamo as Rat #2] • *Meet the Fockers* (2004) [Latinx: Ray Santiago as Jorge Villalobos; Alanna Ubach as Isabel Villalobos] • *Spider-Man 2* (2004) [Other: Aasif Mandvi as Mr. Aziz]

CHAPTER 6

The Menace to Society Archetype

30-SECOND SPOT

- Objectifies criminal element, has criminal tendencies, has "entanglements" with the criminal justice system
- Character threatens White status quo by violating or disregarding social norms
- Marked by intimidating presence and aggressive actions

TRAILER

- WHO: non-White character (archetype)
- WHAT: this person represents a threat (physical or social).
- WHEN: look for this character's threat to be established once the viewing audience is grounded by the protagonist's worldview.
- WHERE: most especially in action/blockbuster movies, this archetype can overlap with Background Figures and serve as convenient henchmen with whom our valiant protagonist must dispense in furtherance of their mission to save the world.
- WHY: this character's principal purpose is to remind the viewer of the protagonist's positive **moral compass.**
- HOW: if a "serious" action movie, then the threat may be a menacing henchman who must be dispensed with; if dispensed with early in the movie, the non-White character's defeat informs the audience of our protagonist's skills and abilities that will really have to be put to the test later in the movie (e.g., Jason Bourne knocking out a well-sculpted, foreign opponent with one punch in the beginning of the 2016 film *Jason Bourne*). Conversely if a "action/comedy" movie, then the threat may be a missed social cue or the inability to perform a task initially for comedic effect.

MAIN FEATURE ANALYSIS

The Menace to Society archetype establishes an important aspect of non-White marginalization, whereby many non-White characters appear static in their opposition to "benevolent" mainstream society and their threat to civil "normalcy." Within the universe of mainstream movies, such threats are often defined in terms of the threat they pose to *White* characters, which is ultimately what makes them such a menace. In this respect, the exclusion of Menace to Society figures from full participation in mainstream society is justified, and in some cases required for the security of the common good, further underscoring subtle messages of racial difference.

As we consider threats to society onscreen as embodied by non-White characters, another key vocabulary term directly relevant to this archetype includes the **protective stereotype,** which comprises exaggerated images of White bigotry or hatred (think clueless Klansmen in the 2012 *Django Unchained* or the 2018 *BlacKkKlansman* films) that allow common White audience members to distance themselves from such abnormal and obvious displays of antisocial behavior—especially when those negative behaviors involve racially discriminatory behavior. Whereby Black and Latinx male "criminal elements" hardly require contextualization within mainstream movies, protective stereotypes are "protective" of White characters in that they mask more subtle and commonplace representations of discrimination or racial microaggressions more likely to be prevalent within contemporary society. The protective stereotype works only because it is designed to be obvious and clear although uncommon in real life.

BLACK MIRROR

Under the HARM Theory rubric, just as archetypes are designed to marginalize non-White participation, and prototypes are designed to glamorize White participation, it is important to bear in mind that every archetype has a corresponding prototype with which to juxtapose behavior observed onscreen. For instance, the Menace to Society archetype likely contrasts the most with the Hero or Romantic prototypes. Most especially when the Menace to Society poses an immediate, physical threat, they are likely most diametrically opposed to classic Hero imagery, where the Hero is a welcomed and appreciated sight. In contrast, Menace to Society figures can represent negative energy that need to be navigated or worse, vanquished for the plotline to proceed. Their presence thus becomes expendable or a "necessary evil" to endure en route to the payoff of seeing the hero or heroine come into their own.

Menace to Society characters are also juxtaposed against Romantic prototypes if only because Romantic characters communicate that not only are they within the visible continuum capable of finding love, but, more importantly, are worthy of love as well. Everyone can laugh at a joke. But not everyone is willing to cry publicly. If the goal of moviemakers is to create a connection to a character whereby movie patrons would indeed be induced to tears, then time must be invested in creating a reason for such a connection. In other words, here principles of **interiority** apply whereby White characters routinely have their character arcs fortified with back stories, revelations about their unique personalities, along with insight on the deepest, most personal relationships that govern or explain most of their behavior seen onscreen. By taking time to set up exploration of character arcs, chances increase of an emotional connection being made with a fictional character "trapped" within a two-dimensional space. However, from *Bambi* to *Spider-Man: No Way Home* to *Avengers: Endgame*, such connections are in fact made more often than we may realize (e.g., note how one fan ended up in the hospital after crying so hard after witnessing Spider-Man's "death" onscreen in *Avengers: Endgame* [Russian, 2019]).

Moreover, Menace to Society archetypes can take upon more subtle forms outside of an armed burglar frothing at the mouth sticking a sawed-off shotgun in between our protagonist's fourth and fifth rib. The "threat" can also be more subtle and assumed as negative attitude or disruptive social behavior.

MENACE TO SOCIETY ARCHETYPE EXAMPLES FROM THE TOP TEN

Asian

Film: Jurassic World *(2015)*
Top Ten Ranking: #8
Character: Dr. Henry Wu (BD Wong)

In *Jurassic World,* like the plotline in the original 1993 *Jurassic Park* film, some unscrupulous scientists chose to profit off the seemingly unfathomable concept of prehistoric life. Whereas the corrupt scientist distinction went to Wayne Knight's character Dennis Nedry in the 1993 version, the evil honors go in the 2015 remake to BD Wong. The only issue here is that Nedry's evil White male character had other images of White males to counterbalance, if not outweigh his negative image:

- paleontologist and principal character Dr. Alan Grant (Sam Neill)
- principal character Dr. Ian Malcolm (Jeff Goldblum)
- park owner Hammond (Sir Richard Attenborough)

Yet, BD Wong's Dr. Henry Wu character stands alone with no other significant Asian characters (male or female) seen speaking onscreen. His isolation is only increased by his socially deviant behavior whereby he agrees to sell such volatile technology for personal gain.

Black

Film: Star Wars VII: The Force Awakens *(2015)*
Top Ten Ranking: #5
Character: Finn, formerly FN-2187 (John Boyega)

FN-2187 was the original name bequeathed to Finn as a member of the evil Galactic Empire's First Order. By definition, he was a Menace to Society who was wreaking havoc upon defenseless communities.

Latinx

Film: Spider-Man: No Way Home *(2021)*
Top Ten Ranking: #7
Character: Dr. Octopus (Alfred Molina)

Molina reprised his 2004 villainous role from *Spider-Man 2* as Dr. Octopus.

Other

Film: Star Wars VII: The Force Awakens *(2015)*
Top Ten Ranking: #5
Character: Tasu Leech (Yayan Ruhian)

Yayan Ruhian's Tasu Leech character in *Star Wars: The Force Awakens* appears to be in a standoff with our favorite, smooth-talking intergalactic smuggler, Han Solo (Harrison Ford). Mr. Solo is apparently in debt (again) and is attempting to negotiate his way out of another awkward transaction. At one point, Solo is onboard his trusted "bucket of bolts" (i.e., Millennium Falcon smuggling spaceship freighter), in the middle of a passageway whereby two mercenary groups are also onboard, vociferously demanding their money at opposite ends of the hallways. Even though Ruhian is from West Java in Southeast Asia, he is included here in the "Other" category. In contrast to the other Scottish-speaking mercenary, Bala-Tik, played by White male Brian Vernel, Ruhian's Tasu Leech character was speaking in an alien, foreign language as an attempt to "other" him and his scraggly, mustachioed look, complete with long hair in contrast to Bala-Tik's more clean-cut, "normal" appearance. When Bala-Tik confronts Han Solo over the 50,000 credits he loaned Solo, Bala-Tik also references a 50,000 sum Solo owes the other gang headed by Leech, Kanjiklub, to which Solo replies, "You know you can't trust those little freaks." "Little freaks" implies "other" even in a realm where alien life is normal (hint: think seven-foot-tall roaring, furry spaceship copilot named Chewbacca).

Also onboard the Millennium Falcon are some large, people-eating, tentacled beasts called Rathtars, which Solo was smuggling for personal profit as clandestine cargo. Adding to the drama of Solo owing large sums of money to at least two different parties on his ship, Rey accidentally released three ravenous Rathtarsfrom their cargo hold, and the beasts start wrecking havoc onboard. For whatever reason, even though the Rathtars loose aboard the Millennium Falcon decimated numerous gang members, while Leech was last seen from behind shooting and running, Bala-Tik somehow survived and reported (in English) to the First Order that the BB-8 droid they were looking for was aboard the escaped Falcon ship.

Questions for Questing	
Define	• Define the Menace to Society archetype. • List 2–3 examples of Menace to Society figures you have seen within the past year. • Which Top Ten Menace to Society archetype example stands out to you the most?
Discuss	• Which White ethnic groups are usually associated with organized crime or dastardly deeds? Are British or "Americans" a part of this group? Why or why not? (Hint: Review *Amistad*. Which White ethnicity is depicted as involved in the slave trade? Aesthetically, how are they depicted?) • Which stereotypes is the Menace to Society figure most closely associated with? In which ways is the Menace to Society archetype more acceptable and less offensive? • Which Top Ten Menace to Society movie examples had you seen before? Did you notice this archetype upon your initial viewing? If not, do you agree or disagree with the analysis?
Decide	• What is the difference between a scheming mastermind and a two-bit violent thug? • List movies with majority non-White casts and White villains. • Do Menace to Society archetypes represent stereotypes or slices of life? • Have you seen the same non-White actors reprise the same Menace to Society archetypes in different roles?
Discover	• *Die Another Day* (2002) [Asian: The evil henchman Zao as played by Rick Yune] • *Lethal Weapon 4* (1998) [Asian: The evil henchman Wah Sing Ku as played by Jet Li] • *Rules of Engagement* (2000) [Other: Assorted Yemeni "protesters"] • *Rush Hour 2* (2001) [Asian: The evil henchman Ricky Tan as played by John Lone] • *Training Day* (2001) [Latinx: Assorted gang members]

CHAPTER 7

The Physical Wonder Archetype

30-SECOND SPOT

- Primarily valued for physical prowess
- Explicit acknowledgment of physical stature, talent, or skill set
- Overly sexualized; often bare-chested, scantily clad, or nude

TRAILER

- WHO: non-White character (archetype)
- WHAT: specimen of demonstrable physical skill, size, or ability
- WHEN: look for this character to be established early in the movie.
- WHERE: most especially in action/blockbuster movies that feature large ensemble casts
- WHY: this character's physical contributions are valued but at the expense of emotional or intellectual capabilities seen onscreen.
- HOW: look for cues and clues from other characters to see whether this archetype character is valued for more than what their body can do.

MAIN FEATURE ANALYSIS

The Physical Wonder archetype encompasses a broad range of non-White characters. With respect to non-White males, the Physical Wonder archetype places an emphasis on the brute strength, size, or speed of the character, as if they were a specimen for the audience to marvel and behold. With respect to female non-White characters, the Physical Wonder includes characters who are regarded for their sexual prowess, with a negligible focus on their romantic capabilities or complicated relationship interests. For both sexes, the Physical Wonder archetype speaks to characters endowed with special physical talents or skills, which typically explains or justifies the non-White character's utility to the plot or involvement with the central characters.

BLACK MIRROR

Under the HARM Theory rubric, just as archetypes are designed to marginalize non-White participation, and prototypes are designed to glamorize White participation, it is important to bear in mind that every archetype has a corresponding prototype with which to juxtapose behavior observed onscreen. For instance, the Physical Wonder archetype most likely counters the Intellectual prototype best. The Physical Wonder is typically blessed with physical gifts at the expense of intellectual or emotional contributions of note during the visible continuum. This archetype speaks to the theme of power and control in the sense that from a physical standpoint, perhaps the character should have more access to power and control than what is depicted—usually that power is wielded by someone who has the requisite rank to tell the person's body literally what to do. Conversely, White Intellectual prototypes do not need to rely upon their physical stature or ability to accomplish their goals—they instead have the ability to exercise free thought to influence their own destiny or the free will of others.

PHYSICAL WONDER ARCHETYPE EXAMPLES FROM THE TOP TEN

Asian

Film: Avengers: Endgame *(2019)*
Top Ten Ranking: #2
Character: Akihiko (Hiroyuki Sanada)

When Black Widow attempted to recruit Hawkeye back into the Avengers camp after "the Blip," or Thanos's finger "snap" that eliminated half the world's population, he was depicted as being in the middle of a paid gig as a contract killer. Hawkeye (now going by the name of "Ronin") was chasing after a skilled Akihiko who demonstrated remarkable sword skill and battled his competent opponent publicly within Tokyo's streets. The Yakuza member demonstrated the ability to jump over roofs and crash through doors unharmed and displayed what could only be perceived as mastery, thereby fulfilling the Physical Wonder archetype in wielding his sword. Yet, this figure is ultimately killed by Hawkeye, presumptively with Scarlett Johansson's Black Widow watching patiently nearby. Hence, while skilled, this Physical Wonder archetype existed only to demonstrate that an even more skilled Hawkeye was up to the task of stopping this Asian male character as a threat. Akihiko's character also overlaps with the Background Figure archetype as his character has limited screentime and virtually no dialogue; there is little other reason provided onscreen for the audience to care for this Asian male character.

Black

Film: Jurassic World *(2015)*
Top Ten Ranking: #8
Character: Barry Sèmbene (Omar Sy)

Barry is the proverbial Black "best friend" of White male protagonist, Owen Grady (Chris Pratt). While Barry is also a co-trainer of the Velociraptors, the audience immediately sees a disparity in Barry's and Owen's skill and mastery for the task at hand. During Owen's introductory scene, he appears to have some semblance of control by having the dinosaurs he named (Echo, Delta, Charlie, and Blue) seemingly respond to his audible cues, aided by the reward of dead Rodentia. Owen even presages what is to come by pausing significantly before rewarding Blue, who eventually goes "rogue" later in the movie. Yet, if the audience was unsure of Owen's mastery and control, a mere two minutes later, this idea is underscored, italicized, and imprinted in bold when another worker falls into the open area with the dinosaurs and without hesitation, Owen jumps into the yard and gains control of the situation only using vocal commands—with no weapons—long enough for them both to escape to safety.

In contrast, despite his physically imposing stature (French actor Omar Sy is 6′3″ in real life) and assumed skill as a Velociraptor co-trainer, he is nonetheless unable to leverage his intellect to solve the problem of his own survival and escape during crunch time. Once chaos breaks out at the Jurassic World complex and the Velociraptors are out loose, Blue turns on his former trainer Barry and attempts to attack him. Barry finds refuge inside of a large hollow log but finds himself screaming on his back with a pistol that seems so small in the face of the Velociraptor's fast-moving claws and teeth. Further, Barry hesitates with his gun as it appears he is having difficulty mustering the courage to shoot—even if to defend himself from a deadly attack. While Barry gets Blue to momentarily pause after calling out her name from his prostrate position, he is clearly not as effective as Owen, as she quickly returns to her business of clawing through the log to presumably finish attacking Barry. Fortunately, Owen comes to Barry's rescue; Owen successfully distracts Blue further by essentially commanding Blue to follow him on his motorcycle after catching her attention with his patented training whistle.

Latinx

Film: Avatar *2009)*
Top Ten Ranking: #1
Character: Tsu'tey (Laz Alonso)

Laz Alonso qualifies as an Afro-Latinx actor, having been raised by Cuban immigrant parents although born in Washington, DC. In the first *Avatar* movie, Alonso provided the voice for the Tsu'tey character, who introduced himself to the audience largely through his physicality, initially coming across as boisterous and supremely confident in his physical abilities. Except that by the movie's end, it is Jake Sully's character who is physically able to conquer the most difficult task in contrast to Tsu'tey, who as an indigenous Na'vi member should have assumed the leadership mantle without question.

But to rewind briefly, early in the movie Jake (and the audience) are exploring this fascinating new, fluorescent world of Pandora. The scene before Tsu'tey's introduction is nothing shy of spellbinding fantasy! It is evening time and Jake and his new local friend Neytiri (Zoe Saldaña) are walking through an enchanted, foreign forest that has neon lights and dazzling illuminating effects. After sharing a tender "moment" with future love interest Neytiri, Jake innocently asks, "What's your name?" before his foot is suddenly snagged by a rope bolas and falls down to the ground. Immediately thereafter, Tsu'tey and his compatriots charge in aggressively on Jake, literally sitting high on their horses with arrows drawn. The "What's your name?" line also meant that Tsu'tey's masculinity was potentially challenged in having another potential suitor distract Neytiri's focus away from his assumed bid or claim for Neytiri's hand as the resident "alpha-male." It is clear that Tsu'tey was only communicating through brute force, physicality, and intimidation—and did not utilize intellect or strategy to navigate the novel situation of discovering a foreign Na'vi avatar appear in his land. Further, in support of the idea that the archetypes are not mutually exclusive, Alonso's Tsu'tey character also exhibits traits of the Utopic Reversal archetype (see Chapter 8).

Other

Film: Avatar *(2009)*
Top Ten Ranking: #1
Character: Eytukan (Wes Studi)

If the destruction of the sacred Na'vi Home Tree by invading forces was not painful enough, Neytiri discovers that her father and leader of the clan, Eytukan, was mortally wounded after being impaled by a fragment of falling wood in the aftermath. In his final words to his daughter, he commands, "Take my bow; protect the people." These six words indicate that his physicality as expressed through military prowess was most important to him, even as he spoke with his dying breath.

Also, notice the relatively brief amount of time the audience spends "grieving" his death during the visible continuum as opposed to the considerably time period (and larger number of people) spent grieving the "death" of White female character, Dr. Grace Augustine (Sigourney Weaver).

Questions for Questing

Define	• Define the Physical Wonder archetype. • List 2–3 examples of Physical Wonder figures you have seen within the past year. • Which Top Ten Physical Wonder archetype example stands out to you the most?
Discuss	• How many mainstream non-White actresses have been paired romantically with a White male onscreen? What does this suggest about non-White female sexuality? • Which stereotypes is the Physical Wonder figure most closely associated with? In which ways is the Physical Wonder archetype more acceptable and less offensive?

	• Which Top Ten Physical Wonder movie examples had you seen before? Did you notice this archetype upon your initial viewing? If not, do you agree or disagree with the analysis?
Decide	• List mainstream movies featuring Asian males who *do not* engage in martial arts. • Are Physical Wonder archetypes fact or fiction? • To what extent have you seen the same non-White actors reprise the same Physical Wonder archetype in different roles?
Discover	• *Dirty Pretty Things* (2002) [Black: Sophie Okonedo's prostitute role] • *Hustle & Flow* (2005) [Black: Taraji P. Henson's prostitute role] • *Payback* (1999) [Asian: Lucy Liu's prostitute role] • *Sin City* (2005) [Black/Latinx: Rosario Dawson's prostitute role; Asian: Devon Aoki's prostitute role]

CHAPTER 8

The Utopic Reversal Archetype

30-SECOND SPOT

- Occupies a high-ranking position, usually in isolation from other minorities
- Authority or power is not fully exercised or recognized onscreen
- Rarely depicted in informal, personal, or romantic settings

TRAILER

- WHO: non-White character (archetype)
- WHAT: powerless or compromised
- WHEN: look for this character to be affiliated early in their scenes with some larger power structure—whether it be a corporation, military, or educational institution.
- WHERE: most especially in mainstream movies purposely set in large metropolitan settings
- WHY: this character's principal purpose is often to demonstrate the protagonist's ability to manipulate.
- HOW: while initially affiliated with power, by movie's end this character's power is usurped, undercut, or undermined during the visible continuum.

MAIN FEATURE ANALYSIS

A vocabulary term that is of particular relevance to this Utopic Reversal archetype is the **unclean hero.** In contrast to many alpha White males who have effectively scored the Hollywood Trifecta—that is, (1) to get the goal, (2) to get the gold, and (3) to get the girl—this non-White "hero" is somewhat successful, or at least has a more complicated and checkered record when it comes to emerging as the clear victor with the three unofficially observed components above. In contrast, the unclean hero represents a non-White protagonist who is indeed the driving force of a movie, yet does not experience the pure moral, financial, and/or sexual victories typically associated with White mainstream heroic character success. The unclean hero is significant in that it demonstrates the penetrating power and reach of the HARM Theory rubric, for even when non-White protagonists are central to the action, their actions may not measure up to larger narratives of heroism familiar by many mainstream movie audience members.

Along these lines, the Utopic Reversal archetype is perhaps the most difficult to detect since it is the most deceptive in its function and appearance. Much like the Angel Figure, the *individual* character may not appear to have any overtly negative characteristics. It is only when viewed from a macro-perspective that moviegoers can recognize the limitations of this character. The overall effect of the Utopic Reversal archetype is similar to that of the "illusion of inclusion" associated with the Background Figure. Despite both archetypes communicating that diversity is present and fully accounted for onscreen, the impact of the character types are very different, with Utopic Reversals initially possessing "power" while Background Figures initially possess presence onscreen. Both types of non-White characters are designed to give the viewer the impression that diversity and power are spread evenly among the movie's characters, but the authority of these Utopic Reversal archetypes is frequently usurped, undermined, or undercut by movie's end.

While the Utopic Reversal archetype's impact is often minimized by limited screen time and dialogue—likely to counterbalance the idea that if only onscreen for brief periods, when onscreen, this character has some type of respectable social rank—this character also has limited displays of authority, especially in relation to the character's job title or seemingly high social position. This character's ineffectiveness is often heightened when lower-ranking White characters trump or usurp this character's authority as a matter of due course in fulfilling their objective during the movie. Think of the 2016 film *Zootopia*, where a White detective (Judy Hopps, as voiced by White actress Ginnifer Goodwin) defied her higher-ranking Black police chief (Chief Bogo, as voiced by Black actor Idris Elba) to successfully solve the case. Also consider scenarios where the White partner does all the "heavy lifting," crafty strategizing, or the most significant sleuthing work in an otherwise equal Black/White buddy-cop pairing such as White actor Mel Gibson and Black actor Danny Glover in the 1998 film *Lethal Weapon 4*.

BLACK MIRROR

Under the HARM Theory rubric, just as archetypes are designed to marginalize non-White participation, and prototypes are designed to glamorize White participation, it is important to bear in mind that every archetype has a corresponding prototype with which to juxtapose behavior observed onscreen. For instance, the Utopic Reversal archetype likely can be contrasted sharply with the Assumed Affluent or Manipulator prototypes. Utopic Reversal characters always start from a position of power—either within a recognized system generally, or at least by having some sort of edge over the protagonist. Hence, this character is imbued with authority simply by rank alone—if depicted as a judge, high-ranking military officer, or a CEO of a company, then the audience need not make any assumptions about this individual having paid some sort of dues within a local community to obtain an above-average promotion. Yet, this dynamic does not last as under the "Cat in the Hat" thesis, power and control are restored back and away from the non-White individual before movie's end. Therefore, while a Black female character can be cast as a judge, due to the White protagonists' interaction with the judge, the viewing audience may soon learn that she is not a *competent* judge, thereby whittling away the respect likely given to the judge character when initially seeing her in a Black. It is rare to find a mainstream (blockbuster) movie where a non-White character grows in power and control in their dominion over other White characters during the visible continuum (recall, in the 2018 *Black Panther* movie, the titular character did not exercise *black power* over other White characters onscreen).

Meanwhile, we have seen examples of the opposite, with Top Ten movies like *Avatar*, for instance, providing a reminder of how a White male as a non-Indigenous outsider can eventually navigate his way to the top of the clan's hierarchy. Where Utopic Reversal characters realize a loss of power, position, or place as they typically are undercut, undermined, or usurped in some way, shape, or form, Manipulator prototypes demonstrate the opposite. The resulting messaging is that not just despite the circumstances but *in spite of* the circumstances, White characters are almost always able to engineer creative solutions. Examples range from "serious" missions to travel back in time to save the world from destruction in *Infinity War* to milder form of "child's play" when the two youths from *Jurassic World,* Zach and Gray, "innocently" ignore signs about entering a restricted area while feeling emboldened in their choice to violate park safety policies and protocols in the name of curiosity and exploration. In the latter case, Zach and Gray's safety violations become secondary to the overarching goal, which is to save them rather than condemn or criticize these precocious youth for putting themselves in a dangerous scenario in the first place.

UTOPIC REVERSAL ARCHETYPE EXAMPLES FROM THE TOP TEN

Asian

Film: Jurassic World *(2015)*
Top Ten Ranking: #8
Character: Katashi Hamada (Brian Tee)

In *Jurassic World*, based upon the character's lead-in, Lt. Hamada initially and immediately creates an impression of competence and confidence. Initially accompanied by a musical score that underscored his military acumen, this purported skillset is usurped when he is dispatched in relatively short order by the Indominus Rex. Lt. Hamada's death therefore not only undercuts his presumed military expertise and training, but it also highlights and dramatizes even more so the successful heroism by untrained (and unarmed) Chris Pratt on his motorcycle and unsuspecting Claire Dearing (Bryce Dallas Howard) running in heels to distract ginormous, carnivorous beasts in order to save the day.

Black

Film: Star Wars VII: The Force Awakens *(2015)*
Top Ten Ranking: #5
Character: Finn, formerly FN-2187 (John Boyega)

In *The Force Awakens,* the Utopic Reversal comes from a potential subtle setup that was months in the making. For months before the movie's release, trailers leaked that hinted at Finn being "force sensitive," or having the untrained but gifted ability to wield the force as a future Jedi knight. All spokes led to this Black male taking on a prominent role within the force. But alas, it was not to be. And if viewers assumed that the initial tension between Rey and Finn onscreen was sexual in nature, and that it might lead to an eventual romance, then they would be wrong again. Purely platonic relationships onscreen are certainly fair game, but in looking at other Top Ten movies such as *Avatar* (i.e., Jake Sully and Neytiri), *Titanic* (i.e., Jack and Rose), or *Jurassic World* (i.e., Owen and Claire), it is interesting to see similar "cannot get along but *do* get along" romantic dynamics that emerge between principal characters as the movie story develops that did not develop in this movie between a White female and a Black male character.

Further, similar to the "twist" in Disney's *Frozen,* whereby "an act of true love" did not involve a man being paired with a woman, *The Force Awakens* had a similar trajectory in that it was actually Rey as the female protagonist who turns out to be badass and heroic. She usurped Finn's presumptive male-dominant positionality, loudly exclaiming twice, "I don't need you to hold my hand!" when Finn attempted to take control of the situation shortly after the two first met and were immediately identified and pursued by First Order enemy soldiers. It just so happens that when electing to depart from male-dominated and male-led narratives within a blockbuster action film, the male whose positionality is directly challenged is a visibly identifiable Black male. This establishing scene set the tone of the power and control hierarchy, which was put in motion a few moments earlier when Finn, after being spotted by Rey not long after crash-landing on Jakku, attempts to elude Rey unsuccessfully when she appears seemingly out of nowhere (essentially besting him) and knocks him on his hind quarters.

Finn's declination on the power scale only continued to accelerate—at least in relation to Rey, who grew stronger in her agency, heroism, and, of course, "the force," as the movie progressed. Despite being a career soldier trained in combat for all his life, Finn offers little in the visual display of confidence and bravura typically exhibited by our blockbuster hero types. The culmination of his impotence was crystallized during the movie's climactic scene when he and Rey had to face down their evil nemesis, Kylo Ren (Adam Driver). Initially, Rey engaged Kylo Ren, was thwarted by her fiercer opponent, and appeared to be knocked out when thrown up against a tree. However, as Finn picked up Luke Skywalker's light saber to avenge and defend his friend in fulfilment of the idea that he was "force sensitive," he was easily bested in less than a minute, notwithstanding his primal yells suggesting the opposite would occur.

Not only was Finn temporarily defeated by Kylo Ren (who insulted Finn by calling him "Traitor!"), but he remained unconscious for the remainder of the movie, not to be heard from again until *Episode VIII*. In contrast, although Rey was also thwarted by Kylo Ren at first, the audience soon sees that such a setback was *temporary*, as she rose again and leveraged the force to command control and hold legendary Luke Skywalker's light saber. Whereas Finn's duel with Kylo Ren lasted for roughly a minute, the moviemakers decided to use roughly three minutes of film time to demonstrate the intensity of the battle between the two truly force-sensitive opponents. Fortunately for the fate of the universe, Rey proved strong enough to injure, scar, and defeat Kylo Ren. Thus, when it came to the Black character of Finn, the force simply could have been stronger with this one.

Latinx

Film: Avatar *(2009)*
Top Ten Ranking: #1
Character: Tsu'tey (Laz Alonso)

Upon discovering Jake in his territory, Tsu'tey dismounts with an angry look and, in reference to Jake, declares that "these demons are forbidden here." When Neytiri challenges him, stating, "This is a matter for the Tsahik," his silence and compliance underscored that he as a warrior—who is trained to defend his people and their territory—ultimately had no power to decide unilaterally what to do with this potential threat. Technically, Tsu'tey was not wrong, in that foreign humans invade and eventually destroy Home Tree, or their spiritual and physical home later in the same movie.

But what really solidifies Tsu'tey's status as Utopic Reversal is that he actually assumes the mantle of leadership as Omatikaya's clan leader after Neytiri's father Eytukan was killed in the battle of Home Tree. In the original movie, Tsu'tey's death at roughly the 2:18:37 mark is relatively brief and succinct, an exit and death that almost betrays his status as the fiercest warrior within the whole clan. Tsu'tey jumps onto the open bay of a flying enemy warship and dispatches several combatants before being gunned down, only to tumble backwards, over and out of the open airship into the abyss below. Perhaps the clues to the audience in real time that Tsu'tey has been eliminated is that his last fighting scene takes place in slow motion (complete with what might be classified as soft "tribal" vocals playing in the background), right before our Latina fighter pilot, Trudy Chacón, is also taken out by the major warship, followed by a visual of a Direhorse creature running while on fire. These events together combine to paint a picture of despair as Neytiri felt overwhelmed, isolated, and defeated right before Sturmbeests came to the rescue by way of reinforcements sent by the larger spirit in which they believe, Eywa.

Additionally, Tsu'tey's death was tacitly recognized when shortly after his slow motion free fall out of the plane to his death, Jake, while flying in battle on his Toruk Makto, attempts to communicate with both Tsu'tey and Chacón—"Tsu'tey! Brother, do you read? Rogue One, you copy? Trudy?"—with his inquiries met with silence. For whatever it is worth, in qualitatively assessing the visual value of life, White male character Norm Spellman (Joel David Moore) was also shot and injured during the "all is lost" sequence that featured the deaths of Tsu'tey, Trudy Chacón, and the Direhorse. Spellman's avatar was injured to the point that he is seen in his human form exiting the transfer pod, gasping for breath, but nonetheless still alive, whereas the other three suffered terminal fates.

I digress.

If time is a necessary ingredient for character arc development, then the small amount of time spent "processing" Tsu'tey's death communicates his relative importance to the overall plotline and story development. If anything, Tsu'tey's originally filmed death scene was much more involved, as he was mortally wounded in battle and not only asks Jake—his prior nemesis and primary challenger—to take over, but he also asks for Jake to help end his life with a mercy killing. However, this scene was only included in the movie's 2010 re-edited version that included nine minutes of previously cut footage. Said *Avatar* director James Cameron of Tsu-tey, "[H]e kind of falls off the back of the shuttle and that's the last that you see of him but here we follow through" (Ziegbe, 2010, para. 3). But even with the added scene, consider how the power dynamic is completely flipped from Tsu'tey's over-the-top bravado in physically intimidating Jake during his introductory scene as a means to exert dominance, to him ultimately in a supine and powerless position asking Jake to complete the *ultimate* task of ending the most precious thing he has: his life.

Also, notice the amount of time "grieving" Tsu'tey's death as opposed to the time (and number of people) spent grieving the "death" of the White female character Dr. Grace Augustine (Sigourney Weaver).

Other

Film: Jurassic World *(2015)*
Top Ten Ranking: #8
Character: Simon Masrani (Irrfan Khan)

In *Jurassic World,* the owner, Simon Masrani, indicated early in the movie that he was taking pilot lessons as a newfound hobby. He may want a refund. During a key scene when flying Pterodactyls were causing commotion among harried parkgoers, Irrfan Khan's character was unable to navigate the situation and crash-landed and died. This is a Utopic Reversal because we must compare this "pilot error" to contrasting instances where our hero, so hell-bent and focused upon completing their mission, would get into a vehicle and "learn" how to pilot it on the fly based upon their intelligent association with other similar crafts. For example, Poe in *Star Wars: Episode VII* indicated he had no prior experience flying a TIE fighter jet but managed to do quite well despite an inauspicious start that saw their escape almost thwarted by a connecting cable. Rey also demonstrated the ability to "learn" how to navigate a craft when she took over the Millennium Falcon. Just consider how it would be virtually impossible for us to imagine an A-list White male actor perishing in a movie due to his inability to properly navigate.

Now the archetypal analysis portion has concluded. Before we shift attention to how White characters are consistently glamorized in mainstream film, by way of review, Table 8.1 illustrates how older, more obviously offensive or racially stereotypical ideas have been massaged into a more palatable and digestible format (i.e., archetypes) over time, thanks to Racism 2.0.

Table 8.1. Racist Tropes Updated Via Racism 2.0

	Racism 1.0 *(overt, obvious, offensive)*	Racism 2.0 *(subtle, suave, sophisticated)*
Angel Figure	"Mammy"	Renders aid or assistance
Background Figure	"Know your place"	Limited presence and impact
Comic Relief	"Coon"	Still the butt of jokes or "doesn't get it"
Menace to Society	"Mandingo"	Represents "threat," or "doesn't get it"
Physical Wonder	"Buck"	Physically, but not intellectually imposing
Utopic Reversal	"Jezebel"	Untrustworthy or incompetent

Questions for Questing

Define	• Define the Utopic Reversal archetype. • List 2-3 examples of Utopic Reversal figures you have seen within the past year. • Which Top Ten Utopic Reversal archetype example stands out to you the most?
Discuss	• List mainstream movies where you have seen a non-Black, non-White in a position of unquestioned and uncompromised authority. • Why are such a high proportion of mainstream movies featuring non-Whites in powerful positions biopic movies? • Which stereotypes is the Utopic Reversal figure most closely associated with? In which ways is the Utopic Reversal archetype more acceptable and less offensive? • Which Top Ten Utopic Reversal movie examples had you seen before? Did you notice this archetype upon your initial viewing? If not, do you agree or disagree with the analysis?
Decide	• Do the vast majority of moviegoers have non-White authority figures in their "real" lives off screen? • Are Utopic Reversal archetypes respected or rejected? • To what extent have you seen the same non-White actors reprise the same Utopic Reversal archetype in different roles?
Discover	• *Analyze This* (1999) [Other: Aasif Mandvi as Dr. Shulman who provides an incorrect diagnosis] • *Bruce Almighty* (2003) [Black: Morgan Freeman starts off the movie as "God," but he essentially abdicates his holy throne, and it is Jim Carrey's Bruce who we see leveraging the Almighty's omnipotent powers during the visible continuum]

- *Collateral* (2004) [Latinx: Emilio Rivera as Paco, or the police officer who is unfortunately stopped (and killed) before being able to stop hitman Vincent played by Tom Cruise]
- *Gothika* (2003) [Black: Charles S. Dutton as Dr. Douglas Grey, who turned out to be part of a kidnapping/raping criminal ring]
- *The Last Samurai* (2003) [Asian: Ken Wantanabe as Katsumoto, or the second-to-last samurai]

CHAPTER 9

The Assumed Affluent Prototype

30-SECOND SPOT

- Impoverished state is temporal/transitory.
- Opportunistic access to improved resources/assets/status
- Unburdened by practical financial considerations (i.e., property destruction)

TRAILER

- WHO: White character (prototype)
- WHAT: access and opportunity
- WHEN: ever-present throughout the entire character arc
- WHERE: clues for this prototype can be found in bits of dialogue (e.g., think how Tony Stark, when verbally sparring with Steve Rogers in *Avengers,* retorts "Genius, billionaire, playboy, philanthropist" in response to "Take that [armor] off, what are you?")
- WHY: this prototype helps Hollywood take plenty of storytelling shortcuts—viewers may have fewer questions about how or why events occur or come to be when one compelling explanation is "unlimited resources."
- HOW: do take note of context clues in material objects and destinations leveraged onscreen.

MAIN FEATURE ANALYSIS

Financing Fantasy

America is a capitalistic society. Therefore, the accrued accumulation of capital, or the process of its acquisition, has been a subject of interest ever since Hollywood began. The projection of "rags to riches" stories writ large provided flesh and coursing blood for the skeletal Horatio Alger story that served as the backbone for many family origin stories in this country. Accordingly, movies such as *The Grapes of Wrath* (1940) or *On the Waterfront* (1954) were intentionally created to appeal to working-class audiences who were just now discovering how to enjoy the newfound fruits of leisure time and disposable income, byproducts of urbanization and industrialization—two rails that kept American machinery on track on the road to progress.

The Hollywood "star system" also played into this psychology, whereby the allure of riches (not necessarily wealth) only made the lifestyles of the real-life robber barons all the closer in mind, but so far out of reach in reality. The astronomical wealth of such "titans of industry" like John D. Rockefeller, Cornelius Vanderbilt, J. P. Morgan, and Andrew Carnegie only verified that while it was indeed *possible* to achieve the American Dream, the sobering reality was that it was not *plausible* for everyone—most especially if you were an Irish, Italian, or Jewish immigrant and suffered severely from limited economic opportunities due to cultural discrimination. It is not hard to see how such economic ostracization might lead to crime, or alternate means of securing income; the fodder for numerous Hollywood films involving Irish or Italian "gangsters"—*Casino, Goodfellas,* and *The Irishman* being but a few modern examples. And God help you if you were Black eking out a survivalist existence within an institutionally and systemically racist, Jim Crow society.

But Hollywood proved to be the "manna from above," or the salve that kept many people's pistons from burning out by not just making the American Dream *possible* for everyone, but by going even further by making it *real.* Documented information in the form of newsreels certainly had a niche audience, but what kept people in lines at movie theaters was fueled by fantasy. In fact, going to the movies was the height of technology. "Back in the day" before cinema, one could explore the hallowed spaces of one's imagination through literature and art. But most mediums were limited to two dimensions, with a painting on a wall or a book in one's hand serving as gateways. Of course, the rigid limitations of working with inanimate objects such as a blank canvas or a piece of paper tested and pushed many artists, from those ingenious artisans who played with perspective dating back to the Renaissance Era to determined sculptors who attempted to demonstrate movement in a solid form with innovative carving and casting techniques. And we still marvel, with many hanging pieces such as the DaVinci's famed *Mona Lisa* attracting 10 million visitors a year just to catch a glimpse of this famous picture.

But if a picture is worth a thousand words, how much is a moving picture worth?

According to Hollywood, quite a few *Pennies From Heaven.* Although the early film industry started off as a neglected nickelodeon, it quickly blossomed into a burgeoning behemoth that commanded weekly audiences as large as 90 million—even during the Great Depression (Geiling, 2013). Similar to the Gold Rush in the 1840s, many flocked West to California and could not get into the moviemaking business fast enough. And for good reason, as the film industry has only continued to grow. Statista Research Department observed that "in 2021, the global box office revenue added up to 21.3 billion U.S. dollars, up from 11.8 billion dollars a year earlier—an annual growth of 80.5%. Still, the 2021 figure amounted to little more than half of the 42.3-billion-dollar revenue recorded in 2019, before the COVID-19 outbreak" (Statista, 2023c). People continue to be stimulated and fascinated by this new medium globally.

Yet, artisans of old were no match for the medium of film, or at least as effectively marketed by Hollywood. Opportunists in Hollywood movie studios saw how film could make fantastical ideas "come alive" in exciting new ways that a statue could not—no matter how marvelously carved. After all, when beholding the (potentially controversial) but critically acclaimed masterpiece sculpture *David* by Michelangelo (Smith, 2023), the vascularity seen in David's right arm suggest that more coursing blood presages a bodily movement in the near and not-too-distant future. *David* is an homage to the protagonist in the biblical story of the smaller, younger shepherd David, who slayed the large, manly Goliath with just his slingshot and no armor. Michelangelo not only "rendered David taller, more handsome, and more muscular than Bible passages suggested" (Brinkof, 2021) by portraying him as full of vim and vigor, but in working with the dense material of marble, he nonetheless had to choose a singular moment in time sliced out of a larger story.

In contrast, moving pictures are just what they say—they take these slices of time and move them together in front of a light source projected to the viewer rapidly to provide the illusion of movement. Hollywood titans then took the illusion of movement and created a movement of illusion. What would it look like to explore planets in galaxies far, far away? Go back to the future? Or imagine what it would be like to see dinosaurs in the here and now? Or how about not just seeing an extraterrestrial but making friends with it? (N.B.: If you were thinking about movies like *Star Wars, Back to the Future, Jurassic Park,* or *E.T.,* so was I!) As more characters from new places came into existence, Hollywood only became more sophisticated in developing techniques to make such fantasy become real, whether it be with proper sound and lighting, more intricate sets, or special effects ranging from fiery explosions to computer-generated imagery (CGI).

Ironically, movies are still experienced by viewers within a limited, two-dimensional space—whether it be a rectangular television at home or a large 70-foot screen at the local movie theater. However, unlike the *David* sculpture that suggests potential movement, this movie medium shows actual movement unlike any painting or sculpture ever could. Whereas imaginations may have to labor a bit to envision a destination such as *Harry Potter*'s Hogwarts Castle from reading its description in the books, in watching the film *Harry Potter and the Sorcerer's Stone*, viewer imaginations do not have to labor nearly as much to see previously described ideas "come to life."

As I write this book in 2023, our society is on the verge of new, unexplored horizons with the advent of virtual reality potentially intersecting with artificial intelligence. In other words, while we may one day soon see another medium as more advanced in bringing us closer to experiencing our artistic ideas, the "movie magic" many an audience currently experiences is the best of what we have to date. "In recognition of the powerful impact of this unique environment, it is not coincidental that early theaters were hallowed, palatial spaces that reflected the capacity of the austere experience moviegoers could expect" (Gooding, 2020, p. xix).

Hollywood studios constantly seek to improve their ability to tell stories and sell the "movie magic" of making the fictional images onscreen seem "real"—at least for a few precious moments. It follows that the moviemakers have done their job in showing the strength and advantages of this medium (say over a book) when they "reduce the labor" normally required to believe in a fantastical, fictional story. If I told you that outside right now there was an eight-foot, green, and extremely muscular individual with torn purple pants smashing public property, would you believe me? Probably not. But if you and I sit down and watch *Avengers: Endgame* and seek the Incredible Hulk talking and interacting with others onscreen *as if he were real,* would this cinematic experience at least be more convincing than my mere verbal description? My "naked" description still puts the onus on you to think about what I described as you process its possibility according to existing laws of nature you know. Within the cinematic space, I can show you the Incredible Hulk—and to the extent that his movements and behaviors are believable, the "movie magic" kicks in with the only remaining barrier to the Hulk being "real" is your willingness to believe. This is what Hollywood is absolutely good at; it has made fantasy more accessible, or "real," for so many, and is so beloved as a result.

Whenever we enter a theater, our ticket purchase indicates a Faustian fantasy bargain, which references a trade of something important in exchange for additional benefit or power. Here, in cinematic terms, on a base intellectual level we all know from the moment we park our car in the movie theater parking lot and proceed to enter a large windowless room with other strangers that on some level that what we are seeing is not "real." Yet, we are willing to trade in, or suspend our "normal" belief system in exchange for the opportunity to have our imaginations inspired, invigorated, or intrigued. Further consider how the conditions of a typical theater experience contains several ingredients to help fuel the imagination as it launches into flight: a quiet and darkened theater where loud distractions are politely admonished, comfortable seating, tastebuds excited through comfort foods, and larger-than-life images—all of which add up to an individual whose mind state is more likely receptive to the potentially pleasurable fantasy experience. "In fact, when the moviemakers perform their task correctly, viewers can *get into* a movie and possibly forget—for at least 90 minutes—where their car is parked or even who is seated directly to their left or right inside the theater" (Gooding, 2020, p. xviii, emphasis added).

With this Faustian fantasy bargain, we become all the more willing to play along or participate in the fantasy, *provided the movie does its part* to give us something worthy of believing. Hence, a "serious" movie set within medieval times will lose credibility and makes the exchange more difficult if characters are spotted wearing contemporary sneakers and jeans beneath their royal raiment. Here is where fans are converted into *stans*; when the universe depicted within the movie's visible continuum is believable enough, that the dedicated and faithful will "return" to this world, rewatching and returning to this fantasy space on multiple occasions. The more than 30,000 people who trekked to London for the Star Wars Celebration 2023 conference—many taking part in cosplay, or fashioning costumes like their favorite character—are likely a testament to such a successful bargain (Subano, 2023). It is unlikely whether millions of fans and stans worldwide would make as deep a "real" connection to the franchise if creator George Lucas originally fashioned the spaceship backgrounds on set out of cardboard and tinfoil.

However, as matters of the mind are delicate, this bargain or exchange can be broken at any time—whether accidentally when a perceptive viewer spots a sound gaffer reflected in a mirror onscreen, or flagrantly ignored or violated with shoddy production techniques (i.e., cardboard and tinfoil). With the latter, it is not uncommon for audiences to feel "cheated" and will respond with their critiques accordingly—just like thousands of Spider-Man fans "feel stupid" after discovering that CGI was used for the signature web slinger's mask covering the faces of Andrew Garfield's and Tobey Maguire's Spider-Man characters (Gibbs, 2022). Again, a simple tour through YouTube will evidence that too many people likely have too much time on their hands as they compose quite cogent and sophisticated critiques of movies they do not like. Yet, in their defense, these members of the paying public invested both their time and money for an experience—and were willing to give up something arguably even more precious: the vulnerability or willingness *to believe* with their imaginations.

Movie studios, which aspire to secure lifelong and even generational customers (as in, how many movies do you enjoy watching with your older and younger family members?), are uniquely incentivized to uphold their end of the Faustian-Fantasy Bargain. In sum, to better sell the idea that one's movie is "real," resources simply must be invested.

Fantasy Financed

Thus, when specifically talking about financing fantasy, or the movement of illusion, Hollywood studios have attempted to appeal to audiences by providing stories that attempt to answer general imaginative queries such as, what would it be like to go back in time and see dinosaurs? Any human being on planet Earth, no matter where they are born or what language they speak, can appreciate that seeing a 99,000-pound beast walk among us currently would be a sight to behold indeed.

And then there are specific, imaginative questions that revolve around capital—namely its loss and acquisition. America, after all, is a capitalistic society. Movies have been made to speak and cater to audiences with an appetite for imaginative questions related to money, such as what would it be like to go from rags to riches? Or what would it be like to live like a respectable mobster, or even pull off a multi-million-dollar heist . . . and get away with it!

The "star system" played into this psychology and helped build "brand" loyalty. But resources were required to create the image and make it "real" on some level. Therefore, if a movie's protagonist is insanely wealthy, like Tony Stark in *Iron Man*, Charles Foster Kane in *Citizen Kane*, or Daddy Warbucks in *Annie*, then shooting on location at a real mansion would certainly help the cause. Having the protagonist emerge from a limousine or expensive car would also help—whether it be a replica or the real thing, resources must be expended.

Traditionally, even in the boundless spaces of our imagination, Hollywood has invested more resources in stories that feature mostly White characters liberated by the *freedom of fantasy*, while most mainstream movies feature non-White characters grounded by the *gravity of reality*, with 80.3% of all Black Oscar nominations consisting of roles dealing with the themes of poverty or racism, for example (Gooding, 2020, p. 234). Thus, in making this investment, the Affluent prototype is present where the plot or a character arc is facilitated by affluence or access to significant capital. This prototype covers a broad span that stretches from the overt "sacrifice" and scheming that White characters willingly engage in with the hoped-for reward of a financial prize (e.g., *Bringing Down the House*) to the unstated and unquestioned source of fantastical opulence (e.g., *Mr. Deeds*). If anything, the Affluent prototype lends credence to the theory that it is easier to create storylines that are lubricated by the presence of capital, since insufficient funds cannot finance high-speed boat chases, swanky dinner parties, and exotic poolside arguments.

Except for *The Lion King,* all of the Top Ten movies have majority-White human casts. As the lone exception, *The Lion King* is a computer-animated film, which means that the majority-Black cast is heard, but not physically seen as we behold talking animated animals onscreen for whatever it is worth. So, with respect to the Top Ten earning movies of all time, the overwhelming majority are summer action blockbusters that feature hundred-million-dollar production budgets and multi-million-dollar, well-polished-and-oiled multinational marketing campaigns (see Table 9.1). Such a large scale of investment is virtually necessary to recoup revenues in the hundreds of billions.

The bottom line is that movie studios can simultaneously communicate to audience members messages of financing fantasy on two levels: (1) first as a *viewer*, the practical understanding that resources were invested to create a lasting impression by making the visual text as legible as possible—whether it be shooting a James Bond scene set in Phuket, Thailand, on location in the actual city of Phuket, Thailand, or shooting a scene in the north African country of Tunisia, doubling as the *Star Wars* "planet" of Tatooine, and (2) as a *voyeur,* or the emotive aspiration of connecting fully with the material and message within the "universe" glimpsed during the movie's *visible continuum*, if taken as "real" on some level. The latter part of this equation is a bit more amorphous and difficult to negotiate consistently, but traversing this space is made infinitely more facile when one's unbridled and unbounded imagination is provided a roadmap, or hint or suggestion of just what it possibly might look like to [fill in the blank].

To wit, the *Star Wars* franchise may not be a household name today if it were not for the quality of production—from concepts (e.g., hyperspace and parsecs), to impressive costumes (e.g., Darth Vader), to technology (e.g., light sabers), to machinery (e.g., Millennium Falcon), to belief systems (e.g., "the force")—that made the viewing experience that much more "real" and therefore enjoyable. Hollywood studios have learned to invest in high-quality fuel if they want their movie products to "catch fire" and burn long and bright at the box office, which is exactly what the most successful movies do—they continue to make money over time as they can be enjoyed repeatedly *ad infinitum*.

While many movies have been made specifically about the concept of money itself (e.g., *The Wolf of Wall Street*), analysis here is focused upon examples from mainstream movies that feature characters enjoying affluence—whether indirectly through the viewer lens of being in a million-dollar home staged to look like a "normal" middle-class abode or more directly through the voyeur lens of a recognized onscreen character of means and ability who turns audience members into vicarious participants who agree to yield and emotionally follow the protagonist as they direct the movie's enriched "experience."

What follows are some Top Ten examples of characters explicitly enjoying the freedom of fantasy as financed by the fruits of affluence in contrast to the gravity of

Table 9.1. Top Ten Highest Grossing Films of All Time Internationally With Production Budgets

	Title	*Gross*	*Year*	*Budget*
1	*Avatar*	$2,923,706,026	2009	$237 million
2	*Avengers: Endgame*	$2,799,439,100	2019	$356 million
3	*Avatar: The Way of Water*	$2,315,057,233	2022	$350–$400 million
4	*Titanic*	$2,261,385,180	1997	$295 million
5	*Star Wars VII: The Force Awakens*	$2,071,310,218	2015	$447 million
6	*Avengers: Infinity War*	$2,052,415,039	2018	$316 million
7	*Spider-Man: No Way Home*	$1,921,847,111	2021	$200 million
8	*Jurassic World*	$1,671,537,444	2015	$150 million
9	*The Lion King*	$1,663,075,401	2019	$260 million
10	*The Avengers*	$1,520,538,536	2012	$220 million

reality that constrains storytelling possibilities for numerous non-White characters, as reflected by the high percentage of Black actors in Academy Award–nominated roles concerned with poverty or racism as referenced earlier.

BLACK MIRROR

Under the HARM Theory rubric, just as archetypes are designed to marginalize non-White participation and prototypes are designed to glamorize White participation, it is important to bear in mind that every prototype has a corresponding archetype with which to juxtapose behavior observed onscreen. The limited character arcs of archetypes such as the Background Figure contrast sharply against the arc of the Assumed Affluent prototype. For instance, the Assumed Affluent prototype's presumptive access to power and control speaks to larger ideas about hope, redemption, and a deeper value and worth than what meets the surface. For otherwise, the movie would not last long if the protagonist were truly stymied by an obstacle depicted in the movie. The issue regarding non-White characters is that given their more limited character arcs, when a non-White character confesses that they do not know how to complete a task, they may be right, and they may not receive the benefit of the time and resources necessary to build their character arc back up.

ASSUMED AFFLUENT PROTOTYPE EXAMPLES FROM THE TOP TEN

N.B.: To show the strength of the prototype pattern, just as there were at least four non-White examples for each of the six archetypes, four prototype examples will be provided to mirror, or reflect back, the ubiquity of the pattern.

Affluent Example #1

Film: Avengers *(2012);* Avengers: Infinity War *(2018);* Avengers: Endgame *(2019)*
Top Ten Ranking: #10, #6, #2
Character: billionaire Tony Stark (Robert Downey, Jr.)

In any of the three *Avengers* movies that made the Top Ten of all-time list, Robert Downey, Jr.'s Iron Man character was and always will be super-smart savant and billionaire Tony Stark. I mean, it is one thing to be rich, but to have a wealth of knowledge on how to work important principles of math and science? The combination can surely make for good chemistry, with capital serving as the catalyst for such imaginative scenarios as Stark's artificial intelligence, JARVIS, politely bantering with him with all the measured restraint of a third-generation English butler. For instance, in *Avengers,* the concept of unlimited resources helped make the scene "more believable" when Stark's new Mark VII Armor Iron Man suit not only was able to fly on its own to approach a freefalling Stark hurtling off the side of a skyscraper (built with his money), but it accelerated to approach his falling body, transforming and enveloping him with a *metallic,* flying power suit that allowed him to fire up his jets and stop his fall—right before going right back to battle the evil Loki. Such fantasy is fueled not only by expensive CGI animations onscreen practically for us as viewers, but also onscreen for us as voyeurs watching an undoubtedly expensive piece of technology magically move right before our very eyes—if we "believe" what we see, that is.

Affluent Example #2

Film: Star Wars VII: The Force Awakens *(2015)*
Top Ten Ranking: #5
Character: The Empire (assorted cast members)

While it may be comforting to think of resources being used for altruistic means, capital is still capital, and it is interesting to see how our imaginations can be stretched to think of untold resources leveraged for the forces of evil. Specifically in *The Force Awakens,* we learn from a military strategy meeting held with General Leia Organa that the Rebel Alliance has the unenviable task of slowing down a new militaristic flex by the First Order called the Starkiller Base. The antecedent to the Starkiller Base was the Death Star, first introduced in Episode IV as a massive, spherical human-made weapon constructed by the Empire that appeared to be as big as a moon itself; moreover, and more unfortunately, the Death Star demonstrated its power when Lord Darth Vader used it to destroy the planet Alderaan, home of Princess Leia. Onscreen during the strategy briefing, after the Starkiller Base is first mentioned, someone calls out, "Hey! Don't you mean Death Star?" A computer graphic hologram is then projected showing images of both and demonstrating the ominous difference by way of scale.

From a "viewer's perspective," even if one does not subscribe to the idea that a seven-and-a-half-foot-tall, hairy, growling creature can copilot spaceships, one may appreciate that clever computer graphics were used to create the convincing illusion of an actual moving hologram seen onscreen. However, if one adopts a "voyeur's perspective," then the same graphic takes on entirely different meaning. For if one takes in what they are seeing as "real," then one cannot help but be impressed as the projected image of the Starkiller Base makes the Death Star look like a diminutive tennis ball sitting coolly in the shadow of a sphere the size of a beach ball.

What is unspoken and unsaid, but perhaps understood just the same, is that this Empire must be powerful if they have access to the resources (and technology) sufficient to create a human-made structure that defies all bounds of scale as we know it. After all, if space is endless, then there is no limit to the size that human beings can build when fueled by the twin engines of creative imaginations and unlimited resources. The glimpse of the scale of this Starkiller, which can destroy other planetary systems harnessing energy from other stars, sends a clear message about influence: the Empire's power is not based upon political might alone; economics play a profound part in the equation. The Empire equips a large and formidable military with Imperial Star Destroyers, All Terrain Armored Transport (AT-ATs), and Starkiller Bases because they have the resources to do so. What we see with the evil Empire is simply not the byproduct of an impoverished and fledgling group of loosely organized space vigilantes trying to take over the universe, but rather the output of finely tuned and well-oiled high-tech imperial machinery.

Affluent Example #3

Film: Titanic *(1997)*
Top Ten Ranking: #4
Character: Rose DeWitt Bukater (Kate Winslet)

The price tag to finance and produce the movie *Titanic* was indeed significant. For the movie to still be ranked as the fourth-highest grossing movie of *all time* over 25 years later suggests that it was successful in communicating to viewers that care was taken to produce believable replicas of the well-known sunken ship as accurately as possible, with realistic underwater scenes *not* filmed at the local YMCA indoor swimming pool. For voyeurs who felt that, due to good casting choices and an adequate storyline, the movie felt "real" to them, the opulent lifestyle that was supposed to be on display—a lifestyle notably devoid of non-White participants—was likely also seen as a real and "authentic" depiction of wealth. After all, *Titanic* is based upon a true story of a luxury ocean liner launched during the Jim Crow era. It is no one's "fault" that in retelling an accurate historical story, the story does not prominently feature non-White characters. This analysis is simply pointing out yet another instance where rich White characters are a routine and necessary part of the storyline, as with Kate Winslet's Rose character.

Affluent Example #4

Film: Jurassic World *(2015)*
Top Ten Ranking: #8
Character: Claire Dearing (Bryce Dallas Howard)

In *Jurassic World*, the movie begins with two brothers, Zach and Gray, being shipped off to visit their Aunt Claire (Bryce Dallas Howard) at her job at Jurassic World.

While the boys appear half-annoyed and suspicious of a boring time, we cannot overlook what is right in front of us. Both of the young males are White and have apparent access to an incredible amusement park experience. The park is located in the fictional realm of Isla Nubar, which still is some ways (we can imagine) from where the protagonists live as it is located "somewhere" off the coast of Central American destination Costa Rica. In other words, from a voyeur's perspective, if what we see is real, we can still appreciate that the transportation alone to this "international" destination may not have been serviced by typical "no frills" airline carriers that refuse to even serve pretzels on board. As to whether the parents or Aunt Claire paid for the transportation, no mention is made of this "detail"; suffice it to say that spending thousands of dollars on a nonessential expense (especially when the kids are not your own!) is not something that most members of the viewing audience can afford to do.

Questions for Questing

Define	• List additional examples of Assumed Affluent sightings you have seen in mainstream movies within the past year. • Define the Assumed Affluent prototype in your own words. • Which Top Ten Assumed Affluent example stood out to you the most?
Discuss	• What role do resources or access to resources play in mainstream movies you watch and enjoy? • Have you noticed when money is mentioned or discussed by White characters, and in what context?
Decide	• Can you think of a mainstream movie where the principal White protagonist started off the movie impoverished and ended the movie in that same state without ever experiencing a change in status? Consider in contrast movies featuring non-White characters that appear "locked" in such impoverished conditions.
Discover	• *50 Shades of Grey* (2015) • *Billy Madison* (1995) • *Casino Royale* (2006) • *Hitch* (2005) • *Wedding Crashers* (2005)

CHAPTER 10

The Family Tied Prototype

30-SECOND SPOT

- Familial or personal relationships directly referenced onscreen
- Personal sacrifice, decision, or tribute for a family member
- By movie's end, the interpersonal bonds are stronger.

TRAILER

- WHO: White character (prototype)
- WHAT: ability to bond
- WHEN: look for this character to be established early within their character arc.
- WHERE: most especially in action/blockbuster movies that feature large "realistic" crowds (i.e., urban setting)
- WHY: such personal connections typically explain or justify most of how we see the protagonist operate the rest of the time onscreen.
- HOW: often through scenes designed to facilitate White interiority—or moments away from the din of life where we as the viewing audience have an opportunity to peer into the featured character's life story a bit more past the superficial observation of another person in a crowd. Interiority scenes are often set up through tight or close-up camera shots and are often accompanied by a shift to "mood music," or nonlyrical, instrumental melodies (e.g., soft and slow piano, violin, or classical music) that cue the viewer into the importance of the character's facial expression, with time to reflect upon the character's thoughts.

MAIN FEATURE ANALYSIS

White characters serve as the universal default for most mainstream roles, and the White family unit most often serves as the emotional **anchor** that grounds the movie. The Family Tied prototype stresses the strength and value of relationships between White family members. This prototype maintains the eventual reunification or continued preservation of the core family unit as a consistent goal, despite the onset of various conflicts and tensions endured during the course of the movie. It is striking to observe how many mainstream movies depict White characters as having larger abiding connections to the people they care about, developing their humanity and character arcs in the process.

BLACK MIRROR

Under the HARM Theory rubric, just as archetypes are designed to marginalize non-White participation and prototypes are designed to glamorize White participation, it is important to bear in mind that every prototype has a corresponding archetype with which to juxtapose behavior observed onscreen. The Angel Figure archetype contrasts sharply against the Family Tied prototype as Angel Figures are typically depicted in isolation, with their primary relationship being the one depicted onscreen with the White protagonist. Conversely, the Family Tied prototype is dominant in all of the Top Ten movies with the exception of *Lion King*. There is nothing wrong with White families sticking together, but the contrast is glaring. In the other nine movies that round out the Top Ten list, the non-White characters not only have minimal presence, but their presence is socially isolated away from close personal relationships that limit key character arc development that can help the audience understand the character as being more than a two-dimensional stick figure. For usually, the three-dimensional, more intimate portraits, are reserved for principal White characters that we learn about their personal life, professional life, and their relationship to power and control.

FAMILY TIED PROTOTYPE EXAMPLES FROM THE TOP TEN

Family Tied Example #1

Film: Avengers *(2012);* Avengers: Infinity War *(2018);* Avengers: Endgame *(2019)*
Top Ten Ranking: #10, #6, #2
Character: Assorted principal characters

With the case of Tony Stark (Iron Man) and Pepper Potts; Clint Barton (Hawkeye) and his family; or Scott Lang (Ant-Man), Janet van Dyne (Wasp), and their family, through thick and thin, family bonds prove strong, even when everything seems to be going wrong.

Family Tied #2

Film: Avatar: The Way of Water *(2022)*
Top Ten Ranking: #3
Character: Jake Sully (Sam Worthington)

With the case of Jake Sully (voiced by Sam Worthington) as the patriarch of his family created with partner Neytiri (Zoe Saldaña) in the movie *Avatar: The Way of Water*, through thick and thin, family bonds prove strong, even when everything seems to be going wrong, as repeated in the refrain: "Sully's stick together." It is important to note that while Jake's family represent a blended family of sorts, from human to Na'vi, from paraplegic to able-bodied, we are also talking from a viewer's perspective that we are pairing a White male voice in a romantic context with the voice of an Afro-Latina voice.

From a voyeur's perspective, we have a quadriplegic White male who has fallen in love with a 10-foot blue humanoid figure who does not "sound" Afro-Latina, but rather sounds Na'vi. Based on historical treatment of Hollywood's Third Rail, or "informal policy prohibiting sexual contact between a Black male and a White female, most especially an A-list actress" (Gooding, 2020, p. 115), it is difficult to speculate on whether a family dynamic featuring a Black male human as the patriarch of a family and an A-list White actress spouse, complete with children, would sell. Meaning, would such a storyline as we see in *Avatar: The Way of Water* also be financed to the tune of nearly a quarter of a billion dollars if the protagonist were not White? Would the powerful storyline and visual effects be just as appealing in drawing people to the theaters? Perhaps we shall never know. What we do know is that *Avatar: The Way of Water* is near the top of the Top Ten earning movies of all time—and the patriarchal protagonist just happens to be a White male.

Family Tied #3

Film: Star Wars VII: The Force Awakens *(2015)*
Top Ten Ranking: #5
Character: Han Solo (Harrison Ford), General Leia (Carrie Fisher)

With the case of Han Solo and General Leia in *Star Wars: The Force Awakens*, through thick and thin, family bonds prove strong, even when everything seems to be going wrong.

Family Tied #4

Film: Avengers: Endgame *(2019)*
Top Ten Ranking: #2
Character: Thor (Chris Hemsworth), Loki (Tom Hiddleston)

Here, with the case of Thor and Loki in *Avengers: Endgame*, through thick and thin, family bonds prove strong, even when everything seems to be going wrong. What is interesting to note here is that outside of the traditional romantic context that prioritizes hetero-dominant relationships presaged upon the traditional Hollywood Trifecta of getting the (1) goal, (2), gold, and (3) girl, we have here an example of Family Tied that goes beyond the presumed male-female-plus-kids-equals-love equation, and also challenged by protagonists like Rey in the third *Star Wars* trilogy or by the sisters in the Top 20 grossing movie of all time, *Frozen*. Here, it is a brother's love for his brother that is of note here.

One "detail" we wish not to overlook is that after Thanos killed Loki to obtain the Space Stone, Thor became enraged and wanted revenge on Thanos. Understandable, but this brotherly love apparently overshadowed in that instant all of the nonbrotherly actions Loki took in the first *Avengers* movie, which saw Loki wreak havoc on the streets of New York (or Cleveland, depending upon your voyeur/viewer perspective). This prototype overlaps with the Assumed Affluent prototype in that Loki's destructive and *murderous* shenanigans likely cost millions of dollars to common taxpayers, much like the ones seated in the theater watching *Avengers* onscreen. However, these previously destructive acts are not even mentioned as a barrier to prioritizing their familial bond over anything else. Meanwhile, in real life, many relationships we have as everyday people might be adversely affected if we owed a family member millions of dollars due to our destructive actions.

Questions for Questing	
Define	• List additional examples of Family Tied sightings you have seen in mainstream movies within the past year. • Define the Family Tied prototype in your own words. • Which Top Ten Family Tied example stood out to you the most?
Discuss	• How many non-White Family Tied examples can you think of that occurred in mainstream movies released within the last year? • What do Family Tied prototypes say about larger themes of security and belonging within society?
Decide	• Consider the 2018 film *Incredibles 2* and its $1.2 billion dollar box office performance. Is there a comparable example of a mainstream movie featuring an "everyday" nuclear non-White family unit that is not only widely marketed and promoted, but is also widely consumed and patronized at the box office?
Discover	• *Bringing Down the House* (2003) • *The Day After Tomorrow* (2004) • *Flightplan* (2005) • *Saving Private Ryan* (1998) • *War of the Worlds* (2005)

CHAPTER 11

The Hero Prototype

30-SECOND SPOT

- Assumes mantle of leadership
- Ability to overcome seemingly difficult odds
- Valiant actions contextualized as benefiting greater good

TRAILER

- WHO: White character (prototype)
- WHAT: ability to succeed
- WHEN: look for this prototype to be established very early in the character arc; to make the viewing experience more "real," establishing scenes are a great starting point to contextualize and explain future (heroic) actions typically consummated by the movie's climax.
- WHERE: chiefly through dialogue referencing their skill or an early, brief demonstration of their "responsibility" to presage additional or increased activity later in the visible continuum
- WHY: once our Hero's "responsibility" to pursue a certain goal is uncovered, discovered, or acknowledged by the Hero early in the movie, this "responsibility" unlocks, unzips, and empowers the Hero to adopt a means-to-an-end philosophy, wherein all death, destruction, and mayhem they leave in their wake is justified by the movie's cathartic end. The Hero, through keen wit or physical skill, not only presumptively helps others, but is now justified in helping herself do whatever it takes to succeed in the process of becoming a Hero.
- HOW: however, if the movie features a cisgender "alpha" White male character (e.g., Jake Sully, Tony Stark, Steve Rogers, Bruce Banner, Thor, Peter Jason Quill, Clinton Barton, Owen Grady, Peter Parker, Jack Dawson) the Hollywood Trifecta may very well be spotted—where our beloved, if not bedraggled, Hero still somehow (1) gets the goal, (2) gets the gold, and (3) gets the girl by movie's end.

MAIN FEATURE ANALYSIS

The Hero is commonly personified by a cisgender White male and enjoys a status elevated far above that of your run-of-the-mill protagonist. The Hero is the destined one, the chosen one, the lucky one, or the smart one who, while maximizing his wits, is authorized to do whatever is necessary to complete his objective (which typically includes saving the world or making it better). Forceful, aggressive, and decisive actions usually accompany this role. Virtually any action movie containing A-list White males like Chris Pratt, Ben Affleck, Tom Cruise, Daniel Craig, or Jason Statham, to name a few, satisfies this prototype. Frequently, the Hero shoulders the "White Man's Burden" to save the world or a large group of individuals to which the Hero often has no direct personal ties. Such a responsibility is commonly vested in White characters we see dominating the Top Ten list; in contrast, consider how (Black) protagonist Simba's heroism within *The Lion King* only applied to a particular group of animals somewhere in Africa (presumably, not Wakanda), and was not applicable or demonstrated as valuable to larger groups of people.

BLACK MIRROR

Under the HARM Theory rubric, just as archetypes are designed to marginalize non-White participation, and prototypes are designed to glamorize White participation, it is important to bear in mind that every prototype has a corresponding archetype with which to juxtapose behavior observed onscreen. For instance, the Hero prototype contrasts sharply with Angel Figure archetypes in that while Heroes often do sacrifice for the greater good, it is typically not exclusively at their own expense. Iron Man/Tony Stark did sacrifice his life in *Avengers: Endgame* and knowing his acumen, this was likely a premeditated act. Jack Dawson from *Titanic* also met a tragic end in his valiant attempt to keep his love alive. Also, both Stark and Dawson's deaths did not come "first," but rather came at the very end of the movies in which they starred. However, Hero figures from all other Top Ten movies survive and thrive. Hero prototypes also contrast against Background Figure archetypes that are far removed from questions of power and control. Heroes also contrast against Comic Relief archetypes in that their ideas are taken and treated seriously. Heroes contrast against Menace to Society characters in that rather than pose a threat to civil normalcy, their actions—even though they may be physically destructive—are justified so long as the greater good is behind the character's actions.

For instance, jumping on an overturned car in the street normally would be frowned upon by the owner, but when Captain America must do so like he did in *Avengers* to save the greater good, then we do not think twice about his valiant actions from which the collective "we" all benefit. Hero prototypes also contrast against Physical Wonder archetypes in that as opposed to lacking intellectual or emotional capacities, these characters possess the emotional and intellectual intelligence to communicate and execute effectively. Lastly, Hero prototypes contrast against Utopic Reversal archetypes in that they take on the mantle of leadership that the audience agrees to concede, making them the new locus of power and control by movie's end. In contrast, Utopic Reversals consist of non-White characters who by movie's end are devoid of the power they initially appeared to have due to not being fully vested within the system of power and control to which they purportedly had access.

HERO PROTOTYPE EXAMPLES FROM THE TOP TEN

Hero Example #1

Film: Titanic *(1997)*
Top Ten Ranking: #4
Character: Jack Dawson (Leonardo DiCaprio)

Even on a sinking ship with the love of his life on his mind, Jack found time for heroism in *Titanic*. Audiences melted upon seeing Jack sacrifice for Rose, valiantly promising to stay alive in freezing cold water on the hopes that his flames of passion would keep him warm enough to survive. Jack held on to Rose but was unable to join her on the floating wood panel that was only strong enough for one in the aftermath of the *Titanic* sinking. Jack's behavior contrasted sharply with the cowardly, deceptive acts of the affianced villain Cal (Billy Zane), who lied to seek shelter on a lifeboat, claiming to be the father of a surviving child.

Hero Example #2

Film: Star Wars VII: The Force Awakens *(2015)*
Top Ten Ranking: #5
Character: Rey (Daisy Ridley)

If Luke Skywalker was the face of the first *Star Wars* trilogy, then it is safe to say Rey is the face of the third trilogy. Despite a marketing campaign that may have suggested a "traditional" storyline featuring a male protagonist (e.g., says one fan on Reddit: "Please tell me I'm not the only one who thought Finn was going to be the main character of *The Force Awakens* before it came out. I mean the main trailer ended with a shot of him with the lightsaber about to fight Kylo Ren and all the posters showed him with the lightsaber" [Pixarfan1, n.d.]), it is she who emerges in the end as the heroine capable of channeling the force and defeating Kylo Ren, in addition to saving her friend Finn.

Speaking of our friend Finn, for additional cross-reference, see the analysis provided for Finn under Utopic Reversal in Chapter 8, whom Rey instructed in no uncertain terms, not to take her hand (and lead her) earlier in the movie. Rey also displayed heroism in being able to adroitly pilot the Millennium Falcon with minimal training, as well as leverage the famed "Jedi mind powers" on First Order stormtroopers. In fact, when Poe and Finn reunite to "help" Rey, Poe smirks as he sees her scaling down the side of a wall (without any apparent bungee equipment or ropes) as she engineered her own escape.

Hero Example #3

Film: Avengers *(2012);* Avengers: Infinity War *(2018);* Avengers: Endgame *(2019)*
Top Ten Ranking: #10, #6, #2
Character: Take your pick

Heroism is displayed in many ways by many superhero characters we see within the visible continuum of the *Avengers* movies. Some of the superheroes featured, such as Captain Marvel, Black Panther, and Wong, are all examples of individuals who do not appear to be White males. But, with such limited time to go around for a 157-minute movie, not every superhero can share the spotlight equally. Particularly within a large ensemble cast, the superheroes who command the most time are those with more significant and developed character arcs. Whether the audience deems these characters as "more important" is a matter of choice, but the moviemakers certainly make it easier to draw that conclusion when White heroes Hulk (i.e., White male Bruce Banner), Iron Man, Thor, and Captain America, along with humans Black Widow and Hawkeye, have been in all four *Avengers* movies sharing most of the screen time in the process.

We have yet to verify but presume that all superheroes are indeed creatively created equal, perhaps with some superheroes being more super than others. So, while it would be wholly inaccurate to say that a non-White superhero such as Black Panther was not included, the question is, what about the quality of such inclusion? Did Black Panther himself and not his army, per se, play a pivotal, prominent, or important role in the resolution of the central problem? Given Black Panther's absence from the first *Avengers* movie entirely, his death in *Infinity War* and limited cameo in *Endgame*, it is not to say that his contributions were not important, but, due to limited character arc development, they may not have risen to the level of being classified as instrumental.

If we were to randomly pick another superhero from the *Avengers* series—for example, Captain America—a different analysis may be found here. It is impossible to have the same trilogy of movies read as the same if one were to cut out all of his scenes. Speaking of which, maybe it has nothing to do with his name, but Captain America shows remarkable resilience in the face of daunting challenges. His other superhero peers look to him for guidance and military strategy, frequently asking, "What's the plan, Cap?"

It is no secret that off-screen, our actual American military does indeed have "an arrangement" with Hollywood whereby, in exchange for access, the military will offer advice on how best to use equipment (Turney, 2023). Just like a savvy journalist who must be very careful about couching their critiques for a celebrity they wish to interview again, Hollywood movies often take care not to depict the American military in an unfavorable light—most especially for summer action blockbusters, and not independent films like *Jarhead* designed to have a more penetrating social commentary.

Hence, in *Endgame*, Captain America appears to be the last one standing in his attempt to defeat the all-powerful and mighty Thanos. Even with the six infinity stones, notice the symbolism of how Thanos significantly *damaged* but did not *destroy* the shield belonging to Captain America. In fact, after a pregnant pause in the action, where it appears that defeat is indeed imminent, and the near future is grim, Captain America tightens the laces on his battered shield further, still ready to fight and defend until the end. It is at this very moment when, out of the wilderness, he hears from his Black best friend Falcon (Anthony Mackie) and the bevy of reinforcements come to turn the tide in the eventual defeat of Thanos.

From a practical "viewer perspective," audiences do not see the lone superhero literally representing the United States of America—complete with consistent colors and stars and stripes symbology—being physically vanquished to the point of ultimate defeat. Further, from an emotional "voyeur perspective," if what the viewer is seeing is "real," then they cannot help but marvel (ahem) that this gritty soldier absolutely *must* be strong if he is somehow able to withstand an assault by the most powerful person in the universe on screen! It just so happens that this gritty individual has "America" in his name and also just happens to be a White male.

Speaking of a strong individual, we would be remiss to overlook Captain Marvel's brief, but impactful appearance. During the climactic battle scene in *Endgame*, like a lightning bolt, this White female character suddenly shoots straight out of the sky and with one, solitary motion or movement through Thanos's relatively large mothership floating ominously in the sky like overcast clouds, pierces through the armor, causing the entire spaceship to self-destruct. This act of heroism speaks to her significant strength and power even though she does not have as much screen time as other superheroes. Supporting superhero Falcon (played by Black male Anthony Mackie) is seen flying around the battlefield as well during the battle royale, but with much different results.

Hero Example #4

Film: Jurassic World *(2015)*
Top Ten Ranking: #8
Character: Claire Dearing (Bryce Dallas Howard)

In *Jurassic World*, Claire demonstrated heroism when she executed her idea to bait the Tyrannosaurus Rex into a battle with the Indominous Rex who was terrorizing the park all movie long. Rather than be terrified of both creatures, the thinking that one prehistoric beast could be manipulated definitely qualifies as cool, calm, and collected hero-level thinking in the face of danger. Not only does she get the Tyrannosaurus Rex to follow her and her lit flares, but she does so in a badass scene where she is running in heels (in slow motion, mind you)! While this may not be realistic to many viewers, for those invested voyeurs, it only adds to her heroic aura.

Do note, though, that similar to Margot Robbie's Jane character in the 2016 *The Legend of Tarzan*, that as the movie progressed, Claire's character was possibly more sexualized the more she developed in her heroic role over the course of the movie. She starts off the movie fully dressed in professional attire and by movie's end has stripped down to a tank top. Perhaps the running with heels scene demonstrated that our heroine did not have to sacrifice her femininity to help save the day—but her business attire was certainly sacrificed at the very least.

Questions for Questing

Define	• List additional examples of Hero sightings you have seen in mainstream movies within the past year. • Define the Hero prototype in your own words. • Which Hero example stood out to you the most?
Discuss	• What do you think about the controversy over **cross-casting**, whereby a traditionally White role is now occupied by a Black body, like in the 2022 Disney remake, *The Little Mermaid*? If it is the same heartwarming story, why the resistance to heroism represented in a different body? • Do audiences respond at the box office to support non-White heroes? If so, what are some examples you can conjure? If not, why not?
Decide	• Think about how the "hero" Black Panther literally has the adjective "Black" in his title—how soon until there is a mainstream movie that earns hundreds of millions of dollars featuring a non-White "Hero" that is considered "normal"? After all, Indiana Jones and John Wick are not specifically labeled as "White" heroes, when in fact, that is what they are. • Given that *Black Panther* arguably is the highest-grossing movie featuring a Black protagonist—in contrast to more "traditional" White male alpha superheroes who have more universal aims for their superpowers—how does Black Panther stack up? Can you specifically describe his powers as seen during the visible continuum and specify how he leveraged his powers to save the greater good (other than his personal battle for power internally within his community generally and against Killmonger specifically)?
Discover	• *Ad Astra* (2019) • *Batman Begins* (2005) • *Erin Brockovich* (2000) • *Finding Nemo* (2003) • *The Lord of the Rings: The Fellowship of the Ring* (2001)

CHAPTER 12

The Intellectual Prototype

30-SECOND SPOT

- Unique expertise established (usually during character's introduction)
- Able to experience an epiphany
- Offers key and crucial information central to movie's plotline or story development

TRAILER

- WHO: White character (prototype)
- WHAT: the central theme undergirding this prototype is the ability to solve.
- WHEN: look for this prototype to be established very early in the character arc; to make the viewing experience more "real," establishing scenes are a great starting point to contextualize and explain future (potentially heroic) actions typically consummated by the movie's climax.
- WHERE: chiefly through dialogue referencing their skill or an early, brief demonstration of their acuity to presage additional or increased activity later in the visible continuum
- WHY: why would most people enter the theater if they knew the protagonist was going to fail? Most mainstream movies (most especially the summertime action blockbuster hits) feature protagonists who emerge as successful despite their inauspicious beginnings.
- HOW: even though teams of writers research and cross-reference the realities of life as an oil rigger (*Armageddon*), an astronaut (*The Martian*), or a brave Marine—except where the actual hero was a Black male seeing how for the movie *World Trade Center*, director Oliver Stone cast a White male to play the part of Sergeant Justin Thomas based upon the faulty assumption that the true-to-life hero was White (Associated Press, 2015)—all of this prepackaged, distilled, and organized knowledge often comes off as being normal or natural for our protagonist who is able to impress viewing audiences possibly with their seemingly fierce command of detached reflection in the face of an uplifted knife (as Oliver Wendell Holmes, Jr. would likely attest)—this character is *always* able to think their way out of their scenario—attributes that mesh and blend frequently

with Hero and Manipulator prototypes. This prototype pattern adds value to one's character arc onscreen as, typically and not coincidentally, the most important characters onscreen reveal or discover the most important pieces of information crucial to understanding the storyline. Within the world of mainstream movies—most especially where there appears to be an ensemble, racially "diverse" cast, such characters that provide the most relevant and vital information are most often White.

MAIN FEATURE ANALYSIS

Contrast this character prototype with a lack of intelligence for non-White Physical Wonder archetypes, whereby the Intellectual prototype encompasses the White character who is inherently knowledgeable about anything and everything. Omniscient-like qualities are often displayed when this character takes on a leadership role, instructing and demonstrating others on better ways to do things: fight, build houses, catch a criminal, or even fly planes at the last minute (even if seemingly outside the area of the character's expertise!). Movie audiences are trained and conditioned to look to White characters to provide vital and important information essential to the plot. Since most protagonists in mainstream movies are White characters, audiences by default rely on Whites to deduce and solve the movie's most pressing problems.

BLACK MIRROR

Under the HARM Theory rubric, just as archetypes are designed to marginalize non-White participation, and prototypes are designed to glamorize White participation, it is important to bear in mind that every prototype has a corresponding archetype with which to juxtapose behavior observed onscreen. For instance, the Intellectual prototype contrasts sharply with the Comic Relief and Physical Wonder archetypes as we routinely are reminded about the computing ability of the individuals, and we agree to let them lead us through the onscreen experience. Whereas the Comic Relief is hardly ever taken seriously, and their statements must be greeted with healthy suspicion (think Chris Tucker's character in *Rush Hour*), with the Intellectual we are instructed to reserve deference and respect—even if they conduct silly acts along the way in the name of providing comic relief. Few dramatic romances that make the Top Ten list as action summer blockbusters have the widest appeal to the greatest possible audience. The Intellectual may also mirror the opposite of the Utopic Reversal archetype, who often finds their power drained before it is too late. A quick-witted Intellectual would not only be able to deduce and piece together what conspiracies were in play in real time, but also would be able to channel Manipulator qualities to avoid getting railroaded.

INTELLECTUAL PROTOTYPE EXAMPLES FROM THE TOP TEN

Intellectual Example #1

Film: Avatar *(2009)*
Top Ten Ranking: #1
Character: Dr. Grace Augustine (Sigourney Weaver)

In *Avatar*, what is undoubtedly impressive is the intellectual capacity of Dr. Grace Augustine, played by Sigourney Weaver, who, as viewers, we know has "knowledge" of *Aliens* from a different galaxy. But the science behind transplanting consciousness is likely difficult seeing how no one else has figured out how to do it yet in real life. Yet, we are treated to 157 minutes of spellbinding visual action thanks in part to this genius technology.

Intellectual Example #2

Film: Avengers *(2012);* Avengers: Infinity War *(2018);* Avengers: Endgame *(2019)*
Top Ten Ranking: #10, #6, #2
Character: Dr. Bruce Banner (Mark Ruffalo)

In the *Avengers* series, the other characters make known their respect for Dr. Bruce Banner's intellect. The title of doctor also cues the audience into the fact that this individual, while saddled with an "anger management" issue (a source of the running joke throughout the series, in terms of Bruce's relationship with "the other guy," or the Hulk alter ego), is nonetheless worthy of intellectual respect. Even in *Avengers: Endgame,* it is the Hulk who capably operates time-traveling technology while adorned with a pair of glasses, a generic symbol of intelligence.

Intellectual Example #3

Film: Avengers *(2012);* Avengers: Infinity War *(2018);* Avengers: Endgame *(2019)*
Top Ten Ranking: #10, #6, #2
Character: Tony Stark/Iron Man (Robert Downey, Jr.)

Tony Stark arguably has the Hollywood Trifecta down pat. He certainly has the gold, being a billionaire. He has "the girl" in being married to the effervescent Pepper Potts (played by blonde A-list actress Gwyneth Paltrow). And he usually gets his goal accomplished on account of leveraging his physical resources with his intellectual ones. Part of Tony Stark's character profile is that he is smart and smug and is not hesitant to let others know—to the point that he can come across as annoying, often causing mild tensions around the strategy table.

Also, the fact that he is able to engineer so many solutions, from advanced weaponry encoded in his innovative flying armored suit, to the contraption that keeps his heart pumping, to figuring out the NPF algorithm (as in Nonlinear Predictive Filter—duh!) to crack the code for traveling through time, audiences from a voyeur's perspective know and "have confidence" that with a person so smart, it just *might* be plausible that he could indeed make his inventions. Just ask at any local middle school cafeteria if Iron Man could be real. . . .

Intellectual Example #4

Film: Avengers *(2012);* Avengers: Infinity War *(2018);* Avengers: Endgame *(2019)*
Top Ten Ranking: #10, #6, #2
Character: Captain America/Steve Rogers (Chris Evans)

In the same *Avengers* series, Captain America demonstrates intellectual capacity with his sound battle-ready stratagems. He confidently gives commands based upon a firm understanding of what needs to be done. Captain America's sound militaristic intellect positions the Avengers for success, even when facing off against a formidable opponent.

Questions for Questing	
Define	• List additional examples of Intellectual prototype sightings you have seen in mainstream movies within the past year. • Define the Intellectual prototype in your own words. • Which Top Ten Intellectual example stood out to you the most?
Discuss	• When was the last time you saw an A-list White actor made to look flat-out incompetent and incapable in a non-comedic role? • Consider how many times within society that you were asked to revere the intellectual production of a non-White individual—just like we are informed at an early age of the intellectual brilliance of a Thomas Jefferson, even though despite his charming intellect, he could not deduce that owning over 300 individuals as enslaved laborers without pay and fathering at least six children by Sally Hemings, an enslaved concubine he took to Europe (with Hemings bearing the first child at the tender age of 14 years old, justifiably raising questions about consent versus rape), just might be in conflict with his noble and time-honored intellectual ideals?
Decide	• How does the Intellectual prototype intersect with historical, more problematic narratives about measuring intelligence in society, from SAT tests to the measuring of craniums in the name of "scientific" eugenics?
Discover	• *Good Will Hunting* (1997) • *National Treasure* (2004) • *Oppenheimer* (2023) • *The Silence of the Lambs* (1991) • *Star Wars: Episode I—The Phantom Menace* (1999)

CHAPTER 13

The Manipulator Prototype

30-SECOND SPOT

- Able to personally change their circumstances.
- Able to influence the actions of others.
- Able to perform unusual acts in justification of their goal.

TRAILER

- WHO: white character (prototype)
- WHAT: ability to navigate
- WHEN: look for this to be fully developed toward the end of character arc within the visible continuum
- WHERE: toward the climactic scene; most especially in action/blockbuster movies where the Manipulator or protagonist is able to prioritize their immediate objective by any means necessary
- WHY: this typically demonstrates resolution of issues or ideas made aware to the viewing audience by primary characters onscreen
- HOW: by adopting a "can do, will try!" attitude, we find there are very few obstacles our empowered protagonist cannot overcome. Consequently, there are very few actions that our empowered protagonist cannot do publicly or privately—especially when the necessity of such actions are contextualized and justified through interiority (think of the lack of social and criminal consequences for our protagonist who must escape "bad guys" in a "foreign market" and plows through several boxes of produce while being chased on a motorcycle, looking back over his shoulder only every so often, of course, because obviously what he is doing or where he is going is more important.

MAIN FEATURE ANALYSIS

Another qualitative measuring point is how—if and when—our White protagonist comes into contact with "the law," how much more fluid and flexible the law can be. Such (fictional) depictions differ dramatically from the reality off-screen that could be the stuff of horror movies! Just consider how horrifying it would be to be playing video games in your own home with your nephew, as Atatiana Jefferson was, and then suddenly and without warning, have real individuals in real military gear turn the violence from your video game into a harrowing experience, whereby an unarmed and innocent Jefferson ends up shot dead (warrant "served" on wrong house). Or consider how horrifying it would be to be shot dead in your own residence by a mistaken "and fatigued" officer, as Botham Jean was? Or to make simple contact with police just yards from your Prairie View campus en route to a new life and then end up dead, like Sandra Bland? Or to have officers kneel on your neck for 9 minutes and 29 seconds over a possible $20 counterfeit bill, like George Floyd? The reality is that for some of us, making contact with the police is no light, nor laughing, manner. Yet, when it comes to Manipulator characters, these White characters often appear to be free of such concerns, demonstrating considerably more plasticity.

Moreover, Manipulator prototypes are important character patterns since they frequently display or evidence growth in one's character arc. White characters are frequently depicted moving from a position where they lack control to the point where they become the primary person in control, unlike non-White characters whose character arcs may remain flatter and steadier. Consider *Avatar's* Jake Sully growing in stature to become Toruk Makto, or an individual with a "pure soul" able to connect with and fly one of the most feared and fearsome flying creatures the Omatikaya clan reveres (not to mention, the largest and most colorful).

Sully becomes only the sixth ever in clan history to do so—even though he starts the movie as an outsider completely foreign to the culture. In contrast, the Academy Award–winning role of Minny, the Black female maid portrayed by Octavia Spencer in *The Help,* featured her in a maid outfit performing maid duties in her final scene onscreen—just as she was on her first scene onscreen—despite arguably being one of the driving protagonists of the movie. Unlike Jake Sully's character, Minny's character arc did not shift or change considerably with respect to how she negotiated *power* with the larger establishment (e.g., become president of a unionized group of domestic workers, or use "proceeds" from the sale of her story to move and retire to Florida, opening a side business selling chocolate pies and living "happily ever after") during the visible continuum.

BLACK MIRROR

Under the HARM Theory rubric, just as archetypes are designed to marginalize non-White participation and prototypes are designed to glamorize White participation, it is important to bear in mind that every prototype has a corresponding archetype with which to juxtapose behavior observed onscreen. For instance, the Manipulator prototype contrasts very strongly against the Background Figure archetypes who, in most instances, we presume have little access or ability to definitively answer questions concerning power and control. The whole point of the Manipulator prototype is to leverage change based upon the personal autonomy to move and to behave based upon a willingness to risk and explore. The willingness to risk and deviate from protocol ironically may come when individuals feel intimately connected and part of a group, not necessarily ostracized. It is because the individual is *invested* that they wish to influence.

The Manipulator prototype may also contrast from Angel Figure archetypes in that rather than sacrifice for someone else, whatever labor in which the character engages is designed also to benefit them personally as opposed to an altruistic sacrifice with no hint of a direct return. Finally, Manipulators likely contrast Utopic Reversal characters who are slowly removed from central questions concerning power and control. Manipulators are constantly questioning and challenging such questions, often to find answers in their favor. Think of the 1984 classic *Ferris Bueller's Day Off* that built up tension over the proper care of a rare sports car and was the source of much angst throughout the movie for the main characters—a tension that crescendoed with the car's total destruction—but was merely shrugged off as an existential lesson for a teenager on how to self-improve with no visible evidence of serious consequences during the movie's visible continuum.

MANIPULATOR PROTOTYPE EXAMPLES FROM THE TOP TEN

Manipulator Example #1

Film: Avatar *(2009)*
Top Ten Ranking: #1
Character: Jake Sully (Sam Worthington)

In *Avatar,* we see how our protagonist is able to grow in power, literally starting off during the visible continuum as one who was learning how to merely walk in his new 10-foot-tall blue avatar body. While these bodies presumptively may connect the user to ideas, thoughts, knowledge, wisdom, and stories indigenous to the land and people, the blue avatar is introduced to the audience almost like a new bike or car that an excited young customer is eager to test. Yet, the audience learns that one indigenous legend is that of the Toruk, which is the hardest flying beast to match with. As demonstration of his (eventual, if not inevitable) leadership of the clan, Jake masters the hardest bird ever. More importantly, the subtle implication is that either the Na'vi culture was very open or Jake was awfully sophisticated to manipulate and master that which native and indigenous members could not for centuries.

Manipulator Example #2

Film: Avengers: Endgame *(2019)*
Top Ten Ranking: #2
Character: Dr. Bruce Banner (Mark Ruffalo), Tony Stark (Robert Downey, Jr.)

Nothing speaks to the ability to manipulate than by figuring out how to go back in time! In *Avengers: Endgame,* great minds Tony Stark and Dr. Bruce Banner deduce this precisely as a means to recover the infinity stones that Thanos successfully collected before decimating half the world's population in *Infinity War.* Don Cheadle's James Rhodes character "didn't get it," much like the viewing audience who have never time-traveled before. Rhodes's Black male character evinced through his dialogue that he doubted the ability of our heroes to do precisely what everyone in the theater paid admission to see them do, so others had to explain to him that they were not actually traveling through time but were manipulating time to flow through them.

Manipulator Example #3

Film: Jurassic World *(2015)*
Top Ten Ranking: #8
Character: Owen Grady (Chris Pratt)

In *Jurassic World*, Chris Pratt's character, Owen, is seen granting implicit access to opportunity by letting Claire's "bored" nephews hang out with him behind the scenes. As an employee, Owen was likely in an area with restricted access, as members of the paying public were out in the main designated spaces. The youngest, Gray, asks Owen the names of four Velociraptors, who responds, "There's Delta, Charlie, Bravo." In response, without skipping a beat Gray asks, "Where's Alpha?"

What is significant about this two-word line is that the young White male demonstrates acuity by following the military practice of utilizing code words to clearly communicate distinct letters with minimal confusion. Hence, "Delta" represents the letter "D," "Charlie" represents "C," while "Bravo" represents "B." As this young boy instantly processes the verbal pattern casually communicated by an adult, he immediately asks "Where's Alpha?" in recognition of the unnamed first letter, "A." Even better, Owen responds, "You're looking at him kid," to acknowledge his ability to manipulate and control wild animals, let alone prehistoric ones. As proof and further evidence of his manipulative ability, later in the movie, a famous scene develops where he purposely lets them loose and "joins" them riding a motorcycle as if one with them.

Manipulator Example #4

Film: Spider-Man: No Way Home *(2021)*
Top Ten Ranking: #7
Character: Peter Parker (Tom Holland)

In *Spider-Man: No Way Home*, Peter Parker is quite frustrated that his identity has been made public, shielding him from the anonymity that not only he desires, but needs for the safety and protection of his paramour, MJ (Zendaya), and best friend, Ned. This young kid needs a solution. So, what to do? He calls upon fellow superhero Dr. Strange (Benedict Cumberbatch) to cast spells and manipulate time on his solitary behalf. Of course, the viewer understands that logically, there is no movie without: (1) entertaining the idea that a Dr. Strange exists, and (2) without Dr. Strange entertaining Spider-Man's idea. That being said, this "simple" request leads to several unintended consequences, including the introduction of two other Spider-Man characters played by Andrew Garfield and Tobey Maguire (who played Spider-Man in the earlier movie series released in the early 2000s). The bottom line is that asking and prevailing upon Dr. Strange to alter time for personal gain is a sign of manipulation. Adding insult to injury, Spider-Man even tricked and trapped Dr. Strange in the Mirror Dimension so he could still do what he wanted to do.

Questions for Questing	
Define	• List additional examples of Manipulator sightings you have seen in mainstream movies within the past year. • Define the Manipulator prototype in your own words. • Which Top Ten Manipulator example stood out to you the most?
Discuss	• How does the Manipulator prototype play out in real life? • Have you witnessed real-life scenarios or situations where White people have "refused to take 'no' for an answer"? To what degree does this ability to protest and demand change in a civil manner suggest access to power and control?
Decide	• When was the last time you saw a blockbuster movie whereby the non-White protagonist was able to commit a major federal crime (i.e., commit a successful heist of a cognizable Las Vegas casino like we saw in *Ocean's Eleven*) and get away with it?
Discover	• *Anger Management* (2003) • *Home Alone* (1990) • *Legally Blonde* (2001) • *Minority Report* (2002) • *Mission: Impossible—Dead Reckoning Part One* (2023)

CHAPTER 14

The Romantic Prototype

30-SECOND SPOT

- Seen being emotionally affectionately with other characters
- Initiates physical touch
- Romantic relationship is part of character's arc.

TRAILER

- WHO: White character (prototype)
- WHAT: ability to love
- WHEN: look for this part of the character arc to be established early in the movie.
- WHERE: through dialogue and scenes exploring interiority—sound and music can be a powerful cue to interiority; for instance, soft violin strings in the background clues the viewer into the idea that whatever the character might be thinking or experiencing is important or conversely, the quieting of all "normal" sound allows the viewer to myopically focus on the character at the center of their attention.
- WHY: this dimension adds depth to character, making the character more "real."
- HOW: primarily by establishing interiority, of which is *de rigueur* when this prototype is exhibited in the protagonist, which is most often White, as frequently seen within the Top Ten–grossing films of all time

MAIN FEATURE ANALYSIS

Interiority here is key, because this means that life within the visible continuum is being governed by the complex set of rules and boundaries set by our protagonist who has a perspective that orients and grounds the viewer—all actions are essentially adjudged from this perspective. Otherwise, the "evil" element—whether it be a supervillain from another world or a "mean" opponent from a team dance or singing tournament—takes on a different meaning if we adopt a different lens or framework. The idea that the concepts of "good and evil" are general principles many audience members share, but are not absolute, is reflected in a mainstream movies like *Joker* or *Cruella,* whereby audiences were previously introduced to these characters as villainous, but the remakes center their stories and do not exactly justify their evil deeds for which they are known, but within the visible continuum of the remake, their actions are "better contextualized" by providing additional insight into their backstories, or originating perspectives.

Consider the case of Cruella, the famous half-black– and half-white–haired fashionista who first came on the mainstream scene as a ruthless, self-centered egomaniac in Disney's 1961 animated film *101 Dalmatians.* However, if you were given up and essentially abandoned by your natural blood mother, who also murdered your loving and doting stepmother, and had to resort to a life of crime merely to eke out an existence and survive, would you not also harbor some resentment and find it challenging to formulate lasting and substantive, emotionally rich relationships? The 2021 movie *Cruella* is an excellent example of interiority whereby we take two whole hours to make what appears to be simple (e.g., portrait of a villain) and make it decidedly more complex (e.g., possible empathetic victim?).

Not to mention in the case of casting Emma Watson as the younger Cruella, undoubtedly, having the "face of evil" represented by an otherwise attractive, well-known A-list actress may blur the moral line even further, with many leaving the theater as invigorated "fans" of Cruella who now are ready to defend the character's overall villain narrative profile as being "misunderstood" (Hassenger, 2021). Investing considerable resources into backstories of White villains is not limited to the big screen, as the multi-million-dollar musical theater production *Wicked,* demonstrates. *Wicked* suggests very heavily that the Wicked Witch of the West from the 1939 Hollywood classic *The Wizard of Oz* was perhaps not that wicked at all, once you got to know her "on the inside."

In other words, even villains have the capacity to love, *and be loved* by fans in the paying audience through principles of interiority.

BLACK MIRROR

Under the HARM Theory rubric, just as archetypes are designed to marginalize non-White participation, and prototypes are designed to glamorize White participation, it is important to bear in mind that every prototype has a corresponding archetype with which to juxtapose behavior observed onscreen. For instance, the Romantic prototype contrasts sharply against Background Figure archetypes, of whom we often know very little. Romantic prototypes, if they are to work, necessarily must command empathy and feeling from viewing audience members. This is what makes the nonunion between Rey and Finn all the more interesting. Within the same franchise, Han Solo and Princess Leia had a relationship that initially appeared as if it would not work. The two could not get along but did end up getting along to the point where Leia tells Solo "I love you" in Episode V, to which he famously retorted in return, "I know."

If new awareness about professionalism in the workplace in the aftermath of the 2017 social media campaigns #metoo or #timesup, designed to raise awareness about male employees within Hollywood industry circles that incorrectly operate with a sense of entitlement, then no, simply working professionally with another woman does not obligate the woman to reciprocate any nonprofessional exchanges or overtures. Yet, *Jurassic World* was made the same year as Episode VII (2015), and featured two leading protagonists, Owen and Claire, who could not get along but ended up navigating the sexual tension that developed over the course of the movie toward a relationship—the same happened to Stark and Potts before we saw them in 2012's *Avengers*. Yet, in *The Force Awakens*, any so-called sexual tension was not acted upon, nor explored, even though it was hinted at when Finn aggressively took Rey by the hand twice when they first met in Jakku, and also when he tenderly held her head in his hands after Kylo Ren used the force to knock her out temporarily by throwing her against a tree. Up until that point in the movie, the proverbial "romantic door was still open," but was never entered. Based upon so many movies made that feature protagonists who end up kindling a romantic spark by movie's end, for whatever reason, the moviemakers decided against exploring this possibility onscreen with the White female character Rey and the Black male character Finn (and Poe, too). In this instance, the focus was on friendship.

ROMANTIC PROTOTYPE EXAMPLES FROM THE TOP TEN

Romantic Example #1

Film: Avatar *(2009)*
Top Ten Ranking: #1
Character: Jake Sully (Sam Worthington)

In *Avatar*, even as an outsider from a foreign species, it is Jake who finds romance with indigenous Na'vi woman Neytiri (Zoe Saldaña). Neytiri appears to have the most to give up in the relationship, getting her father to accept, but Jake gets his way and runs the clan once dad and brother are removed from the equation. *Avatar: The Way of the Water* continues the story with him depicted as a "family man."

Romantic Example #2

Film: Avengers *(2012);* Avengers: Infinity War *(2018);* Avengers: Endgame *(2019)*
Top Ten Ranking: #10, #6, #2
Character: Hawkeye/Clint Barton (Jeremy Renner)

Whereas Iron Man demonstrates a romance that grew over a decade's worth of movie releases since the time the first *Iron Man* movie released in 2005, over the course of the *Avengers* series Hawkeye sprouted a romance that cultivated in a family and children—a romance that still motivated this character's actions.

Romantic Example #3

Film: Avengers: Infinity War *(2018)*
Top Ten Ranking: #6
Character: Wanda (Elizabeth Olsen), Vision (Paul Bettany)

In *Avengers: Infinity War*, the romance from Wanda and Vision was palpable from the beginning when Vision first is perturbed by signals from the stone in his head inside the bedroom he appears to be sharing with Wanda during evening hours. A potential solution to slow down or stop the rampaging Thanos that grows in power with the acquisition of each of the six infinity stones was to destroy the one inside of Vision. Captain America has an idea that such technology to extract the stone without sacrificing Vision can be found in technologically advanced Wakanda. Because Vision is important to the team, his superhero friends go to Wakanda to defend him from Thanos while the operation is complete. Alas, Thanos beats them to the punch, however not before Wanda professes her love to Vision onscreen and vice versa.

Romantic Example #4

Film: Avengers: Endgame *(2019)*
Top Ten Ranking: #2
Character: Steve Rogers (Chris Evans)

In *Avengers: Endgame*, after the team bonds together to successfully defeat Thanos at Tony Stark's expense, Captain America agrees to go back in time and return the stones. Yet, he exhibits signs of the Manipulator prototype and "returns" to the present in a much older form, thereby deciding to give up the Captain America shield to Falcon (one of the few "heroes" who wears glasses in hero form, by the way).

Wearing glasses or goggles is not a crime, but it provides a low-level barrier between the audience and his "naked" facial expressions, which presumably allow for the audience to better connect with the character. Even though Iron Man wears a full mask, his entire face is displayed from the movie perspective of "inside" the mask. Second, the glasses remind the viewer that the character is not a superhero who possesses remarkable eyesight naturally and leverages it to complete their tasks.

But the movie ends with Captain America forever happy in time, dancing with his true love, seemingly happy for all eternity (a story one may know if they followed Captain America's backstory). This depiction definitely qualifies as romance.

Bottom Line #2

[Part II, *Color Me Bad*: Chapters 3–14]

Hollywood mainstream movies routinely present a limited view of non-White characters, in stark contrast to the more developed spectrum of White characters.

QUESTIONS FOR QUESTING

Define	• List additional examples of Romantic prototype sightings you have seen in mainstream movies within the past year. • Define the Romantic prototype in your own words. • Which Top Ten Romantic example stood out to you the most?
Discuss	• Name financially successful romantic comedies or dramas featuring non-White actors—*The Notebook* or *Bridget Jones's Diary* come to mind as comparison cases. • To what degree does romance suggest interiority? To what degree are non-Whites depicted as capable of bonding with others, or more importantly, depicted as being *worthy* of bonding with others?
Decide	• Name the last movie you saw that contravened Hollywood's Third Rail, whereby a non-White male actor is depicted as being romantically *and intimately* involved with an A-list White actress.
Discover	• *How to Lose a Guy in 10 Days* (2003) • *The Proposal* (2009) • *Something's Gotta Give* (2004) • *Trainwreck* (2015) • *What Women Want* (2000)

What the Black Guy Dying First Means

Movies generally utilize a three-act structure to tell a story: (1) introduction, (2) conflict and climax, and (3) resolution. Given this manuscript's focus on mainstream movies, it is only fitting that this book follow that formula and use this final chapter as a means to achieve resolution of the numerous concepts and ideas presented in the book's first two parts. Just like a riveting Hollywood movie, the hope here is that in this section any loose ends will obtain denouement. Of course, if the reader is curious to engage with the topic further, Hollywood is producing more material as we speak that will likely warrant or justify a sequel.

For this text, which set out to explore the question, "Why Does the Black Guy Die First?," the "Black guy" can be seen as anyone who is not White and serves as shorthand for an individual who visibly departs from or challenges the White aesthetic as normal. Further, the Black guy "dying first" does not have to be limited to the literal order in which characters permanently exit the stage. Rather, "dying first" can generally refer to a diminishing of the non-White character's status or person (with the logical extreme being death), resulting in their being marginalized in contrast to more principal White characters. Ultimately, the concern is that consistent marginalization of "Black guys dying first" underscores the uncomfortable but unstated premise that White characters are generally "more important" to the storytelling narratives Hollywood produces for all audiences to share onscreen. Hence, examining the phenomenon of dying first opens the door to larger questions about mainstream movie images and the power of such iconography to reflect and reinforce psychosocial dynamics present within society. In other words, this intellectual shorthand can help bolster qualitative discussions by inserting yet another data point with which to measure how characters may be treated or depicted onscreen differently relative to their race.

This book's contribution to media literacy is primarily to illustrate how Hollywood has operated in a fairly predictable and formulaic manner when it comes to race onscreen. Ultimately, implied and implicit in the rhetorical question, "Why Does the Black Guy Die First?" is a larger social commentary about the value and visibility of diverse or non-White images onscreen. For any educator, film practitioner, or general movie fan who wishes to increase and improve their media literacy skills, this lens will aid and assist you by providing concrete racial rubrics to apply to mainstream movies in order to better assess the iconography we often ingest whole without taking time to digest and parse out its layered meaning.

Now, if my metaphoric use of "dying first" is unsatisfactory and you were hoping for more concrete examples, before you "leave the theater," stick around for the

Appendix appearing after this Conclusion—you can think of it as a bonus scene—where I dig down to the root of the book's provocative subtitle by offering one more "Top Ten" list of movies that absolutely subscribe to the premise that the Black guy dies first!

USING LOGIC WITH EMOTION PICTURES

Movie studios leverage mainstream movies to illustrate in spectacular fashion the greatest aspects of human nature. Would heroic movies such as *Batman Begins, Lord of the Rings, Harry Potter,* or *Pirates of the Caribbean* have been as successful at the box office if the protagonists failed in saving the world from evil, and the audience knew beforehand that failure was the imminent outcome? Probably not. We watch movies like *La La Land*, *Seabiscuit*, and *Miracle* not just for their entertainment value but also for the inspiration provided by the protagonists' triumphs in the face of the seemingly insurmountable obstacles that they had to overcome.

Studios knowingly exploit the **identification process** for millions of Americans who otherwise do not know each other, but who otherwise share and identify with a common denominator by being members of a global, Hollywood audience. Membership in the Hollywood audience has paid dividends with respect to providing a common context and source of communication. Unfortunately, within the shared memory of the Hollywood audience, studios have yet to consistently invest in the creation of non-White characters or actors who convincingly depart from marginalizing non-White archetype character patterns.

Meanwhile, the shared memory of mainstream Hollywood productions worldwide contains positive associations for White protagonists, to the virtual exclusion of non-White characters, who remain marginalized in their status and importance. If anything, White characters' participation in mainstream movies is consistently glamorized through more developed character arcs, thereby making their appearance and presence "more important" to viewers than non-Whites sharing the same screen. Further, archetypes and prototypes as outlined in the HARM Theory rubric have the significant potential to affect perceptions offscreen, the same way images of smoking, violence, drug use, or nudity can be deemed inappropriate for viewers of younger ages according to the ratings system employed by the Motion Picture Association of America (MPAA). In fact, the entire ratings system (e.g., "G" for "general audiences," "PG" for "parental guidance is advised," etc.) that many viewers absent-mindedly take for granted still exists and persists due to the belief that the mere exposure to images has the ability to influence behavior. Following this logic, if violent images from a fictional, "made up" movie are believed to have the ability to influence, then why should the same not be true for racially disparaging images contained within mainstream movies? Would they not also have the ability to make an impression and influence behavior as well? Provided racially problematic imagery has the same potential to influence viewers, then studio-generated imagery from mainstream movies may help form and reinforce presumptions of non-White irrelevance that are not limited to the boundaries of the walls inside the movie theater.

The common tendency of mainstream moviegoers to identify with central White characters, whether through deliberate choice or out of "necessity" due to the paucity of mainstream movie options showcasing non-White characters in prominent, protagonist roles undergirds the slow, steady, and subtle construction of a racial hierarchy in the minds of millions. When moviegoers consistently identify with White prototypes and protagonists over time, the cumulative effect is that viewers automatically distinguish White characters as "important" and worthy of attention. Meanwhile, non-White characters become further entrenched and confined to the more limited and marginalized world of the formulaic archetype patterns.

Based upon principles surrounding the identification process and a related concept called the **connective switch**, which refers to the ability of a viewer to adopt the perspective of a character to form an emotional connection with that character, it is not without coincidence that the top-grossing movies of all time contain a limited non-White presence and are primarily driven by White characters with whom majority White audiences can identify. For instance, it is not surprising to see that Disney's *Frozen* series (featuring White female protagonists Elsa and Anna) garnered over $2.6 billion at the box office, in contrast to Disney's *Princess and the Frog* (Black female protagonist) or *Wish* (Afro-Latina protagonist), which totaled $271 million and $233 million, respectively. The bottom line is that major movie studios are intensely sensitive to the sensibilities of the "girl next door" when greenlighting movie projects designed to appeal to the greatest possible audience. The fear is often that non-White characters may challenge audience members to individually identify or connect with the protagonist voluntarily within a fantasy space when in actuality they may not have to do so within their real life off screen.

After all, in reconsidering the principle of the 3Es, or the concept that most people are good in the world but are simply limited by a lack of (1) education, (2) exposure, or (3) experience, it may still be difficult for societal members to reconcile with how, in the course of living their otherwise good lives, they may still be existing within nominally racially segregated bubbles. Notions of merit, achievement, and *laissez faire* marketplace policies may only muddy and cloud the waters further when trying to parse the line between individual and institutional acts of racism that precipitate conditions whereby there is "only one" non-White individual living on one's street or working in one's building. If the reality is that our society is not fully integrated off screen, then we must ask ourselves as viewers whether Hollywood literally attempts to sell the fantasy of tension-free race relations—whenever convenient, that is. For in comparing the box office sales of Disney's *Frozen* to *Wish*, numerous factors may logically be at play to help explain the differing box-office performances—from the quality of the script, to the quality of the songs showcased, to the quality of the animation. However, I argue in this book that we should also consider race as an additional *factor*.

As avid movie lovers, we appreciate Hollywood movies and their social function—in spite of their racial imperfections—because they are an important part of American culture. Thus, with the HARM Theory rubric, the ability to consistently detect patterns and make relational associations on a large scale is vital since mainstream Hollywood must be judged by its total body of work, and not by singular cases or exceptions. Although you will now walk away with a heightened sensitivity about mainstream movie images, you will nonetheless be able to enjoy movies while simultaneously recognizing the subtle patterns and imagery that shape the racial landscape of mainstream movies—even if the "Black guy" dies first!

BUT IT'S JUST A MOVIE, RIGHT?

Researchers at Harvard University and other institutions have conducted prodigious research on implicit bias, though many members of society find it incredible to believe that nonetheless *they themselves* can possibly harbor bias even if they intellectually and morally disagree with overt racism (Lopez, 2017). If theories of implicit bias are to be believed (as strongly supported by quantitative data), then it is also logically possible to believe that even *A Beautiful Mind* can produce inspiring, riveting, and entertaining movies that may unwittingly create images that reflect ugly implicit biases. Thus, while Hollywood is a fiercely creative space that nurtures our boundless imaginations to travel as far as our creativity can take us, the reality is that much of what we see created is still bound by what we know here on planet Earth.

The good news is that society has mostly moved on from the social concept of legalized segregation, most likely owing its growing unpopularity and decline to an incredibly influential Civil Rights Movement that crescendoed globally in the 1960s. Therefore, in our modern era, unless it is a period piece made with the express intent of illustrating "old" racism (i.e., *12 Years a Slave*), examples of mainstream movies gratuitously featuring scenes of brazen acts of racism are few and far between. Conversely, the bad news is that the persistence of implicit bias continues to produce more developed character arcs for White characters, which collectively communicate subtle differences of value that prioritize or elevate White imagery above non-White characters within mainstream movies.

Critics and skeptics may retort, "But, it's just a movie!" in response to the suggestion that messages communicated by movies actually have the ability to influence viewer behavior. My response would be twofold: (a) tell that to the military and b) tell that to Hollywood studios. Starting with the military, if Hollywood producers wish to have access to authentic U.S. military equipment for a summer blockbuster movie like *Transformers,* it has to be done in accordance with existing standards that will not make the military look silly or foolish. Hollywood producers routinely consult U.S. military officials, seeing as how "the Pentagon's [Department of Defense] Entertainment Media office is staffed by two former US servicemen" and "each of the six US military branches have their own operators and office" (Turney, 2023). Since a blockbuster movie has the potential to be seen by a myriad of audiences worldwide for decades on end, numerous military official may disagree with the premise, "but it's just a movie." Such a partnership between Hollywood and the armed services evidences that the military has a vested interest in accomplishing their objectives of penetrating numerous minds with a "positive" image—call it positive propaganda or a productive partnership.

"But it's just a movie" may also not suffice when we turn our attention to the actions of Hollywood studios themselves. With the average cost of investment rising to produce a high-quality blockbuster that will reap dividends in return, many movie studios currently actively seek out financial partnerships to help defray rising production costs. Again, no causation, but there appears to be a correlation behind product placement within movies and corresponding rising sales off screen, as was seen with Hershey's Reese's Pieces candies after their prominent product placement in the movie *E.T. (Extra Terrestrial),* Ray-Ban sunglasses from the *Men in Black* series, and Ford Explorers from *Jurassic Park,* to name a few examples. There was even a spike in sales of clownfish after the release of *Finding Nemo*! The idea is that once numerous individuals are exposed to an idea or image, many may be influenced by it. Does this not help explain why so many "fans" take pleasure in the art of cosplay, where they labor relentlessly to acquire all the accoutrements of an "authentic" outfit in honor of a fictional character they admire at comic book conferences the world over?

Consistent with the concerns and logic that buttress the MPAA's rating system, and the evident effect that movies have on consumer behavior, I argue that the subtle image patterns present in mainstream movies today that devalue non-White imagery, when consistently consumed, can have serious consequences beyond the walls of the theater. Again, as Hollywood is a flexible and creative space, so should we be. Is an image only racially problematic if it is obvious and offensive, like a hanging noose from a tree or a uniformed (or costumed) card-carrying member of the Ku Klux Klan domestic terrorist group? What if the concept of racial difference is nonetheless communicated, but just in a less explicit manner? A strange but perhaps appropriate question is whether we as viewers are *creative enough* to observe and detect Racism 2.0 in its new manifestations outside of "traditional" (or dated) imagery of hooded klanspersons.

This book tested the strength of this thesis by applying the HARM Theory rubric to the Top Ten–grossing films of all time (as of print) to effectively illustrate how subtle messages of racial difference can remain "hidden in plain sight." Very few examples profiled in this book contain overt, obvious, or offensive depictions of racism. However, upon a closer look at many of these top-performing movies through the bi-focal lens of archetypes and prototypes, what becomes magnified is the subtle yet significant differences in how White character arcs are developed in contrast to non-White characters onscreen. No matter how you cut it, if the White characters are more developed during the story narrative, it follows that these White characters are simply "more important" to the story narrative displayed during the movie's visible continuum. Thus, whether analyzing top-grossing summer blockbuster movies or movies just released this past weekend, we must continue to ask ourselves: (a) whether the non-White characters we observe in such movies are also the valiant heroes for whom we fear and cheer *if and when* they survive until the very end, or (b) "Why does the Black guy die first?"

ADDING UP THE BOTTOM LINES

The bottom line of this analysis is not to suggest that a controversial movie like *Tropic Thunder*, which as recently as 2011 featured a White male in blackface for most of the movie as a "joke," will spell the end-all, be-all for race relations. But by considering the two related concepts of **premium of proportion** and racial capital, such disparaging images can have a disproportionate effect. This becomes clear when we simply "add up" the *bottom lines* given at the end of Parts I and II of the book:

- Bottom Line #1: White Screens, Dark Theaters (Part I: Introduction–Chapter 2). *Although Hollywood consistently produces lucrative mainstream movies designed to appeal universally to large, broad audiences of all races, it remains a White-dominated industry.*
- Bottom Line #2: Color Me Bad [Part II: Chapters 3–14]. *Hollywood mainstream movies routinely present a limited view of non-White characters, in stark contrast to the more developed spectrum of White characters.*

These two summary statements help build toward the conclusion that was actually already presented, or "hidden in plain sight," to the reader in the Introduction. The fact that Hollywood currently remains White-dominated in creative power and content is not a sin unto itself, *per se* (institutional barriers to opportunity and access notwithstanding). But such a data point becomes all the more concerning when coupled with qualitative data demonstrating a consistent contrast of more developed White characters onscreen versus a more limited or marginalized view of non-White characters. Given Hollywood's extensive global reach and extensive economic impact, these two factors combine to precipitate conditions whereby mainstream movies, through the use of consistently marginalized non-White images, reflect and reinforce messages of racial imbalance worldwide.

While movies have the seemingly magical capacity to inspire, encourage, and enlighten they also have the power to discourage, disparage, and demean. When absorbing mainstream movies, we must continue to ask critical questions to better understand and decode all implications of their visual vocabulary—some messages that perhaps are "hidden in plain sight" without the proper perspective to see what remains unseen or unspoken. This book represents a call for viewers to not only measure the *quantity* of racial representations on screen but also think seriously about the *quality* of the images we often digest whole without a second thought. My goal in producing this work is to have movie patrons first consider *if and when* they encounter a non-White character in a mainstream movie, how to apply the HARM Theory and its archetype and prototype rubrics as a means for consistent racial analysis. For, when it comes to both the intent and impact of potentially problematic racial images proliferated worldwide, we must continue to ask ourselves:

If a picture is worth 1,000 words,
then how much is a moving picture worth?

My Non-Horror Top Ten Movies for "Why Die First?!"

In none of the - 10 movies listed below does the Black character in question survive until the third act, which is typical of the overwhelming majority of White protagonists and main characters highlighted and detailed throughout this text.

	Movie	Brief Commentary	Time of Death
#1	*300* (2006)	The Persian messenger (portrayed by Black male actor Peter Mensah) was kicked into a large gaping hole that, apparently, he did not see or notice, though he was standing directly in front of it. Our Hero, played by an absolutely "abtastic" Gerard Butler, famously applies foot clad with sandal to the middle of the messenger's chest and the Persian becomes the first casualty of war as Butler yells the infamous battle cry, "This is Sparta!"	This death occurred within the movie's first act.
#2	*The Other Guys* (2010)	Similar to *Scream,* the moviemakers purposely killed off cognizable stars as a plot device to draw the viewers into the story. The resident "badass" policing duo played by Black male Samuel L. Jackson and multi-ethnic wrestling star crossover Dwayne "The Rock" Johnson meet their demise quite quickly—especially after being so badass as to threaten "putting my hand up your ass if I want you to speak." After the two men of color are removed, our unassuming and unlikely White duo (along with a Prius) were able to save the day. This is significant in that there are hardly any other Black characters with speaking parts the rest of the movie.	Very early, movie's opening act.
#3	*Terminator Salvation* (2009)	In this movie, cognizable Hollywood regular, Black male actor Terry Crews, who not only bravely went public with his story of male sexual harassment during the 2017 #MeToo movement campaign and, as of print, was the host (not judge) for the television show *America's Got Talent*, must have had to pick up the kids early from school the day of shooting or something, because his character indeed made an early exit—through death, that is. As in, his lifeless body is viewed by John Connor in the *opening scene*. Crews was actually not happy with the diminished role of his character, especially since it came as a surprise to Crews while screening the movie for the first time along with general audiences. Crews had filmed more scenes that unfortunately all ended up on the cutting room floor. Perhaps emboldened by his speaking out on #MeToo, Crews himself posted on the social media platform Twitter (now known as "X") in 2019: "I was a dead body in *Terminator Salvation*" (Crews, 2019).	As in *very* early, as in the movie's opening scene.
#4	*Expendables* (2010)	Here, Black male Somali pirates can be seen holding several non-Black people hostage (note the visual contrast heightening the idea of "othering," or foreign danger). Their initial appearance onscreen is marked by untranslated and frantic yelling (presumptively in their own, "foreign" language), again underscoring their "othering." Yet, despite their chiseled, sweaty physiques and large, intimidating machetes, they grow silent when they realize that several infrared beams are pointed in their direction. Yes, one should not become a pirate in the first place (unless you aspire to the fun-and-rum-loving kind as depicted by Johnny Depp in Disney's multi-billion-dollar franchise, *Pirates of the Caribbean*), but similar to the fate of the reminiscent dark-skinned, raving	Early in the movie's first act.

		pirates in *Captain Phillips*, matters do not end well for these pirating Black bodies. As in, not only are they vanquished cleanly and relatively quickly, but before they meet their demise, alpha male White actors Jason Stratham and Sylvester Stallone "debate" which method of delivering death to these offending menaces is most efficient: guns or knives. This pregnant moment is extended in humorous fashion when Stratham's character receives an incoming phone call. All this dialogue and drama is not normal, as you and I would likely have made a full deposit of yesterday's meal into our undergarments by now, given the incredible stress of the life-and-death hostage situation—but as we are in a Hollywood movie, normal rules are suspended as the moviemakers go out of their way to hyperbolize and illustrate just how badass our heroes really are. To have the presence of mind to "compete" while saving lives demonstrates mastery indeed—this is the takeaway that is most important. Meanwhile, more than cannon fodder, the Black bodies serve the technique of **canvassing**, whereby their character roles serve as a blank canvas onto which are painted the true colors of White heroism—even if red blood from Black bodies must be employed.	
#5	*Monster's Ball* (2001)	This award-winning movie made Halle Berry the first Black woman to win the Best Actress award since the Academy Awards began in 1929. According to *Entertainment Weekly*, "In the two decades since Berry's historic win, no other woman of color has been victorious in the category" (Nolfi, 2023). There are two Black guy deaths of note in *Monster's Ball*—the first of which was Berry's onscreen husband, Lawrence Musgrove, as played by crossover music mogul Sean Combs. The movie's title speaks to Musgrove's predicament on death row as a convicted murderer, for which the audience has little context, since a "Monster's Ball" consists of a get-together by those correctional officers excited to witness the literal execution of justice. Musgrove is the first "Black guy" to go, and by removing Berry's love interest, this "opens the door" for her to be available for the "real romance" the audience has come to see between correctional officer Hank Grotowski (played by Billy Bob Thornton) and Berry's Leticia Musgrove. Not to mention, with this interracial "romance," it is interesting how it just so happens that it is a Black female body that is *canvassed* for visual representations of rough and raw sex onscreen for the viewing pleasure of mainstream audiences—so much so, that Thornton later shared that those scenes he filmed made his then-marriage to A-list actress Angelina Jolie "tough" (News24, 2013). In view of Hollywood's strict observation of the third rail, where specifically Black and generally non-White males are *not* paired romantically with A-list White actresses, it is difficult to envision this scenario in reverse—that is, a Black male ravishing an A-list actress within borderline X-rated sex scenes that are far from criticized and condemned, but are critically acclaimed, garnering the actress one of the highest honors for acting at the Academy Awards.	Black male is executed early in the movie, during the movie's first act.

(*continued*)

	Movie	Brief Commentary	Time of Death
		I digress to the earlier point that all of this "romance" would not be possible if Berry's onscreen husband was still in the picture—for according to Hollywood's loose moral compass, if her legal husband (i.e., Lawrence Musgrove) was still alive and they were still married, it would cast the romance in a completely different light—it would now take on a more dubious, adulterous nature that ultimately can have damaging consequences for all parties involved; thus, the plot device of removing the Black male so that the "true romance" focused on during the visible continuum can take place without any moral qualms stirred in the viewing audience. For, by technical reading of the script, "romance" potentially existed at some point in time between Berry's character and her husband to the extent that they had a child together, Tyrell Musgrove (played by Black male actor Coronji Calhoun), who also met his untimely fate when run over by a car in the street. Admonished and abused for being "other," or obese and dark-skinned Black, he too was depicted as a burden on his mother. While she may have been morally incorrect to entertain this thinking, Leticia nonetheless is depicted as having an opportunity to pursue her happiness now that she has found a "liberating romance" with Thornton's character by movie's end. Grotowski is also a broken man, dealing with the suicide of his son, which arguably helps explain their unlikely connection. Recall, the movie's final scene of the two eating ice cream with the White male reassuring the Black female that they will be okay.	
#6	*The Princess and the Frog* (2009)	In case you missed it, Black female protagonist Tiana had a Black male father (voiced by Terrence Howard) who was killed off in battle during World War I. This movie represented Disney's first concerted effort to showcase a Black princess in a departure from the traditional White female seen in narrative vehicles such as *Sleeping Beauty, Cinderella, Alice in Wonderland, Snow White, Beauty and the Beast, The Little Mermaid,* and others. Yet, some details to observe are that Tiana's name originally was to be Maddie, and rather than be a restaurant worker, she was originally slated to be a maid (Misick, 2020). In the aftermath of organic advocacy and newfound corporate awareness that sprouted from the global protests against the dastardly killing of George Floyd in May 2020, *The Princess and the Frog* characters will now grace the Splash Mountain amusement park ride found in Disney parks, replacing the cast of characters from the blatantly racist and problematic *Song of the South*, which featured James Baskerville as good ol' Uncle Remus who sang colorful songs to White chilluns on the plantation. The movie is deemed to be so offensive that Disney refuses to release the material to its online streaming platform Disney+, launched in 2019. So, in other words, *The Princess and the Frog* is certainly now included, but only as a replacement. Contrasting that with the several Disney rides that were engineered with a specific story or character	During movie's first act.

		in mind (e.g., Cinderella's Castle, Mr. Toad's Wild Ride) perhaps provides yet another qualitative clue as to how important or valuable the image of a Black "princess" is to the Disney brand. Moreover, while the movie's title certainly contains the word "princess," Tiana spends significantly more time onscreen as a frog than as a princess—further, her princess status came via proxy, upon marrying Prince Naveen (voiced by Brazilian actor Bruno Campos). Not only is this type of storyline considered more "traditional" and not as progressive in contrast to the 2013 billion-dollar franchise *Frozen* (with the third installment, *Frozen III* slated for a 2025 release date), whereby one of the princess sisters was saved by "an act of true love" that did not (shockingly) involve a cisgender male saving a cisgender female, but the mode of technology was more traditional as well, as it represented a "return" to hand-drawn cel animation reminiscent of the Disney movies made in the 1950s. Since its acquisition of Pixar animation studios in 2006, Disney has made a nice mint off of movies that have employed the latest computer animation technology, with the *Frozen* franchise, *Tangled*, and *Brave* as examples. For whatever it is worth, while the first *Frozen* movie made $1.28 billion, *Princess* made $271 million, with no announced plans for a sequel. For those keeping score at home, *Frozen II*, the 2019 sequel, made a cool $1.453 billion. Apologies once again are in order, as I digress—Tiana's Black male father played an instrumental role in her story in that she shared a dream with him to open a restaurant—something she eventually accomplishes as princess during the movie's denouement. For the movie's visible continuum, his contribution was short—but *savory* (if we are being true to the New Orleans Cajun cuisine that Tiana's restaurant would likely serve).	
#7	*Soul* (2020)	Hmm. Where to begin? Similar to *The Princess and the Frog*, this movie was hailed as being a trendsetter, for it was a Disney animated film that prominently featured a Black male protagonist, Ray, as voiced by Academy Award–winning actor Jamie Foxx. While Foxx's character Ray is present throughout the duration of the movie, the movie claims its title from the fact that Ray loses his human, mortal life early in the movie when he absentmindedly walks into an open manhole in the middle of the street and enters the realm of "the Great Beyond" (the day after the best jazz saxophone performance in his life, incidentally). Hence, the rest of the movie deals with Ray wrestling with the identity and purpose of his being, or "soul." It is difficult for this author to proclaim and designate Foxx as the central protagonist, for a valid argument can be made for Tina Fey's "22" character as being just as central, if not the driving force of the movie, for it is she who actually inhabits Ray's body for most of the second act of the movie. Eerily enough, the very thought of White people dispossessing Black bodies and transplanting their consciousness in order to have a pleasurable existence through the physical form of an actual Black body was the stuff of horror when Jordan Peele released the surprise hit, *Get Out* in 2017.	Very early, during movie's first act.

(*continued*)

	Movie	Brief Commentary	Time of Death
		Yet, this very same premise was central to the plot of a "children's film" in 2020. I put "children's film" in quotations only because, in stark contrast to the teenaged or youngish heroes and heroines common in many successful Disney movies (e.g., *Frozen, Tangled, Inside Out*), here, within the space of the first Disney movie that specifically focuses upon a Black male protagonist, Ray is a bespectacled, single, mustachioed, middle-aged middle school jazz teacher. Despite his slender legs, he also sports a bit of a "pooch" in his belly unlike our traditionally fit protagonists we have grown accustomed to marveling at on the big screen. The intention here may have been noble, to be diverse and inclusive, but if going by box office sales alone, the $121 million it made is not only a fraction of the billions generated by other Disney stories that just happen to showcase White protagonists, but more importantly, its revenue fell short of its $150 million budget. In other words, one is unlikely to happen upon stuffed plush toy dolls featuring Ray's likeness at your local Target anytime soon. One further detail is that, similar to *The Princess and the Frog*, whereby the "Black protagonist" spends most of their time onscreen disembodied from their actual Black body, "Ray" spends most of his time onscreen as his blue spirit form, which for whatever reason, has the material attributes of his trademark hat and glasses, but does not mirror or share his distinctive physical attributes, such as his nose and lips—facial features that have been the subject of ridicule and derision historically for members of the Black community for being larger than those of "normal" White persons (White, 2018). The moviemakers may have thought that by muting these features, they would make the character more palatable to a broad audience. However, if "facial remodeling" and popular lip injection procedures, some even named after mainstream media personas (e.g., the "Kylie Jenner package"), are any indication, large lips, once criticized, are now all the rage (Kale, 2019).	
#8	*Crash* (2004)	In this landmark movie that was hailed for directly confronting and engaging the touchy subject of race relations, numerous storylines were employed by director Paul Haggis, who elected to draw upon his own experiences of being carjacked as a means to foster broader conversations. Although initially praised, critics have since sobered up and have come to offer more incisive critiques about how, even in making the noble effort to engage critical questions surrounding race and privilege, White characters and Whiteness were nonetheless ironically privileged in the process of doing so (Lodge, 2018). However, when it comes to the privilege of being first to depart onscreen, the distinction goes to Larenz Tate's Black male character, who is killed "accidentally" in the movie's second act by a paranoid White male officer. The officer mistook Tate's movements as hostile and aggressive, when in actuality he only had a statuette of Saint Christopher he wanted to share before crashing out of the picture.	During movie's second act.

#9	*Jurassic Park* (1993)	In the original cinematic classic that brought so many imaginations to life with arguably the most "realistic" depiction of dinosaurs on film up until that time, the movie also served as a cautionary tale about the risk involved in attempting to manipulate the laws of Mother Nature. The fierce carnivorous dinosaurs of eons ago apparently did not lose their appetite when revived and resurrected millions of years later. This was the case for Mr. Tyrannosaurus Rex, who terrorized Jurassic Park once it broke free of its containment. Among the lives lost in the ensuing mayhem was that of Samuel L. Jackson's Black male Ray Arnold character, who, despite having some modest one-liners as a valued, chain-smoking chief engineer (e.g., "Hold on to your butts!"), was summarily dispensed with without much context or explanation. In another example of canvassing, to illustrate just how "serious" the threat is to the main protagonists, when Laura Dern's White female heroine character is trying to seek safe shelter from terrorizing Velociraptors, at one point she backs into a cage and is relieved by what appears to be the comforting touch of Ray's hand on her shoulder during a stressful situation (e.g., running for her life from a ginormous, menacing, carnivorous beast). Unfortunately, this feeling of relief was short-lived—she turns around to discover that Ray would ultimately not have a hand in helping her as she was only left with his dismembered arm. Consider that we did not even have the "opportunity" to see Ray perish and witness his human struggle to survive. In one scene, he is seen troubleshooting and engaging in problem solving just like our protagonists, and then in the next scene, a dismembered and discolored arm is all that remains of him. And once Ray's death has served its purpose—to show that the Velociraptors are indeed dangerous—the film moves on with the plot and concentrates on what is most important, which is ensuring the safe survival of the "more important" White protagonists.	During movie's second act.
#10	*The Green Mile* (1999)	This entry requires a bit of explanation. As mentioned previously, this book's subtitle *(or Why Does the Black Guy Die First?)* has a more general application than is perhaps indicated. "Black Guy" refers to the larger concept of othering where anyone who is non-White may be immediately visually identifiable, and therefore isolated as a target as a result. Although a Black male's death features prominently in the narrative, the *earliest* exit belongs to convict Arlen Bitterbuck, as played by Indigenous actor Graham Greene. Here, his "other" status serves as a convenient backdrop for his early departure. This movie, made from the best-selling novel by Stephen King, revolves around the story of a misunderstood yet "magical negro"—for those unfamiliar with the term, that's "the trope in literature and movies where a black character appears in a plot solely to help a white character—and then vanishes" (Kelly, 2019). This character trope also fits cleanly within the "helpful" Angel Figure archetype. Black male John Coffey (Michael Clarke Duncan) has magical powers to heal, yet he is ironically serving a sentence on Death Row and scheduled to die. In fact, his discovered powers are deemed to be	Graham Greene's character in the first act; Michael Clarke Duncan's character at the end of movie's second act.

(continued)

Movie	Brief Commentary	Time of Death
	so valuable that White male correctional officers *break him out of jail* to provide healing to the jail warden's ailing White wife. Unfortunately, despite helping others with these healing powers, Duncan was unable to leverage these powers to help himself and negotiate a longer lease on life in exchange for the truth that he was not guilty of the crimes of which he was accused, or at least in exchange for all the free healing he provided. Duncan's death was presaged in many ways and is not a surprise, even though it comes in the movie's second act. Also, I would be remiss if I failed to point out the presence of **one-way culture sharing**, whereby Coffey's magical powers are transferred to White male Tom Hanks, who ends the movie "cursed" with the prospect of living longer than everyone else he knows—a fate which falls right into the same category of accursed blessings as having "too much money."	

Glossary

A-LIST TALENT. An actor deemed über important within mainstream society and worthy of constant attention due to their ability to consistently draw a large following; as a result this actor is able to command and receive significant financial compensation for their work. *Significance*—when analyzing non-White participation in mainstream Hollywood, it is important to take note of how many non-Whites occupy a central space. While many non-White actors who appear in mainstream movies may be well-known, this does not automatically deem the individual to be an A-list actor who is specifically known, regarded, featured, and compensated for their stage presence or acting ability.

ANCHOR The moral, political and social orientation of a character around which events in the movie revolve. *Significance*—many moviegoers may take for granted the fact that they view most movies through the thoughts and emotions of White characters. In the name of formulaic results, many movie studios are reluctant to make a movie without a White anchor who can steady and satisfy the majority-White paying audience that they are trying to reach.

ANGEL FIGURE. A non-White archetype character usually found in a servile position or functioning as a sidekick, serving as a source of spiritual strength, guidance, and support to the central character(s). Frequently, this character occupies a "teacher"-type role, imparting insightful perspectives or life lessons, despite the smaller amount of privilege and screen time that they may command relative to the protagonist. *Significance*—observe how this non-White character is typically isolated from other minorities in the visible continuum of the movie, and usually "fades to black" once their primary function has been served.

ARCHETYPE. A broader character pattern by which individual conduct is classified; this categorization groups characters who manifest a similar set of values and functions in dissimilar settings. *Significance*—archetypes broaden students' understanding of racial patterns. Students are likely more familiar with stereotypes, which are usually more obvious and offensive in character. Students must understand that in our "post-racial" society, archetypes are so very effective because of the very fact that they do not immediately strike the viewer as harmful, although they nonetheless fulfill older negative narratives about non-White participation.

ASYMPTOTE. A non-White actor whose physical attributes approach the White Beauty Standard or allow the actor to portray White characters. As with the mathematical concept that shares the same name, although this actor closely resembles or can be made to resemble the mainstream paradigm for beauty (e.g., for women: long, flowing hair, waifish figure), she cannot reproduce the paradigm completely since she is not White. No matter how much she does externally to try and approach the paradigm, her culture or race still serves as a mark of social distinction. *Significance*—this is Hollywood's version of "having your cake and eating it too." Here, Hollywood gets a "2 for 1" special in that they officially claim credit for casting a non-White actor in a role (which *does not* necessarily mean that the non-White actor *will be cast as* a non-White character) but retain the advantage of keeping the movie universally marketable by not transgressing the "tipping point" and inundating the movie with too many across-the-street minorities.

BACKGROUND FIGURE. A non-White archetype character who is rather inconsequential to the overall storyline and does not perform actions or recite dialogue that advances the plot in any meaningful way; serves as mere "window dressing" onscreen. *Significance*—while this character appears to play an insignificant role, this character is vital to the moviemaker in their attempt to "remind" the audience that diversity has not been overlooked completely.

BLOCKBUSTER. A movie that proves to be an overwhelming financial success at the box office. In common usage, a blockbuster is a movie that has a box office of typically more than $100 million upon its release in North America. *Significance*—the major movie studios that produce the vast majority of mainstream movies are profit driven. How much money a movie makes—especially in contrast to the initial outlay—is a significant component in evaluating a movie's success.

CANVASSING. A storytelling technique whereby non-White character's bodies are used as an open "canvas" or platform to showcase emotional or physical painful scenarios. *Significance*—this technique often "preserves" more central, White characters without causing major disruptions to the flow of the story. Thus, for scriptwriters to demonstrate and establish how "evil" a villain is early in a movie, a non-White character (and potentially Background Figure) can serve as the "canvas" for such heinous behavior to illustrate that the villain "means business." Otherwise, if the villain were to take out such physical aggression on the actual White protagonist so early in the movie, the villain would instantly triumph and there would be no movie to watch.

CATHARSIS. An emotional or psychological release of tension, resulting in revelation or personal growth for a character. *Significance*—despite quantitative measurements that indicate a growing non-White presence in mainstream movies, it is remarkable to evaluate the depth and meaning of such diversity through character catharsis. It is revealing indeed to see what percentage of non-White characters are developed enough to display this character feature.

CHARACTER ARC. The charting of the emotional or psychological change that occurs within a character as they progress through a story. *Significance*—when analyzing non-White characters onscreen, it is important to chart their overall trajectory, or change over time, as opposed to isolating their analysis to one specific instant in time. In contrast to White characters, the vast majority of non-White characters appear more static in their character development, due to limited screen time and limited dialogue, which often prevent the viewing audience from learning more about these characters.

COMIC RELIEF. A non-White archetype character where culture serves as fodder for most the jokes that they are involved in. Typical conduct includes loud, improper grammar; intense emotion; and exaggerated motions and expressions. *Significance*—because this non-White character pattern is defined in a comedic context, humor often serves as a protective veil to defend the use of such racially themed humor. This archetype raises additional questions about who has the privilege or authority to define that which is acceptable to burlesque.

COMMON DENOMINATOR. A broad theme that most people can recognize or relate to based on their general human experience. *Significance*—as with literature, the best movies are often those that can speak to a variety of people in a variety of ways. Due to their ubiquitous distribution, movies and the discussion of them serve as a common denominator.

CONNECTIVE SWITCH. The ability of a viewer to adopt the perspective of a character to form an emotional connection with that character. *Significance*—major movie studios are intensely sensitive to the sensibilities of the "girl next door" when greenlighting movie projects designed to appeal to the greatest possible audience. The fear is often that non-White characters may challenge audience members to connect with the protagonist in different ways as opposed to a White protagonist who may be viewed if anything as more habitual than more acceptable.

CONTRA-JUXTAPOSITION. An exaggeration of an existing non-White stereotype contrasted against "typical" White middle-class norms. *Significance*—humorous situations for minorities often are deemed as comedic if and only because of their contrast to "normal" White status quo conditions. The more that the non-White deviates from the norm, the more humorous the situation is intended to be.

CROSS-CASTING. Wherein a movie studio casts a non-White actor in a role originally slated for, designed for, portrayed by, or written for a White actor. *Significance*—two items to note for this term are: (1) the box office reception of such cross-casting, and (2) the fact that this term even exists (i.e., it acknowledges exclusion at the onset in the contemplation of the script).

EMASCULATION. The process whereby the male identity of a non-White character is overtly compromised or challenged in the face of conventional gender roles. *Significance*—dating back to the era of enslavement, the control of non-White males was deemed instrumental in maintaining law and order throughout society. While emasculation may often be done with humor or with a perfectly logical storyline in mind, the effect of bringing the non-White male "back down to size" is similar. This emasculation trend contrasts sharply with messages of virility, power, and influence commonly exhibited by White characters by movie's end.

***ETHNICITY*.** Specific group affiliation based upon particular cultural ties, often related to a shared country of origin. *Significance*—race and ethnicity are often used as interchangeable terms, but this is an opportunity to parse out with students how these two terms differ in their definitions. Generally, members of the same ethnicity share race, but those of the same race do not necessarily share ethnicity. Have students consider to what extent Hollywood develops space and distinguishes White ethnic groups (e.g., French vs. Italian, Russian vs. British) in contrast to other non-White ethnic groups (e.g., Nigerian vs. Ethiopian).

***FIRST-RUN MOVIE*.** A feature film typically 90 minutes to 3 hours in length that is first exhibited to the public in national and regional movie theater chains. *Significance*—first-run movies are culturally significant since they are heavily advertised in the weeks and months leading up to their release. When fully introduced into the mainstream, they become "what everyone's talking about."

***GREATEST POSSIBLE AUDIENCE*.** The ideal number of available consumers willing to purchase or view a particular mainstream movie. *Significance*—typically, the bigger the initial financial outlay, the more formulaic the movie will be to appeal to the greatest possible audience. Unfortunately for minorities, the more mainstream the production and the more "universal" its appeal, the more likely they are to be marginalized or excluded. A quick review of the highest-grossing movies of all time reflects this dynamic.

***GREENLIGHTING/GREENLIT*.** Process whereby an idea for a movie project receives authorization for filming by a major movie studio, matched with financial backing. *Significance*—a project is considered greenlit once it is determined that money can be made off the packaged idea. Students must think about what other incentives major movie studios have in deciding to go forward with a movie project.

HOLLYWOOD'S ACTING RULE FOR MINORITIES (or non-White characters). Holds that if and when a non-White character appears in a mainstream movie, their character will be compromised in some way, shape, or form. *Significance*—the HARM Theory's novelty is that it tasks students with a rebuttable presumption that students are free to challenge. To critically analyze Hollywood as a whole, students must ask themselves the converse of the HARM Theory, meaning, when has Hollywood gone out of its way to purposely glamorize non-White characters?

***HOLLYWOOD'S RACIAL MAKEUP*.** Refers to the five racial categories consistently acknowledged by Hollywood onscreen in mainstream movies: Asian, Black, Latinx, Other, and White. *Significance*—these categorizations are based on the most frequent and prominent races that mainstream Hollywood overtly depicts consistently on the silver screen and are not to be taken as an exhaustive detailing of all possible racial images that may appear onscreen.

***HOLLYWOOD TRIFECTA*.** This concept represents the ultimate accomplishment for a character within the span of a movie's visible continuum, most usually reserved for White males. *Significance*—the character is able to: (1) get the goal (completed, whether saving the world or vanquishing the villain, whatever it may be), (2) get the gold (most protagonists obtain some sort of reward for their labors), and, of course, (3) "get the girl" (need we explain?).

IDENTIFICATION PROCESS. The method and manner by which the moviegoer physically, emotionally, and psychologically connects with a character who resembles the viewer's physical, emotional, and psychological profile. *Significance*—it is unknown to what degree White moviegoers have considered that every weekend that they have been alive in the United States, there was always a movie *starring* a character that looked like them or someone who they were related to (i.e., of the White race). Non-White moviegoers do not have the same luxury, and therefore if they wish to enjoy Hollywood movies, they *must* agree to identify as a White person for the purposes of the movie.

INTERIORITY. This concept speaks to the effort exhibited by moviemakers to draw viewers "inside" the lives of central (usually White) characters. Techniques include flashback scenes (where the viewing audience becomes privy to the character's internal and private memories) or close-up shots of facial expressions or of depicting the character outside the public eye in their most comfortable environments so that the audience is able to read deeper meaning into the decisions and actions the character makes. Musical scores in the background often will change to cue the viewer in that what the protagonist is thinking or viewing is important as well. *Significance*—interiority is a key component of developing one's character arc, to distinguish this character from a Background Figure that is considerably more dispensable.

MAINSTREAM CULTURE. The prevailing, yet intangible current of contemporary thought within society. *Significance*—viewers must think about what exactly constitutes mainstream culture.

MAINSTREAM MOVIE. A movie designed, produced, and marketed with the purpose of reaching the greatest possible audience. *Significance*—viewers must consider in which specific ways mainstream movies differ from independent or foreign films substantively, aesthetically and stylistically.

MAINSTREAM PIPELINE. The assortment of major media outlets that reach the greatest possible audience due to nationwide marketing and distribution networks. This network consists of radio programs, newspapers, magazines, television shows, and movies that are seen by vast numbers of people throughout the country at or around the same time, thereby serving as an informal means of sharing information, centralizing thought, and organizing loose societal networks. *Significance*—have students think about how hard or easy it would be for them to create a product that would be disseminated through the mainstream pipeline.

MAJOR MOVIE STUDIOS. The corporate conglomerates responsible for the majority of mainstream distribution. As of print, the six major distributors and producers of movies are: (1) Buena Vista Pictures Distribution (The Walt Disney Company), (2) Paramount Pictures Corporation, (3) Sony Pictures Entertainment Inc., (4) Twentieth Century Fox Film Corporation, (5) Universal City Studios LLP, and (6) Warner Bros. Entertainment Inc. The chairpeople and presidents of these companies all serve on the board of directors for the MPAA. *Significance*—have students consider the breadth and scope of these major movie studios. Take the time to sensitize your students to the history behind these companies, for many of your students may be readily familiar with their product but unfamiliar with their corporate profiles.

MASKING. Whereby an actor is able to hide their racial identity on- or off-screen and blend in with the White majority through a superficial change (e.g., bleaching of hair, change of surname). *Significance*—while related to the asymptote, this term differs in that the focus is placed squarely on the actor's actions off-screen to better interface with the White majority as opposed to the asymptote that is more of a marketing decision by the moviemakers to create and appeal to a certain visual aesthetic.

MENACE TO SOCIETY. This non-White archetype character is portrayed as possessing a value system that poses a threat to civil "normalcy," through violence (or potential violence) and/or moral corruption. *Significance*—this archetype is significant in that it often blurs the line between perceived and actual criminality by minorities. These non-White characters usually are not developed and therefore the threat they represent to society is often taken for granted.

MINSTRELSY. A wildly popular form of entertainment that denigrated Blacks and lampooned their status as victims of systemic racism. Minstrel shows frequently featured both Whites and Blacks who donned "blackface" make-up. *Significance*—blackface is all but an afterthought in today's modern cinema. However, the notion that minorities, Blacks in particular, engage in unflattering and wildly overdramatized scenarios designed and conceived primarily by Whites for laughs, hearkens back to the principle undergirding minstrelsy that uses humor as a wedge rather than a bridge for understanding.

MORAL COMPASS. The unwritten rule guiding major studios so that they consistently produce mainstream movies communicating the ultimate victory of "good over bad." *Significance*—in seeking resolution by movie's end, the moral compass often prioritizes White characters and their catharsis over that of non-White characters.

ONE-WAY CULTURE SHARING. Where one racial group's cultural "resources" are exploited chiefly to benefit a White character without a reciprocal exchange. *Significance*—non-White Angel archetypes are usually defined by their level of loyalty and sacrifice to the protagonist. It is telling to see how Angel figures often are *not* in a position of authority or prosperity, which makes their sacrifice all the more poignant, symbolic, and significant.

PHYSICAL WONDER. This non-White archetype character is regarded for their physical or sexual prowess, typically at the sacrifice of intellectual or emotional capacities. *Significance*—this character pattern is exceedingly complex and dates back to the era of enslavement wherein there was often present a perverse fear and fascination of Black slaves. While the Physical Wonder may appear to be lauded onscreen, you may challenge students to see to what degree such "respect" is limited to their physical ability only and have them look to see if the character is valued in any other way by leading White characters.

PREMIUM OF PROPORTION. The amount of impact a character image possesses relative to their entire racial group. Isolated and unfavorably depicted non-White roles disproportionately disparage the overall group image to which the representative character belongs, primarily due to a lack of other available images with which to provide balance. *Significance*—this concept explains in part why consistently disparaging non-White imagery is so impactful. Due to the limited amount of countering images that provide audience members with a more comprehensive view of the non-White experience, more prominent images that marginalize the non-White experience will leave a larger lasting impression upon the viewer.

PROTECTIVE STEREOTYPE. Exaggerated images of bigotry or hatred that allow common White audience members to distance themselves from such abnormal and obvious displays of antisocial behavior. Such a character is "protective" in that it masks more subtle and common representations of discrimination more likely to be prevalent within contemporary society. *Significance*—the protective stereotype works only because it is designed to be obvious and clear, although uncommon in real life.

PROTOTYPES. General patterns of common traits shared or exhibited by White characters in mainstream movies. These overarching character patterns reflect the most consistent methods in which White characters assert an exclusive and domineering presence onscreen. These prototypes prioritize Whites as central characters whose thoughts, feelings, sentiments, and actions become a primary concern for the viewing audience. Moreover, these characters typically serve as emotional anchors for the movies in which they appear, often harnessing and marshaling their stated attributes to achieve some measure of cathartic growth or achieve resolution for their individual character arc. *Significance*—the prototypes are absolutely essential to understanding how Hollywood operates, for non-White marginalization is only one side of the coin. It follows that if minorities are pushed to the periphery, then who remains at the center of the audience's attention?

PSYCHO-SEGREGATION. The concept that while in post–Civil Rights era American society, individuals are no longer legally segregated in public places purely on account of race and formal physical restrictions against freedom of movement have been removed, psychological barriers persist and remain, whereby many members of society harbor and act upon racially problematic constructs. *Significance*—these psychological barriers are difficult to both detect and dismantle, resulting in many persistent and racially problematic patterns "hidden in plain sight" under the auspices of Racism 2.0, which the HARM Theory rubric is designed to discern.

RACE. General group affiliation based upon physically observable characteristics or physical constructs, such as skin color or hair type. *Significance*—generally, members of the same ethnicity share race, but those of the same race do not necessarily share ethnicity. Have students consider trends in how Hollywood represents racial groups as a whole, despite differing ethnic groups.

RACIAL CAPITAL. The amount of power (economic, political, or social) ascribed collectively to a particular racial group. *Significance*—use this term to have students think about race as a "currency"; to what extent does the visual representation of race allow or prevent access based upon a larger, shared "credit history" with other members of the same race?

RACISM 2.0. This concept holds that racism has largely changed in form, but not substance, over the years. Thus, historically familiar instances of racism were overt, obvious, and offensive within a society that recognized legalized enslavement for nearly two and a half centuries followed closely by a Jim Crow period that enforced racial segregation. Harsh and vitriolic instrumentalities used to uphold racist thinking have been modified over the years as new policies designed to combat racism have developed. *Significance*—rather than celebrate the fact that such older and overt forms of racism have largely evaporated from daily public life, viewers must remain vigilant to the possibility that racism has evolved into a form that is more subtle, suave, and sophisticated in nature—so much so that part of the problem is that "there is no problem," thereby leaving racially disparaging messaging within the visual text of Hollywood mainstream movies largely "hidden in plain sight."

STEREOTYPE. A negative classification based upon specific conduct or characteristics ascribed to a particular racial group. *Significance*—stereotypes are typically negative and are more obvious to spot than archetypes. A non-White character may also exhibit stereotypical behavior, particularly in comedies, where such behavior is deemed implicitly acceptable when cloaked in humor, but stereotypes give way to archetypes in other "more serious" genres.

UNCLEAN HERO. Whereby a non-White protagonist represents the driving force of a movie, yet does not experience the pure moral, financial, and/or sexual victories typically associated with White mainstream heroic characters. *Significance*—the unclean hero is significant in that it demonstrates the penetrating power and reach of the HARM Theory for even when non-White protagonists are central to the action, their actions may not measure up to larger narratives of heroism familiar by many mainstream movie audience members.

UTOPIC REVERSAL. Found occupying a high social position (e.g., police chief, judge, etc.), they in actuality are a pseudoauthority figure since their level of power and authority is undercut (either explicitly or implicitly) in relation to other characters onscreen, thereby rendering their authority or position as mostly symbolic in nature. *Significance*—this character pattern is key in understanding the more subtle and nuanced displays of modern racism. This character is deceptively alluring for it gives the appearance of racial progressivism onscreen and instantly satisfies potential attacks for non-inclusiveness. Yet, this character pattern fits within a larger pattern of non-White marginalization since the audience rarely has the opportunity to see this non-White character actualize or utilize their authority.

VISIBLE CONTINUUM. The observable part of a movie's timeline as portrayed and shown to the movie audience between the beginning and ending credits. Note: In theory, there is no beginning or end to a movie since a sequence of events led up until the time when the visible continuum began, and additionally, there will be a future chain of events after the movie's viewing window closes. Oftentimes, this timeline is manipulated, and the audience is allowed to see in the past via flashbacks or glimpse into the future via time travel. The movie's creators must therefore select finite points within a larger story to form the boundaries of the visible continuum, or those segments of time that the audience is allowed to see. *Significance*—this concept reminds students that choices and decisions are constantly made about what to include and what to leave out when telling a story. Students, in the course of analyzing a movie, may refer to the movie's chronology or script as if it were static; this concept teases out the idea that a conscious decision was made on what to showcase.

WHITE BEAUTY STANDARD. Actresses who approach (or are made to approach) the White aesthetic (e.g., small hips and slender build; long or lightened, flowing hair). *Significance*—the White Beauty Standard dominates much of mainstream media and while reviled and criticized in some circles, particularly as it relates to its potential damage to young girls and their developing psyches and esteem, it is still the unquestioned standard by which women are judged, let alone actresses who are handsomely compensated to maintain an attractive appearance.

Watchdog Guide

In addition to the various intellectual exercises contained herein, I presently wish to offer you a working template for consistently analyzing movies as a whole. Feel free to make copies and distribute it liberally among your viewing communities, and feel free to brainstorm ways in which to make it even more effective.

The Watchdog Guide is an innovative tool designed to assist moviegoers to begin analyzing racial imagery in movies. By standardizing an analytical approach, future conversations about racial images in mainstream movies hopefully will be improved with participants having a more qualitatively supported understanding of what it is that they saw. Through this intellectual exercise, we do not make movies look bad, because we do not make movies. Hollywood does its own work. In our intellectual laboratory, the Watchdog Guide merely serves as a group of blades of varying sharpness against which we test certain materials (mainstream movies). For us, the test is not how sharp the blades are, but rather, how resistant the material is that comes into contact with the blades. If, after contact, the material holds up with relatively few puncture marks, it was evidently well made. However, if the material is shredded mercilessly, this guide will help record the data, and let you know why. In the process, we become more consistent and pragmatic in our analysis of a potentially volatile and emotional topic: race.

Feel free to employ either during or after the viewing of a movie. There is no "right" answer; however, this guide will help you focus on the racial imagery within a mainstream movie (if any) for future discussion. To help you gain familiarity with this tool, what follows are some general insights about the structure of the guide itself:

- IS THE MOVIE A MAINSTREAM MOVIE? The six characteristics listed under this category are the six Mainstream Movie Factors detailed in Chapter 1, Have We Seen This Movie Before? This is the threshold question that speaks to the movie's influential quality. In addition, any combination of the bonus features listed helps solidify a movie's mainstream status.
- WHAT TYPE OF MOVIE IS IT? This question speaks to the relative need for the audience to identify with the movie's characters as explored in the connective switch concept in Chapter 15, Using Logic with Emotion Pictures. Recall that typically comedies and the like require a lesser need for a connective switch, whereas romances and dramas require a greater need for a connective switch. Accordingly, movie patrons are less frequently "asked" or required to adopt the perspective of minorities to maximize the

movie's experience, especially in dramas or romances, where the need to switch is greatest.

- WHO IS IN THE MOVIE? This question speaks to the visible racial presence depicted overtly onscreen as delineated and outlined under the HARM Theory rubrics from Chapter 2, Value and Visibility. If the character is animated, list the race of the animated character, or where applicable or able, list the race of the actor providing the animated character's voice. If unknown, list as "character undefined." Also, check the "character undefined" box if you are unable to classify the character's race as it appears onscreen. In selecting the class status for a character, check the box for the character's terminal status, especially where the character undergoes a change in fortune.
- WHAT IS THE QUALITY OF THE ROLE? This question speaks to the impact that a non-White character commands onscreen as explored in Chapters 3 through 14. If a non-White character appears onscreen, it is likely that their role will fall within one of the six archetypal patterns in accordance with the Hollywood Acting Rule for Minorities: (1) Angel, (2) Background, (3) Comic Relief, (4) Menace to Society, (5) Physical Wonder, and (6) Utopic Reversal.
- QUESTIONS FOR ANALYSIS. These questions are designed to help you, the moviegoer, think in concrete terms about the breadth and scope of a non-White role within a mainstream movie. Therefore, the questions inquire into aspects of non-White "life" onscreen that is usually showcased gratuitously by Whites in mainstream movies.
- BONUS CONSIDERATIONS. Chapters 1 and 2 outline some data points that highlight the sobering statistical reality of how non-Whites are overwhelmingly outnumbered in Hollywood, and how that impacts the end product provided to the end user or the neighborhood moviegoer like you. Everyone has an equal opportunity to patronize a movie and support it financially; however, many considerations, including the marketing plan, often dictate a narrower audience that movie studios bear in mind.
- WHAT IS THE LASTING IMPRESSION? This question speaks to the overall impression that you as a moviegoer sustain upon imbibing such imagery into your consciousness. In answering this question, also bear in mind the answer of the individual not from America who has never visited personally but is all the more reliant upon such visual messaging and iconography for a glimpse of what "life might be like" insofar as movies reflect and reinforce our contemporary racial reality—even if purely fictional productions.

MAINSTREAM MOVIE WATCHDOG GUIDE™

Please feel free to complete the following guide to help you analyze the racial images you see within a mainstream movie. Please note that this guide is intended to serve as an analytical tool only and does not offer a review or opinion about the overall quality of a movie.

NAME OF MOVIE:	YEAR OF RELEASE:
YOUR PERSPECTIVE: ☐Asian ☐Black ☐Latino ☐Other ☐White ☐M ☐F ☐Other	DATE OF REVIEW:

Step 1: IS THE MOVIE A MAINSTREAM MOVIE?

(check all factors that apply)

(1) ☐ Full-length, first-run feature? (2) ☐ Widespread distribution? (3) ☐ Large production & marketing budget?

(4) ☐ Large box office sales? (5) ☐ A-list talent? (6) ☐ Mainstream media exposure?

Any Bonus Features?

(a) ☐ product for sale (e.g., toy, video game) (b) ☐ extended promotional lead time (c) ☐ spinoff from book/TV show/movie/etc.

(d) ☐ extremely successful soundtrack (e) ☐ Academy Award nomination/win (f) ☐ corporate sponsorship/promotion (i.e., product placement)

---» IS IT A MAINSTREAM MOVIE? (i.e., 4 or more factors checked) ☐ YES ☐ NO

Step 2. WHAT TYPE OF MOVIE IS IT?

(mark scale accordingly)

« comedy — horror — action/adventure — sci-fi/fantasy — romance — drama »

less serious … *more serious*

Step 3. WHO IS IN THE MOVIE?

(a) Minority character(s) appear in movie? **IF NOT, MOVE ON TO STEP #6** ☐ YES ☐ NO

(check all that apply) ☐Asian ☐Black ☐Latino ☐Other (list if known: ____________________) ☐ Undefined

(b) If so, is the lead character a minority? ☐ YES ☐ NO

i. If so, what is the character's apparent gender? ☐male ☐female ☐other

ii. What is the character's apparent class status? ☐upper ☐upper-middle ☐lower-middle ☐lower/under

(c) What is the impact of any supporting/background minority characters? ☐insignificant ☐significant ☐very significant

(d) How many minority characters do you recall in the movie? (write in number) [__________]

Step 4. WHAT IS THE QUALITY OF THE ROLE?

If any minority characters appeared onscreen, it is likely their role fulfilled an archetype pattern (in box below). Did you observe any character:

(fill in all letters that apply; please note that characters may exhibit combinations of various archetype traits)

(a)☐ offer aid to a White character?	(a)☐ facilitate healing/understanding for a White character?	(a)☐ devoid of relationships outside of a White character?
(b)☐ offer little to no dialogue?	(b)☐ have little to no bearing or influence on plot development?	(b)☐ devoid of close-ups or significant screentime?
(c)☐ 's ethnicity/race used as fodder for jokes?	(c)☐ 's conduct contrasted vs. "normal" White behavior?	(c)☐ use exaggerated gestures/tones/language?
(d)☐ violate any laws/moral codes?	(d)☐ threaten the "White" value system/status quo?	(d)☐ pose a threat for physical harm?
(e)☐ overtly sexualized?	(e)☐ 's physical stature/talent acknowledged directly?	(e)☐ use physical ability as part of their primary skill set?
(f)☐ occupy an uncommonly high social position	(f)☐ 's authority undermined/curtailed/compromised?	(f)☐ devoid of intimacy/familial relationships?

(a) = Angel (b) = Background (c) = Comic Relief (d) = Menace to Society (e) = Physical Wonder (f) = Utopic Reversal

WATCHDOG GUIDE™ (part 1 of 2)

Step 5. QUESTIONS FOR ANALYSIS

a) Did any minority characters have any significant screen time?	☐ YES ☐ NO
b) If so, was their contribution essential to the plot's development?	☐ YES ☐ NO
c) Did any minority characters wield any authority/power over Whites?	☐ YES ☐ NO
d) Were any minority characters justified in destroying property to achieve a goal?	☐ YES ☐ NO
e) Did any minority characters successfully start a romantic relationship and/or reunite their family unit?	☐ YES ☐ NO
f) Were any minority characters depicted inside of their homes?	☐ YES ☐ NO
g) Were any minority characters depicted being intimate with the lead?	☐ YES ☐ NO
h) Were any minority characters depicted as being intimate with whites?	☐ YES ☐ NO
i) Were there any scenes containing exclusively minority characters?	☐ YES ☐ NO
j) Did any minority characters control the pace and action of the movie?	☐ YES ☐ NO

(add up "YES" responses)

White Dominant Movie	Minority Minimal Movie	Minority Flavored Movie	Minority Involved Movie
☐(0-2)	☐(3-4)	☐(5-7)	☐(8-10)

Step 6. BONUS CONSIDERATIONS

a) Is the Director of the movie a minority?	☐ YES ☐ NO
b) Is the Writer a minority?	☐ YES ☐ NO
c) Is the Executive Producer a minority?	☐ YES ☐ NO
d) Are there any themes of romance, family bonding or familial reconciliation for Whites?	☐ YES ☐ NO
e) Who would you consider as the movie's target audience?	☐ primarily for Whites ☐ primarily for minorities ☐ for all audiences

Step 7. WHAT IS THE LASTING IMPRESSION?

☐ **Negative Impression/Marginalization At Stake**

☐ **Fair Representation/Status Quo Maintained**

☐ **Positive Impression/Breakthrough Performance**

COMMENTS

WATCHDOG GUIDE™ (part 2 of 2)

References

Adachi, J. (2006). *Slanted screen: Asian men in film and television.* Asian American Media Mafia.

Aleiss, A. (2005). *Making the white man's Indian: Native Americans and Hollywood movies.* Praeger.

Andrews, T., & Burke, F. (2007, January 1). What does it mean to think historically? *Perspectives on History.* https://www.historians.org/research-and-publications/perspectives-on-history/january-2007/what-does-it-mean-to-think-historically

Associated Press. (2013, January 20). *MLK's "content of character" quote inspires debate.* CBS News. https://www.cbsnews.com/news/mlks-content-of-character-quote-inspires-debate/

Associated Press. (2015, January 13). Mystery Sept. 11 Marine rescuer comes forward after 'World Trade Center' movie. *Fox News.* https://www.foxnews.com/story/mystery-sept-11-marine-rescuer-comes-foward-after-world-trade-center-movie

Barnes, B. (2010, July 26). Marketing 'Tron: Legacy' brings the hardest sell yet. *New York Times.* https://www.nytimes.com/2010/07/26/business/media/26tron.html

Benshoff, H., & Griffin, S. (2009). *America on film: Representing race, class, gender, and sexuality at the movies.* Wiley.

Bergeson, S. (2023, March 1). 'The Blackening' trailer: Jay Pharoah and Yvonne Orji slaughter horror movie stereotypes. *IndieWire.* https://www.indiewire.com/features/general/the-blackening-trailer-jay-pharaoh-slaughters-horror-movie-stereotypes-1234814805/

Bertrand, M., & Mullainathan, S. (2004). Are Emily and Greg more employable than Lakisha and Jamal? A field experiment on labor market discrimination. *The American Economic Review, 94*(4), 991–1013. http://www.jstor.org/stable/3592802

Bogle, D. (2016). *Toms, coons, mulattoes, mammies, and bucks: An interpretive history of Blacks in American films.* Bloomsbury Academic.

Box Office Mojo. (n.d.). *Top lifetime grosses.* https://www.boxofficemojo.com/chart/ww_top_lifetime_gross/

Bradley, B. (2023, March 10). Disney sells out ad inventory for 95th Oscars with pricing slightly down. *Adweek.* https://www.adweek.com/convergent-tv/disney-sells-out-ad-inventory-for-95th-oscars-with-pricing-slightly-down/

Brinkof, T. (2021, October 4). How Michelangelo's David turned Renaissance Italy on its head. *Big Think.* https://bigthink.com/high-culture/michelangelo-david-medici/

Brown v. Board of Education, 347 U.S. 483 (1954). https://www.loc.gov/item/usrep347483/

Castagno, A. E. (Ed.). (2019). *The price of nice: How good intentions maintain educational inequity.* University of Minnesota Press.

Chang, A. (2018, July 31). White America is quietly self-segregating. *Vox.* https://www.vox.com/2017/1/18/14296126/white-segregated-suburb-neighborhood-cartoon

Chiu, A. (2020, January 22). Robert Downey, Jr. on 'Tropic Thunder' blackface: '90 percent of my black friends were like, "Dude, that was great."' *Washington Post*. https://www.washingtonpost.com/nation/2020/01/22/downey-blackface-tropic-thunder/

Coaston, J. (2019, May 28). The intersectionality wars. Vox. https://www.vox.com/the-highlight/2019/5/20/18542843/intersectionality-conservatism-law-race-gender-discrimination

Coleman, R.R.M., & Harris, M. H. (2023). *The Black guy dies first: Black horror cinema, from fodder to Oscar*. Simon & Schuster.

Course, B. (2016, April 14). Black people and Titanic: The reality. *Medium*. https://medium.com/@BrandieCourse/african-americans-and-titanic-the-reality-dbcb185ba691

Crews, T. [@terrycrews]. (2019, August 2). *I was a dead body in "Terminator Salvation"* . . . [Post]. X. https://twitter.com/terrycrews/status/1157339944676814849

Deloitte. (2021, July 22). For millennials and Gen Zs, social issues are top of mind—Here's how organizations can drive meaningful change. *Forbes*. https://www.forbes.com/sites/deloitte/2021/07/22/for-millennials-and-gen-zs-social-issues-are-top-of-mind-heres-how-organizations-can-drive-meaningful-change/?sh=1a83336d450c

Denzin, N. (2002). *Reading race: Hollywood and the cinema of racial violence*. SAGE Publications.

Dred Scott v. Sanford, 60 U.S. 393 (1857). https://www.loc.gov/item/usrep060393a/

Eddington, M. (2022, November 1). Cedar City police investigate teens filmed wearing blackface in Walmart. *The Salt Lake Tribune*. https://www.sltrib.com/news/2022/11/01/cedar-city-police-investigate/

Eggertsen, C. (2017, August 24). 'Terminator 2: Judgment Day' filming locations, mapped. *Curbed Los Angeles*. https://la.curbed.com/maps/terminator-2-movie-arnold-schwarzenegger

Epting, C. (2020, September 11). 12 movies that made more money overseas than in America. *Screen Crush*. https://screencrush.com/movies-that-made-more-money-overseas/

Famuerwa, J. (2020, September 2). John Boyega: 'I'm the only cast member whose experience of Star Wars was based on their race.' *GQ Magazine UK*. https://www.gq-magazine.co.uk/culture/article/john-boyega-interview-2020/amp

Fang, J. (2018, August 8). Yellowface, whitewashing, and the history of white people playing Asian characters. *Teen Vogue*. https://www.teenvogue.com/story/yellowface-whitewashing-history

Geiling, N. (2013, October 6). The Great Depression brought popcorn to the movies. *Salon*. https://www.salon.com/2013/10/06/the_great_depression_is_responsible_for_bringing_popcorn_to_the_movies_partner/

Gibbs, A. (2022, March 10). Spider-Man fans 'feel stupid' after discovering key prop is also CGI. *Newsweek*. https://www.newsweek.com/spider-man-fans-feel-stupid-discovering-cgi-1686705

Gilblom, K. (2021, February 24). How a Barbie makeover led to a pandemic sales boom. *Bloomberg News*. https://www.bloomberg.com/news/articles/2021-02-24/barbie-s-pandemic-sales-boom-followed-yearslong-revamp-at-mattel

González, C., & Aldama, F. (2019). *Reel Latinxs: Representation in U.S. film and TV*. University of Arizona Press.

Gooding, F., Jr. (2017). *You mean, there's race in my movie? The complete guide to understanding race in mainstream Hollywood*. On the Reelz Press.

Gooding, F., Jr. (2020). *Black Oscars: From Mammy to Minny, what the Academy Awards tell us about African Americans*. Rowman & Littlefield.

Gooding, F., Jr. (2023, January 12). Who does 'The Help' help? A curt critique. *The Activist History Review*. https://activisthistory.com/2023/01/12/who-does-the-help-help-a-curt-critique/

Gooding, F., Jr., Greensword, S., & Perkins, M. (2023). *A history to remember: TCU in purple, white and black*. Texas Christian University Press.

Handel, J. (2018, June 21). Diversity among film directors remains low, DGA study says. *Hollywood Reporter.* https://www.hollywoodreporter.com/news/general-news/diversity-film-directors-remains-low-dga-study-says-1122268/

Hannah-Jones, N. (2019, August 14). The 1619 Project. *The New York Times Magazine.* https://www.nytimes.com/interactive/2019/08/14/magazine/1619-america-slavery.html

Harwell, D. (2015, June 12). 'Jurassic World' shows just how weird product placement has become. *Washington Post.* https://www.washingtonpost.com/news/wonk/wp/2015/06/12/jurassic-world-shows-just-how-weird-product-placement-has-become/

Hassenger, J. (2021, June 1). Disney's defanged villains try to pass off brand management as feminist nuance. *Slate.* https://slate.com/culture/2021/06/cruella-maleficent-frozen-disney-villains.html

Hill, C. (2016, June 21). Millennials engage with their smartphones more than they do actual humans. *MarketWatch.* https://www.marketwatch.com/story/millennials-engage-with-their-smartphones-more-than-they-do-actual-humans-2016-06-21

Hollinger, K. (2012). *Feminist film studies*. Routledge.

Howard, J. (2018, March 9). The history of the 'ideal' woman and where that has left us. *CNN Health.* https://edition.cnn.com/2018/03/07/health/body-image-history-of-beauty-explainer-intl/index.html

Howe, N. (2017, January 16). Millennials: A generation of page-turners. *Forbes.* https://www.forbes.com/sites/neilhowe/2017/01/16/millennials-a-generation-of-page-turners/?sh=db14e2919786

Ifill, S. (2021, March 10). How Thurgood Marshall paved the road to 'Brown v. Board of Education.' *Smithsonian Magazine.* https://www.smithsonianmag.com/history/how-thurgood-marshall-paved-road-brown-v-board-education-180977197/

Jim Crow Museum. (2020, October 26). 1950 Blackface performance Vernon & Ryan [Video]. *YouTube.* https://www.youtube.com/watch?v=P3QaLNsWW9M

Jones, E. E. (2019, May 31). From Mammy to Ma: Hollywood's favourite racist stereotype. *BBC.* https://www.bbc.com/culture/article/20190530-rom-mammy-to-ma-hollywoods-favourite-racist-stereotype

Kale, S. (2019, September 23). The unstoppable rise of the 'Instagram face.' *Vice.* https://www.vice.com/en/article/evjpj7/instagram-face-kylie-jenner-package-fillers

Kelly, M. L. (2019, February 11). 'Magical Negro' carries the weight of history. *NPR.* https://www.npr.org/2019/02/11/693587521/magical-negro-carries-the-weight-of-history

Kennedy, M. (2021, February 21). How many people Rambo has actually killed. *Screen Rant.* https://screenrant.com/rambo-kill-count-movies/

Kuperberg, C. & Kuperberg, J. (2022). *Yellowface: Asian whitewashing and racism in Hollywood.* Kali Pictures.

Little, B. (2017, August 16). How the Nazis were inspired by Jim Crow. *History Channel.* https://www.history.com/news/how-the-nazis-were-inspired-by-jim-crow

Littleton, C. (2019, March 19). Disney closes $71 billion 21st Century Fox deal. *Variety.* https://variety.com/2019/biz/news/disney-fox-deal-complete-1203167374/

Lodge, G. (2018, February 15). 'Full of heart but devoid of life': Is Crash really the worst Oscar winner ever? *The Guardian.* https://www.theguardian.com/film/2018/feb/15/crash-worst-oscar-best-picture-winner-three-billboards

London, D. (2019, February 11). Why I still can't stop thinking about Sarah Silverman's blackface moment. *Medium.* https://medium.com/@DIANCALONDON/why-i-still-cant-stop-thinking-about-sarah-silverman-s-blackface-moment-e7c5e1fe3beb

Lopez, G. (2017, March 7). For years, this popular test measured anyone's racial bias. But it might not work after all. *Vox.* https://www.vox.com/identities/2017/3/7/14637626/implicit-association-test-racism

Madigan, R. (2017, September 17). A Russian proverb constantly repeated by Ronald Reagan has never been more important for investors. *Business Insider.* https://www.businessinsider.com/trust-but-verify-has-never-been-more-important-for-investors-2017-9

McDonald, P. (2002). *The star system: Hollywood's production of popular identities.* Wallflower Press.

McGinn, C. (2005). *The power of movies: How screen and mind interact.* First Vintage Books.

McKnight, B. (2015, November 13). How long is Star Wars: The Force Awakens? Run time revealed. *Cinema Blend.* https://www.cinemablend.com/new/How-Long-Star-Wars-Force-Awakens-Run-Time-Revealed-94337.html

Misick, B. (2020, October 29). Controversy over "The Princess and the Frog." *Essence.* https://www.essence.com/news/critics-dispute-princess-and-the-frog/

Moen, M. (2022, March 10). Samuel L. Jackson wants that cussing crown. *Paper.* https://www.papermag.com/samuel-jackson-film-swearing-record

MPR News Staff. (2016, January 5). 'What if I say the wrong thing on race?': How to talk about race. *MPR News.* https://www.mprnews.org/story/2016/01/05/verna-myers-how-to-have-difficult-conversations

Mueller, A. (2022, July 31). Why movies cost so much to make. *Investopedia.* https://www.investopedia.com/financial-edge/0611/why-movies-cost-so-much-to-make.aspx

Munson, O. (2022, October 19). What is the highest grossing movie of all time? The top box-office record breakers. *USA Today.* https://www.usatoday.com/story/entertainment/movies/2022/10/19/highest-grossing-movie-all-time/8062601001/

National Park Service. (n.d.). *The Middle Passage.* https://www.nps.gov/articles/the-middle-passage.htm

Nevels, C. S. (2007). *Lynching to belong: Claiming Whiteness through racial violence.* Texas A&M University Press.

News24. (2013, October 21). *Billy Bob Thornton says sex scenes with Halle made marriage to Angie tough.* https://www.news24.com/life/billy-bob-thornton-says-sex-scenes-with-halle-made-marriage-to-angie-tough-20131021

Newton, D. (2023, February 28). Reel segregation: The revealing racial history of local movie theaters. *The Local Reporter.* https://thelocalreporter.press/reel-segregation-the-revealing-racial-history-of-local-movie-theaters/

Nolfi, J. (2023, March 12). Halle Berry replaces Will Smith as Oscars Best Actress presenter alongside Jessica Chastain. *Entertainment Week.* https://ew.com/awards/oscars/2023-oscars-halle-berry-replaces-will-smith-best-actress-presenter-jessica-chastain/

Oleksinski, J. (2020, May 8). How Chris Hemsworth kills 183 men in one 'Extraction' scene. *New York Post.* https://nypost.com/2020/05/08/how-chris-hemsworth-kills-183-men-in-one-extraction-scene/

Pixarfan1. (n.d.). Please tell me I'm not the only one who thought Finn was going to be the main character of The Force Awakens before it came out [Online forum post]. *Reddit.* https://www.reddit.com/r/StarWars/comments/zzepfl/please_tell_me_im_not_the_only_one_who_thought/

Plessy v. Ferguson, 163 U.S. 537 (1896). https://www.loc.gov/item/usrep163537/

Ramón, A., Tran, M., & Hunt, D. (2023). Hollywood diversity report 2023: Exclusivity in progress. *UCLA Entertainment & Media Research Initiative*. https://socialsciences.ucla.edu/hollywood-diversity-report-2023/

Regester, C. (2005). From the buzzard's roost: Black movie-going in Durham and other North Carolina cities during the early period of American cinema. *Film History, 17*(1), 113–124 .

Regester, C. (2010). *African American actresses: The struggle for visibility, 1900–1960*. Indiana University Press.

Robb, D. (2022, April 6). WGA West Inclusion & Equity Report finds 'significant' gains by women & people of color. *Deadline*. https://deadline.com/2022/04/wga-west-inclusion-report-2022-1234995926/

Russian, A. (2019, April 29). An 'Avengers: Endgame' fan in China was hospitalized for crying too hard. *People*. https://people.com/movies/avengers-endgame-fan-rushed-to-hospital-in-china/

Salmon, C. (2019, October 10). Martin Scorsese is right about Marvel films—they are formulaic fairground rides, not cinema. *Independent*. https://www.independent.co.uk/arts-entertainment/films/features/marvel-martin-scorsese-theme-parks-avengers-endgame-robert-downey-jr-a9150396.html

Sandwell, I. (2022, March 18). *Why 'Spider-Man: No Way Home' isn't available to watch on Disney+*. Digital Spy. https://www.digitalspy.com/movies/a38399475/spider-man-no-way-home-disney-plus-release-date/

Schulz, B., & Guynn, J. (2022, September 18). Is TikTok the new Google? Why TikTok is Gen Z's favorite search engine. *USA Today*. https://www.usatoday.com/story/tech/2022/09/18/google-search-tiktok-gen-z/10361233002/?gnt-cfr=1

Segal, G. & Antonio, S. (2021). *Dramatic effects with a movie camera*. Bloomsbury Publishing.

Semuels, A. (2021, June 21). The U.S. is increasingly diverse, so why is segregation getting worse? *TIME*. https://time.com/6074243/segregation-america-increasing/

Seymour, L. (2017, December 18). Over the last 20 years, Broadway's 'Lion King' has made more money for Disney than 'Star Wars.' *Forbes*. https://www.forbes.com/sites/leeseymour/2017/12/18/the-lion-king-is-making-more-money-for-disney-than-star-wars/#

Shaheen, J. (2012). *Reel bad Arabs: How Hollywood vilifies a people*. Olive Branch Press.

Silverman, S. [@SarahKSilverman]. (2016, July 23). *Menstrual cramps like a mofo* [Post]. X. https://twitter.com/SarahKSilverman/status/756860859486441472

Smith, J. (2023, March 23). Tallahassee principal is forced to resign after parents complained that Michelangelo's statue of David is 'pornographic' and shouldn't be shown to sixth grade art history class. *Daily Mail*. https://www.dailymail.co.uk/news/article-11894493/Tallahassee-principal-fired-parents-complain-Michelangelo-statue-David-pornographic.html

Smith, S. L., Choueiti, M., Pieper, K., Yao, K., Case, A., & Choi, A. (2019). *Inequality in 1,200 popular films: Examining portrayals of gender, race/ethnicity, LGBTQ & disability from 2007 to 2018*. USC Annenberg School for Communication Inclusion Initiative & the Annenberg Foundation's Media, Diversity, & Social Change Initiative. https://assets.uscannenberg.org/docs/aii-inequality-report-2019-09-03.pdf

Statista. (2023a, January 5). *Number of cinema sites in the United States from 1995 to 2020*. https://www.statista.com/statistics/188643/number-of-us-cinema-sites-since-1995

Statista. (2023b, February 13). *Number of movies released in the United States and Canada from 2000 to 2022*. https://www.statista.com/statistics/187122/movie-releases-in-north-america-since-2001/

Statista. (2023c, July 28). *Global box office revenue from 2005 to 2021*. https://www.statista.com/statistics/271856/global-box-office-revenue/

Statista. (2024, January 9). *Average daily internet usage worldwide 2019, by age and device.* https://www.statista.com/statistics/416850/average-duration-of-internet-use-age-device/

Subano, E. E. (2023, April 11). The highlights from Star Wars Celebration 2023. *Lifestyle Asia.* https://www.lifestyleasia.com/bk/entertainment/star-wars-celebration-2023-highlights/

Turney, D. (2023, February 23). How Hollywood and the military work together. *Reader's Digest.* https://www.readersdigest.co.uk/culture/film-tv/how-hollywood-and-the-military-work-together-off-screen

University of Chicago. (2013, October 14). Race and the design of American life: African Americans in twentieth-century commercial art. https://www.lib.uchicago.edu/collex/exhibits/race-and-design-american-life/race-and-meaning-progress/blackface-industry/

Weiss, J. (2017, June 2). Underoos: How an underwear craze got its origin story. *Hollywood Reporter.* https://www.hollywoodreporter.com/movies/movie-news/captain-underpants-how-underoos-got-origin-story-1008804/

White, B. (2018, March 11). How I learned to love my big nose and lips. *Yahoo! Life.* https://www.yahoo.com/lifestyle/learned-love-big-nose-lips-120000554.html

Wilder, C. S. (2013). *Ebony & ivy: Race, slavery, and the troubled history of America's universities.* Bloomsbury Publishing.

WuTangClan-VEVO. (2014, January 21). Wu-Tang Clan—C.R.E.A.M. [Video]. *YouTube.* https://www.youtube.com/watch?v=PBwAxmrE194

Yuen, N. (2016). *Reel inequality: Hollywood actors and racism.* Rutgers University Press.

Zahneis, M., & Supiano, B. (2023, June 9). Fear and confusion in the classroom. *The Chronicle of Higher Education.* https://www.chronicle.com/article/fear-and-confusion-in-the-classroom

Ziegbe, M. (2010, August 7). 'Avatar' re-release to highlight Tsu'tey death. *MTV.com.* https://www.mtv.com/news/sd345d/avatar-re-release-to-highlight-tsutey-death

Index

NOTE: *Italicized* page numbers indicate entries defined in the Glossary section.

About the Author

Frederick W. Gooding, Jr. (PhD, Georgetown University) is the Dr. Ronald E. Moore Endowed Professor of the Humanities and associate history professor of African American Studies within the John V. Roach Honors College at Texas Christian University in Fort Worth, TX. Featured in national outlets such as *New York Times, USA Today,* and *TIME Magazine*, Dr. Gooding is a professor of pop culture who engages audiences on subtle racial patterns "hidden in plain sight." Dr. Gooding has also provided social commentary on CNBC, CBS, and Fox News networks and has reached an international audience through his invited lectures and media writings, which include *Black Oscars: From Mammy to Minny, What the Academy Awards Tell Us About African Americans*, and *Double Crossed: Black Female Intersectionality in Hollywood.*

MULTICULTURAL EDUCATION SERIES

James A. Banks, Series Editor

Race and Media Literacy, Explained (or Why Does the Black Guy Die First?)
Frederick W. Gooding, Jr.

Whiteness in the Ivory Tower: Why *Don't* We Notice the White Students Sitting Together in the Quad?
Nolan L. Cabrera

Culturally Sustaining Policymaking in Indigenous Communities: Partnering to Promote Lasting Change
Aprille J. Phillips

Educating for Equity and Excellence: Enacting Culturally Responsive Teaching
Geneva Gay

Speculative Pedagogies: Designing Equitable Educational Futures
Antero Garcia & Nicole Mirra, Eds.

Seeing Whiteness: The Essential Essays of Robin DiAngelo
Robin DiAngelo

Becoming an Antiracist School Leader: Dare to Be Real
Patrick A. Duffy

The Hip-Hop Mindset: Success Strategies for Educators and Other Professionals
Toby S. Jenkins

Education for Liberal Democracy: Using Classroom Discussion to Build Knowledge and Voice
Walter C. Parker

Critical Race Theory and Its Critics: Implications for Research and Teaching
Francesca López & Christine E. Sleeter

Anti-Blackness at School: Creating Affirming Educational Spaces for African American Students
Joi A. Spencer & Kerri Ullucci

Sustaining Disabled Youth: Centering Disability in Asset Pedagogies
Federico R. Waitoller & Kathleen A. King Thorius, Eds.

The Civil Rights Road to Deeper Learning: Five Essentials for Equity
Kia Darling-Hammond & Linda Darling-Hammond

Reckoning With Racism in Family–School Partnerships: Centering Black Parents' School Engagement
Jennifer L. McCarthy Foubert

Teaching Anti-Fascism: A Critical Multicultural Pedagogy for Civic Engagement
Michael Vavrus

Unsettling Settler-Colonial Education: The Transformational Indigenous Praxis Model
Cornel Pewewardy, Anna Lees, & Robin Zape-tah-hol-ah Minthorn, Eds.

Culturally and Socially Responsible Assessment: Theory, Research, and Practice
Catherine S. Taylor, with Susan B. Nolen

LGBTQ Youth and Education: Policies and Practices, 2nd Ed.
Cris Mayo

Transforming Multicultural Education Policy and Practice: Expanding Educational Opportunity
James A. Banks, Ed.

Critical Race Theory in Education: A Scholar's Journey
Gloria Ladson-Billings

Civic Education in the Age of Mass Migration: Implications for Theory and Practice
Angela M. Banks

Creating a Home in Schools: Sustaining Identities for Black, Indigenous, and Teachers of Color
Francisco Rios & A Longoria

Generation Mixed Goes to School: Radically Listening to Multiracial Kids
Ralina L. Joseph & Allison Briscoe-Smith

Race, Culture, and Politics in Education: A Global Journey from South Africa
Kogila Moodley

Indian Education for All: Decolonizing Indigenous Education in Public Schools
John P. Hopkins

Racial Microaggressions: Using Critical Race Theory to Respond to Everyday Racism
Daniel G. Solórzano & Lindsay Pérez Huber

City Schools and the American Dream 2: The Enduring Promise of Public Education
Pedro A. Noguera & Esa Syeed

Measuring Race: Why Disaggregating Data Matters for Addressing Educational Inequality
Robert T. Teranishi, Bach Mai Dolly Nguyen, Cynthia Maribel Alcantar, & Edward R. Curammeng

Campus Uprisings: How Student Activists and Collegiate Leaders Resist Racism and Create Hope
Ty-Ron M. O. Douglas, Kmt G. Shockley, & Ivory Toldson

Transformative Ethnic Studies in Schools: Curriculum, Pedagogy, and Research
Christine E. Sleeter & Miguel Zavala

For a complete list of series titles, please visit www.tcpress.com/MCE

(continued)

Multicultural Education Series, *continued*

Why Race and Culture Matter in Schools, 2nd Ed.
Tyrone C. Howard

Just Schools
Ann M. Ishimaru

Immigrant-Origin Students in Community College
Carola Suárez-Orozco & Olivia Osei-Twumasi, Eds.

"We Dare Say Love"
Na'ilah Suad Nasir et al., Eds.

Teaching What *Really* Happened, 2nd Ed.
James W. Loewen

Culturally Responsive Teaching, 3rd Ed.
Geneva Gay

Music, Education, and Diversity
Patricia Shehan Campbell

Reaching and Teaching Students in Poverty, 2nd Ed.
Paul C. Gorski

Deconstructing Race
Jabari Mahiri

Is Everyone Really Equal? 2nd Ed.
Özlem Sensoy & Robin DiAngelo

Transforming Educational Pathways for Chicana/o Students
Dolores Delgado Bernal & Enrique Alemán Jr.

Un-Standardizing Curriculum, 2nd Ed.
Christine E. Sleeter & Judith Flores Carmona

Global Migration, Diversity, and Civic Education
James A. Banks et al., Eds.

Reclaiming the Multicultural Roots of U.S. Curriculum
Wayne Au et al.

Human Rights and Schooling
Audrey Osler

We Can't Teach What We Don't Know, 3rd Ed.
Gary R. Howard

Diversity and Education
Michael Vavrus

Mathematics for Equity
Na'ilah Suad Nasir et al., Eds.

Race, Empire, and English Language Teaching
Suhanthie Motha

Black Male(d)
Tyrone C. Howard

Race Frameworks
Zeus Leonardo

Class Rules
Peter W. Cookson Jr.

Streetsmart Schoolsmart
Gilberto Q. Conchas & James Diego Vigil

Achieving Equity for Latino Students
Frances Contreras

Literacy Achievement and Diversity
Kathryn H. Au

Understanding English Language Variation in U.S. Schools
Anne H. Charity Hudley & Christine Mallinson

Latino Children Learning English
Guadalupe Valdés et al.

Asians in the Ivory Tower
Robert T. Teranishi

Diversity and Equity in Science Education
Okhee Lee & Cory A. Buxton

Forbidden Language
Patricia Gándara & Megan Hopkins, Eds.

The Light in Their Eyes, 10th Anniversary Ed.
Sonia Nieto

The Flat World and Education
Linda Darling-Hammond

Educating Citizens in a Multicultural Society, 2nd Ed.
James A. Banks

Culture, Literacy, and Learning
Carol D. Lee

Facing Accountability in Education
Christine E. Sleeter, Ed.

Talkin Black Talk
H. Samy Alim & John Baugh, Eds.

Improving Access to Mathematics
Na'ilah Suad Nasir & Paul Cobb, Eds.

"To Remain an Indian"
K. Tsianina Lomawaima & Teresa L. McCarty

Beyond the Big House
Gloria Ladson-Billings

Teaching and Learning in Two Languages
Eugene E. García

Improving Multicultural Education
Cherry A. McGee Banks

Transforming the Multicultural Education of Teachers
Michael Vavrus

Learning to Teach for Social Justice
Linda Darling-Hammond et al., Eds.

Learning and Not Learning English
Guadalupe Valdés

The Children Are Watching
Carlos E. Cortés

Multicultural Education, Transformative Knowledge, and Action
James A. Banks, Ed.